Understanding Judaism

Teaching Religions and Worldviews

Series Editor: James D. Holt

This series explores the beliefs and practices of the different religions and worldviews alongside pedagogically supported approaches of how knowledge of each religion or worldview could be taught within the primary and secondary classroom, and to enhance teaching of those students in the classroom who practice that particular religion or worldview.

Books in the series explore the beliefs and practices of each religion or worldview as a lived experience in the UK. Aspects of each religion or worldview are explored including the concepts that form the central beliefs, and then the expression of these beliefs in worship, daily life, and the ethics of believers in the modern day. Each chapter will utilize the authentic voice of those who identify with the religion or worldview today through the use of vignettes and provide reflective tasks for the reader to consider the concepts and how they can be taught in the classroom.

Also available in the series:

Understanding Sikhism, James D. Holt
Understanding Hinduism, James D. Holt
Understanding Buddhism, James D. Holt

Understanding Judaism

A Guide for Teachers

James D. Holt

BLOOMSBURY ACADEMIC
LONDON • NEW YORK • OXFORD • NEW DELHI • SYDNEY

BLOOMSBURY ACADEMIC
Bloomsbury Publishing Plc, 50 Bedford Square, London, WC1B 3DP, UK
Bloomsbury Publishing Inc, 1359 Broadway, New York, NY 10018, USA
Bloomsbury Publishing Ireland, 29 Earlsfort Terrace, Dublin 2, D02 AY28, Ireland

BLOOMSBURY, BLOOMSBURY ACADEMIC and the Diana logo
are trademarks of Bloomsbury Publishing Plc

First published in Great Britain 2026

Series design by Charlotte James
Cover image © anand purohit / Getty Images

A catalogue record for this book is available from the British Library.

Library of Congress Cataloging-in-Publication Data
Names: Holt, James author
Title: Understanding Judaism : a guide for teachers / James D. Holt.
Description: First edition. | New York, N.Y. : Bloomsbury Academic, 2026. |
Series: Teaching religions and worldviews | Includes bibliographical references and index.
Identifiers: LCCN 2025040522 (print) | LCCN 2025040523 (ebook) |
ISBN 9781350477544 hardback | ISBN 9781350477537 paperback |
ISBN 9781350477568 epub | ISBN 9781350477551 pdf
Subjects: LCSH: Judaism–Study and teaching | Judaism–Doctrines
Classification: LCC BM70 .H65 2026 (print) | LCC BM70 (ebook) |
DDC 296–dc23/eng/20250923
LC record available at https://lccn.loc.gov/2025040522
LC ebook record available at https://lccn.loc.gov/2025040523

ISBN: HB: 978-1-3504-7754-4
          PB: 978-1-3504-7753-7
        ePDF: 978-1-3504-7755-1
       eBook: 978-1-3504-7756-8

Series: Teaching Religions and Worldviews

Typeset by Integra Software Services Pvt. Ltd.
Printed and bound in Great Britain

For product safety related questions contact productsafety@bloomsbury.com.

To find out more about our authors and books visit www.bloomsbury.com
and sign up for our newsletters.

For Edie …

… as you are wrapped in your parents' arms, so may your life be wrapped in justice and righteousness. As we embrace you today, so may you embrace your traditions and your communities. As your eyes are filled with wonder when you gaze at the world, so too may you be filled with wonder at the everyday miracles of life. As you startle to the world around you, so may you remain ever open both to the happiness and to the pain of those you encounter in the world. As you cry for food and comfort now, so may you one day cry out to correct the injustices of the world, to help clothe the naked and feed the hungry. As your hand tightly grasps your parents' fingers, so may you grasp hold of learning to grow in knowledge and wisdom (*A Grandparent's Prayer*)

Contents

Figures

Tables

Series Foreword

The teaching of religion in schools has an interesting history in the UK. It has been through various iterations and paradigm shifts. There is a suggestion, and quite a loud one, at the moment that we are in the midst of a change of paradigm as it moves from a world religions approach to one that is focused on religion and worldviews. Much is made of this shift, suggesting that it is a seismic landscape-altering approach within the classroom. Against this background it may seem odd to write a series of books that focuses on subject knowledge for teachers of what can be seen as reified religious structures that could be seen to be artificial creations.

Although the nomenclature used in the systematization of religions has changed to include worldviews, I am not convinced that the change is as seismic as has been suggested. The religion and worldviews approach to the teaching of religion and beliefs in schools is, in some ways, a rebranding rather than anything substantive. Effective teaching of religion and belief in schools has, in the recent past, always taken account of worldviews, maybe without recognizing that this is what has been happening. The 'change' to religion and worldviews will still rely on essential aspects of religions/structural worldviews and it is for this reason that this series of books are being written. What is meant by the 'essential' aspects? That will differ between religions and worldviews; it is at this point that a discussion of the positive contributions of a religion and worldviews approach will help frame the writing of this and subsequent books.

There are many ways to discuss what is entailed in a religion and worldviews approach to the teaching of religion and belief in schools and other settings. I often speak about the 'messiness' of religion and worldviews, and this messiness has to do with the two terms: religion and worldviews.

In exploring the term religion, it becomes evident very quickly that the neat structures that we have in our minds, or that are taught in the classroom, are not reflective of the reality that we find in the world today. The various elements that we use in comparative religion enable us to line religions up next to each other and compare various elements, but in some ways in trying to get them to conform to a particular structure of religion we have tried to fit square pegs into round holes. Jonathan Z. Smith noted this:

> 'Religion' is not a native category. It is not a first person term of self-characterization. It is a category imposed from the outside on some aspect of native culture. It is the other, in these instances colonialists, who are solely responsible for the content of the term (2004, 179–180).

In having religions fit an artificially constructed paradigm it is possible to see that both the constituent parts and the whole have been made less, and their vibrancy and meaning have been lost. One such example is in the development of the idea of what Buddhism is in relation to Christianity or, at least, to the religious structure of Christianity has meant that the person of the Buddha, Siddhartha Gautama has developed as the central focus of Buddhism in the West, and certainly the Buddhism that is taught in classrooms. Authors such as Tomoko Masuzawa (2005) highlight that original Buddhism was mined and reified in the nineteenth century with reference to texts in India, with little reference to the lived reality of different Buddhisms in other countries. As a result Donald Lopez (1995) suggests that Buddhism is a 'hypostatised object … created by Europe, [which, in turn] could also be controlled by it, and it was against this Buddhism that all the Buddhisms of the modern Orient were to be judged … ' (7). It remains true to say that the Enlightenment understanding of religion was reinforced as colonial powers sought to make sense of the beliefs and practices that they found among the peoples of the Empire.

In establishing religion as an observable and static phenomenon, the religions themselves began to reflect the structures and emphases of those who studied and wrote about them. While it is possible to see a continued diversity of expression and understanding, certain principles began to be perceived as normative, and as such an orthodoxy (even if only from the outsider's perspective) began to develop and deviance from the constructed norms began to be seen to be peripheral, where in the past it was part of vast panoply of loosely related beliefs and practices. This normafication continues today; in 2021 it was argued, by Kalpana Jain, that Indian Prime Minister Modi was attempting to normalize a particular understanding of the Ramayana, and by association the celebration of Diwali. Establishing a Hindu canon or orthodoxy could be seen to be unifying; yet at the same time eroding the diversity and vibrancy of the Hindu community.

It is this approach that, it is argued, developed a post-Enlightenment view of religion and religions. The history of Sikhism, for example, can also be seen to be a reflection of this process where boundaries were established, and norms enforced. The typology of religions, in the Western mind, prior to the nineteenth century tended to reflect a fourfold model: that of Christian, Jewish, Muslim and Heathen/ Pagan. Christianity was the 'norm' while Judaism and Islam were seen to be related (but ultimately wrong), and everything else was put into the equivalent of the 'other' category. During the nineteenth century religious classifications began to develop further with the first recorded use of terminology such as Buddhism (Boudhism) in 1801, Hinduism (Hindooism) in 1829, Taoism (Taouism) in 1839, Zoroastrianism in 1854, and Confucianism in 1862 (see Josephson, 2012). The nuance of difference within and between religions was not explored in great depth, as is illustrated in the classification of Sikhs as Hindus in the earliest Indian colonial censuses. Up until this point in Sikh history, the self-identification and practice undertaken by Sikhs as followers of the Gurus were seen to be fairly diverse, but also not a matter that needed to be delineated. There was evidence of practices more associated of Hinduism being followed by Sikhs alongside what could be seen to be more Sikhlike elements. It was in the classification of such, that provided the impetus for some Sikhs to begin to establish an orthodoxy that separated the Panth from Sikhism. The publication of Ham Hindu Nahin (We are not Hindus) in 1899 is evidence of Sikhs feeling the need to establish boundaries where previously they were not perceived to be important (greater exploration of this Sikh 'orthodoxy' is explored in the Sikh volume of this series).

To some extent the development of a focus on worldviews within the classroom can be seen to be an effort to counter the colonialization of religions, and return the understanding of them to a richer and more diverse expression that allows for individual expressions of religion. In exploring worldviews The Commission on Religious Education has suggested what they mean:

The English word 'worldview' is a translation of the German weltanschauung, which literally means a view of the world. A worldview is a person's way of understanding, experiencing and responding to the world. It can be described as a philosophy of life or an approach to life. This includes how a person understands the nature of reality and their own place in the world. A person's worldview is likely to influence and be influenced by their beliefs, values, behaviours, experiences, identities and commitments (Commission on RE, 2018, 4).

The Theos Think Tank (2021) video No one stands nowhere suggests that a worldview is a complex amalgam of various influences that are constantly shifting and developing. This means that there are personal and institutional worldviews; and that in these institutional worldviews there is a wide variety of experiences and interpretations. This can be seen to build on the world of writers such as Kimberlé Crenshaw (1989) and bell hooks who have explored aspects of intersectionality. Crenshaw explored what it was to be a Black woman, and how race and gender intersect. This develops into a discussion of worldviews and how they are held by individuals; Trevor Cooling suggests that people 'inhabit' their world view (Cooling et al, 2020, 29).

This is an important development in the study of religion but, as suggested earlier, is not new. People like Robert Jackson (1997) have long suggested listening to the insider or individual voice as a way to understand the complexity of religion. This ethnographic approach recognizes the rich diversity of lived religion. In the wider academic field of Religious Studies writers such as McGuire (2008) and Ammerman (2020) have similarly advocated for a focus on the lived experience of religion in the lives of individuals. If this is what is meant by 'worldviews' then it could be argued that teaching about religion in schools has been doing this. The focus on worldviews as a concept is a timely reminder that the religions that we explore are not neatly packaged, but they are messy and a result of the confluence of influences and identities in a person's life.

In trying to understand I imagine a prism, similar to that found on the cover of Pink Floyd's Dark Side of the Moon album. The prism is the receptacle where our backgrounds, cultures, experiences coalesce to help make sense of life and the expressions and interpretations of new experiences and the development of values and the like. These form a different spectrum of colours for each individual. This intersectionality recognizes and emphasizes that no two people are alike. Simply speaking, in the context of this book, a Jewish brother and sister in the UK would have different perceptions of Judaism despite similar upbringings, because of their gender as well as other experiences that may have coloured their view.

This approach could be seen to problematize the very concept of religion and world-views to such an extent that religion could be seen to lose all meaning. It reduces religion to an individual expression of individual belief system.

The argument and purpose of this series of books are to recognize the messiness, intersectionality and worldviews approach to religions, but in a way that does not dismiss everything that is useful about a world religions paradigm. It will recognize the diversity within each tradition, but will also use what can be commonly termed the 'essential' aspects of a religion or worldview that enables diversity to be recognized. The essential aspects are need to frame the discussions that are taking place. Ben Wood (2020) argues:

> Some argue that 'essentialism' narrows and limits understanding and fails to provide a realistic picture of the world and religion and belief. Others, myself included, accept this to a point, arguing that 'essentialism' may be limited, but it is a necessary part of the process of learning about religions in a progressive manner, in that what is learnt in this phase is essential for progress to more sophisticated learning. (Wood, 2020, 14)

The Commission on RE (2018) suggest that:

> We need to move beyond an essentialised presentation of six 'major world faiths' and towards a deeper understanding of the complex, diverse and plural nature of world-views at both institutional and personal levels. (Commission on RE, 2018, 6)

Although it may be not what they intended, I would suggest that a 'moving beyond' essentialism does not mean that we need to dismiss the existence of the central elements of a religion or institutionalized worldview; rather, that we should utilize aspects that are helpful to frame our study. Moving beyond is studying religion in a framework of intersectionality or worldviews that recognizes the problems inherent in the world religions paradigm. This means that adopting a categorization of all religions as having set commonalities is out of date and does not reflect the lived reality of many people in the world. Any study of religion in schools must begin with a recognition of the diversity that is found within the world.

I argue elsewhere (Holt, 2022) that this diversity is appropriate at every level of the school experience. At the very youngest of ages it is possible to use language such as 'many', 'most', and 'some' when speaking of religious belief and practice. As pupils get older it is possible to introduce the nuances and specifics of diversity. It also serves the purpose of exercising a humility of knowledge when we teach; in the intersectional world of religions it is impossible to know everything about the beliefs and practices of all aspects of a religion; using qualifiers ensures that we are not unconsciously establishing boundaries and norms in religions that do not exist.

One of the consequences of exploring religion and worldviews as a paradigm, is the inclusion of systems of belief that are not seen to be religious. For many years, groups such as Humanists UK have argued for a recognition and inclusion of non-religious worldviews within the classroom. Many schools, syllabi and specifications now include non-religious worldviews; the worldviews approach can be seen to have expanded what might be explored in the curriculum. In recognizing that the 'big six' have traditionally been prioritized it is possible that this shift in paradigm will expand what traditions and worldviews should be studied. I have explored the arguments for the inclusion of religions 'beyond the big six', and also the inclusion of expressions of the big six beyond the mainstream, and that we should expand what we understand and teach (Holt, 2019). It is against this background that this series of books works; while recognizing what can be perceived as the 'normative' it will also recognize and explore aspects of diversity within the religious tradition.

It is this point I feel that it is important that I recognize my own positionality with respect to the religions and worldviews that will be covered in this series. For most of the religions I will be coming from the perspective of an outsider. I recognize both the benefits and hindrances this may bring. I cannot fully understand what it is to live as a Sikh, or as a Buddhist. The spirituality of Islam or of Judaism is not something that I have experienced as a believer. This does not mean, though, that I am unsympathetic. When I present the beliefs and practices of the individual religions I will do so, as best I can, in a way that they would be understood by believers. I understand and appreciate the impact that religions and worldviews can have on the lives of individuals and communities. As an outsider I am also able to recognize debates within the community that may be given short shrift by an insider.

As a teacher, lecturer and professor of religious education over many years I am also able to understand the nuances of what is needed to teach religion and worldviews in the classroom. I will not be able to cover everything, and the selection of material may leave out things that some people think are important. That is the beauty of intersectionality and worldviews; there are a myriad of ways that religion can be understood and presented. It is my hope that this series of books will provide a basis on which to build in the future. I would encourage to discuss the contents of this book with fellow professionals, your students, but perhaps most importantly with followers of the religions and worldviews explored. The authentic voice is central to understanding the beliefs and impact of religion. This book should provide you with a good knowledge on which to develop your teaching and those conversations.

Acknowledgements

There are many people who contribute to the writing of a book. At many different points throughout my life there are people I have met, worked with, and become friends with, who have contributed to my understanding of religion and especially, in terms of this book, of Judaism.

There are many members of the Jewish community who have helped with the answering of questions over the years that have assisted in my understanding that enabled this book to be written. I will not be able to name them all, but Rabbi Daniel Walker and the Heaton Park Ashkenazi Shul community have been particularly helpful over the years, also the old Jackson Row Reform synagogue, Anne Goldstein, and Sara Perlmutter. I take complete responsibility for anything that might not quite be as understood within the Jewish community.

Within my teaching community so many people challenge me and inspire me to be better and understand more. John Rudge, Lesley Wakefield, Emma Watson, Diane Kolka, and Christine Paul have particularly been helpful in my understanding of Judaism. Special thanks are also due to colleagues and students at the University of Chester.

The biggest thanks of all are reserved for my wife Ruth, and our children, Eleanor, Abi, Ethan, Gideon, Natasha and Martha know that sometimes I disappear and hibernate for a while as I write. I am so grateful for their love and support. Special mention must be made of my beautiful granddaughter to whom this book is dedicated who came into our lives during the writing of this book and came to visit grandpa now and again while he was in his office writing.

As with everything I do, all credit goes to God. I am nothing without the influence of God in my life.

Note on Text and Translation

Passages throughout the book from the Tanakh and from the Talmud are taken from the freely available translations on sefaria.org. These also include the commentaries written by Maimonides such as Bereshit Rabbah Sefaria and others such as Rashi on Genesis.

Passages from the Zohar are taken from https://www.zohar.com/zohar

A note about nomenclature is important at this stage. In the rabbinic texts the Tanakh is often referred to as Ha-Sefarim (the books), in other times it was also referred to as Kitvet Ha-Kodesh (the holy writings), and more recently 'the Hebrew Bible'. The term 'bible' comes from the Greek biblia which means books and as such refers to the library of books found therein. Although it is common to find the Tanakh referred to as such within Judaism, this book will use the term Tanakh throughout to utilize terminology distinct to Judaism. One other point should also be noted, there are some Jews who when referring to the Torah do so as a shorthand for the whole of the Tanakh. To avoid any level of confusion in this book, the use of Torah will refer to the first five books of the Tanakh.

Introduction

What is Judaism? Who is a Jew?[1] These are questions that are important in writing a book about Judaism, but they are also important for teachers and also individuals. Simon Schama (2014) begins his BBC documentary Series *The Story of the Jews* in the following way:

> So what, if anything, do we [Jews] have in common? Not the colour of our skin, not the languages we speak, the tunes we sing, the food we eat. Not our opinions – we're a fiercely argumentative lot. Not even the way we pray, assuming we do …

To be a Jew, a person does not fit a stereotype, Jews are as diverse as the sand on the seashore. It might seem that a Jew is a person who follows the religion of Judaism, but there is so much more to explore when considering who is Jewish; there is nuance that seems that just as a definition is made, there is a question mark raised. This Introduction will explore these nuances, but at the same time will underpin the discussion throughout this book. A Jew believes in the Almighty, but at the same time a Jew can be someone who does not. A Jew believes the Torah is the word of the Almighty, or then again someone who does not. A Jew is someone who lives the mitzvot in their lives, or again someone who does not. The diversity of Judaism, as with all religions, is complicated

---

[1] It may seem strange in a book about Judaism that a footnote is included explaining the use of the word 'Jew' to describe those who identify as Jews. Much more will be discussed about this in Chapter 5 but suffice it to say that although 'Jew' has been used as a pejorative term, many people feel it is time to challenge this and reclaim it as it should be used. Dave Rich (2024) makes this same observation:

> To sidestep any potential offence, the word 'Jews' regularly gets replaced with the softer phrase 'Jewish people'. … Despite all of this, Jews say Jew to refer to ourselves, and that shouldn't be a problem … When Jews say the word 'Jew' they just mean a Jew, and when other people say (or hear) the word 'Jew' it may be something quite different that comes to mind. Changing our language is a good start when it comes to reducing antisemitism, but it is the thinking behind the language that needs to shift if we are going to bring about fundamental change.
>
> (5–7)

It is in this manner that 'Jew' and 'Jews' will be used throughout this book. It is a descriptive identifier that should not be loaded with prejudice or negativity. In a similar way to there being no question about the use of Christian or Muslim or Hindu, then there should be no question about its use for Jews. As Rich suggests, society needs to change the meaning with which the words may have become imbued.

in terms of belief and practice. Indeed, how to structure a book on Judaism is equally complex. There are many who would suggest that to begin with beliefs, as this book does, is problematic as the way a Jew lives their life, and practises their religion is so much more important than what they believe. This is exemplified in the words of a 75-year-old Jewish woman responding to the question, 'What do you believe about life after death?':

> I don't really know; I've not thought about it. Let me go and ask the Rabbi.

To the follow-up question, 'Why do you follow the mitzvot then?', she answered:

> It is the right thing to do, it what I have been told to do.

For this lady, the living of her religion was what was important, not any belief that might have underpinned them. Conversely, it is possible to suggest that without under-standing the why, the practices make little sense. This discussion is highlighted in the scene from *Fiddler on the Roof* where the question is asked, among many other ques-tions, 'Why must men dance separately to women at a wedding?' Some are happy just to know that it seems to have always been part of 'Tradition', whereas others need to know the reasons behind for the practice. While there is a sequential order to this book, each chapter can be read independently of others, with any links identified. If a reader wants to explore any aspect of Judaism, then they can do so by reading the chapters in the order they choose.

Judaism is a word that would appear to have its first use in the second century BCE[2] in the book of 2 Maccabees, in the Greek word *Ioudaismos*. Two contrasting examples of its translation and use are found in the Sefaria translation of 2 Maccabees 2:21:

> And the heavenly signs that the strong and zealous saw for the *congregation of Israel*.
>
> (emphasis added)

Whereas in the Oresmus translation of 2 Maccabees 8:1 we read:

> Meanwhile Judas, who was also called Maccabeus, and his companions secretly entered the villages and summoned their kindred and enlisted those who had continued in the *Jewish faith*, and so they gathered about six thousand.
>
> (emphasis added)

This highlights an ongoing discussion of the term in its historical context. While today it is seen as the precursor of Judaism as a religion, there is a debate about whether it referred

---

[2]The dating system common throughout the world using the suffixes BCE and CE is used here for ease of understanding. It should be recognized that there is a Jewish calendar based on the creation of the world (often with the suffix AM – Anno Mundi – the year of creation). It is a lunar calendar, with an additional month every two to three years to more closely align it with the solar calendar. For example, AM 5785, began at sunset on 2 October 2024 and ended at sunset on 22 September 2025.

to those who are associated with, or of, Judaea or whether it refers to religion. Shaye Cohen (1999) suggests that its use of a religious designator is anachronistic:

> We are tempted, of course, to translate [Ioudaïsmós] as 'Judaism', but this translation is too narrow, because in this first occurrence of the term, Ioudaïsmós has not yet been reduced to the designation of a religion. It means rather 'the aggregate of all those characteristics that makes Judaeans Judaean (or Jews Jewish)'. Among these characteristics, to be sure, are practices and beliefs that we would today call 'religious', but these practices and beliefs are not the sole content of the term. Thus *Ioudaïsmós* should be translated not as 'Judaism' but as Judaeanness.
>
> (105–6)

It would appear that this is not as settled as Cohen suggests. There is an argument that in comparing 1 and 2 Maccabees that the first book is very much about the nation and its people, whereas the second focuses very much on the religious identity, reflected in its use of *Ioudaismos* which is not found in the first book (Schwartz, 2021).

Exploring its usage in the early Roman period Morton Smith (1999) suggests that it had three meanings prior to this time:

> (1) one of the descendants of the patriarch Judah, i.e. (if in the male line) a member of the tribe of Judah; (2) a native of Judaea, a 'Judaean'; (3) a 'Jew', i.e. a member of Yahweh's chosen people, entitled to participate in those religious ceremonies to which only such members were admitted.

Smith continues that it then took on a political meaning:

> Now appears the new, fourth meaning: (4) a member of the Judaeo–Samaritan–Idumaean–Ituraean–Galilean alliance. These members we shall call 'Ioudaioi ', but we shall use the term often for the non-Judaean members only.
>
> (210)

This suggests that one affiliated with the Judeans became the more usual meaning. As interesting as this discussion is, it does continue to have modern relevance in a discussion of what is Judaism and who is a Jew. For over two thousand years it appears that the delineation between 'of Judah' or 'Judaean' and the religion of what are now termed 'Jews' has been interchangeable. Fast forward to today and the relationship between Judaism and Israel continues in the same way.

This approach to the definition of Judaism in varying terms is reflected in the responses of Jews today. Consider:

> Identity is internal as much as external … My Judaism, my Jewishness, is my religion as much as it is my culture, ethnicity, or something else. Its not the same thing as having rights as a citizen of a country. One can take on an identity without taking a test.
>
> (Hahn Tapper, 2016, 74)

For me it is an ethnicity
Belonging to a community
I think it is almost impossible to summarise it.
A belief in one God, the Jewish peoplehood and putting the values of the Torah into action.

Defining what Judaism means is a problematic endeavour, even among Jews. Ehrlich (2010) has identified that 'Judaism has three essential elements: God, Torah and Israel' (6). The Torah refers to the Law given to Moses and Israel can be seen to be a land but also includes 'an historic political entity, a people, a nation, a belief system, a social group and a culture' (Ehrlich, 2010, 7). Edward Kessler (2006) has also suggested a threefold typology:

> In fact, there is no single definition of Judaism that is acceptable to all Jews. Some maintain that Judaism is solely a religion, others that it is a culture, still others emphasise nationhood and attachment with the Land of Israel.

> (1)

Both Kessler and Ehrlich come at it from different, but complementary perspectives that will form a tension that will be present throughout this book. Ehrlich mainly focuses on beliefs: God, Torah and Israel, whereas Kessler looks at the lived nature of Judaism: religion, culture and nationhood. Indeed, Matt Greene (2020) suggests the difficulties of definition:

> That Jews aren't really a race is an argument beloved by racists and anti-Semites alike, but a rarer, adjacent truth is that Judaism isn't really a religion. You might think it's semantics but I'd argue it's mechanics. Look under the bonnet of most major religions and you'll find a system of beliefs that's at least internally consistent (the clue's in the name: they're faiths). But the engine for Judaism isn't faith. It's doubt. What keeps the vehicle moving isn't the belief that it will but the heat generated from a thousand simultaneous disagreements ... What Judaism essentially amounts to is a four-thousand-year-old argument.

> (15–16)

Indeed, in exploring how Jews categorized themselves in the UK the Institute for Jewish Policy Research (Graham & Boyd, 2024) highlighted 'religious practice and belief, ethical behaviour, cultural engagement, and sense of peoplehood' (31) as the categories that most Jews' responses fell into. This echoed a previous report of theirs that measured Jewishness in the following scales:

- **Frumness**: [The extent to which Jews] are strictly religious or 'frum' (do not travel or switch on lights on Shabbat; keep kosher outside the home; study religious texts)
- **Social religiosity**: [The extent to which Jews] behave religiously in social and familial settings (belong to/attend synagogue; observe Jewish festivals; observe some aspects of Shabbat; consider prayer and God important)

- **Cultural attachment**: [The extent to which Jews] engage in Jewish cultural consumption (read Jewish news sources and websites; buy and support Jewish artistic works)
- **Ethnocentrism**: [The extent to which Jews] feel that Jewishness is about shared destiny (remembering the Holocaust; combating antisemitism; supporting Israel)
- **Moral ideals**: [The extent to which Jews] believe their Jewishness is shaped by values and principles such as social justice; charity; and volunteering (Graham & Boyd, 2016, 37).

Before exploring aspects of beliefs and expressions of faith, this introduction will provide a background in suggesting how Judaism is understood today by the millions of Jews around the world. The difficulty is how to capture the myriad of different approaches to understanding and living Judaism in a book, rather than in experiencing the lived reality of Judaism in the lives of Jews today. This Introductory chapter will try and provide a working definition that embraces the diversity of approaches within Judaism itself.

Children of Abraham

The suggestion above is that a 'Jew' is a descendant of Judah, but in terms of Jewish identity it would seem to be much more correct to define a Jew as someone who is descended from the Patriarch Abraham, and his son Isaac, and his grandson Jacob (later named Israel), it is only then, with one of Jacob's sons Judah that we get to the definition above. Abraham, it is argued, is the 'founder' of Judaism. What does that mean?

Abram (later renamed Abraham) was born about 4,000 years ago in Ur near the Persian Gulf. He grew up to be a wealthy man and began to believe in one God. This change in Abram's life is believed to mark the beginning of the Jewish faith. Abraham believed in the Almighty, the creator of all. Abraham was chosen to enter a covenant (b'rit) with the Almighty (see Genesis 12 and below Chapter 3). Part of the covenant was that Abraham and his descendants would become a great nation. When both Abraham and his wife were very old, they had a son called Isaac – from whom Jews believe they are descended. This means that all the promises given to Abraham's family are given to all Jews. Abraham is the 'Father' or 'Patriarch' of Judaism; his name, Abraham, means 'Father of the nations'. This is only a very brief summary of Abraham's life and the covenant with the Almighty, but at this point it is important to note these 'founding' events. It is through the lineage of Abraham that the people, who would later become known as Jews, and the religion of Judaism would continue.

The identification of lineage as important suggests Judaism as an ethnicity. Judaism is traditionally seen as being matrilineal; that is, the Jewishness of a person is passed on through their mother. Some are beginning to recognize the possibility of patrilineal Jewish descendancy, though the identity of the mother as an indicator of Jewishness is much more common. Indeed, the complexity of matrilineality was the subject of a case brought before the UK Supreme Court in 2009. In this case, a child was denied a place at a Jewish Faith School because they gave priority to those children who met the criteria of being Jewish by the Office of the Chief Rabbi of the United Hebrew Congregation of the Commonwealth (OCR). The UK Supreme Court (2009) outlined:

> The OCR only recognises a person as Jewish if: (i) that person is descended in the matrilineal line from a woman whom the OCR would recognise as Jewish; or (ii) he or she has undertaken a qualifying course of Orthodox conversion.
>
> (1)

The child's father was born Jewish, and the mother was a convert but within the Masorti tradition. As such she was not recognized by the OCR and the school as Jewish, and neither was the child. The Supreme Court decided that this was discrimination based on ethnic origin, and as such was illegal based on the race relations act. The ruling suggests that someone's Jewishness is indeed an ethnicity, rather than solely being within a religious context. Although no such data exists within the UK, in 2013 the Pew Research Center suggested that 'among Jews in the youngest generation of U.S. adults – the Millennials – 68% identify as Jews by religion, while 32% describe themselves as having no religion and identify as Jewish on the basis of ancestry, ethnicity or culture' (8). This seems to be supported in other data from the Institute for Jewish Policy Research (Graham & Boyd, 2024) who outline such data as only 34 per cent of UK Jews believing in God and the Torah.

Ethnic identity thus becomes a central aspect of what it means to be Jewish among those who might be considered to be secular Jews, and also among those for whom religion is an important part of their life and practice. This will be considered throughout this book as a way of exploring the diversity of belief and practice within Judaism.

Note should be taken about the use of ethnicity rather than race in explaining the identifying of Jewishness. There are different reasons that such a categorization should be avoided. The first is that this is the argument that was used by Hitler in trying to establish racial purity of the Aryan nation. The identification of Jews as a race rather than a religion is shown by the categorization of Jehovah's Witnesses as a religion whose adherents could avoid the concentration camps by recanting their faith. Such an option was not available to Jews. The second reason is to do with race being a social construct. Race seems to be determined on the observable and has no justification in genetics, and is no longer seen to be a helpful classification within biology, genetics and maybe society.

This is not the purpose of the current volume, but as an aside it is important to note the difference between ethnicity and race, as they can often be conflated in their understanding. Though this could be contested, a simple contrast would be:

> Ethnicity is similar in concept to race. But while races have often been distinguished on the basis of physical characteristics, especially skin colour, ethnic distinctions generally focus on such cultural characteristics as language, history, religion, and customs. However, physical and cultural characteristics are often conflated in the identification of

racial and ethnic groups. What begins as an ethnic or cultural distinction often becomes racialized, and racial groups are often identified, in the public mind, with reference to customs and behaviour.

(Bulatao & Anderson, 2004, 9)

Ethnicity could therefore be adopted through conversion, and this is evident within Judaism. Though the eradication of race as a category is contested, as it may erode an important part of social discourse. Michael Yudell suggests that 'While we argue phasing out racial terminology in the biological sciences, we also acknowledge that using race as a political or social category to study racism, although filled with lots of challenges, remains necessary given our need to understand how structural inequities and discrimination produce health disparities between groups' (Gannon, 2016).

Returning to the concept of ethnicity and lineage, it is important to note that ancestry within UK Jews is often seen to be linked with geography. More about the different categorizations of ethnicity within Judaism will be developed below, but at this point it is enough to note that the ethnic background of most UK Jews is either Ashkenazi or Sephardi:

The majority of UK Jews (82%) identify as Ashkenazi, with just 5% identifying as Sephardi, 9% as mixed Jewish ethnicity, and 2% 'other'. A small proportion (2%) do not know their Jewish ethnic background.

(Graham & Boyd, 2024, 79)

This results in slight differences in practice but perhaps are seen to be less important than 'denominational' differences, both of which will be explored throughout this book.

The story of the Jews, the descendants of Abraham, from the time of Abraham until today will help provide a background to what might be seen as a contiguous identity, but it is not without its nuance.

History

What ties us together is a story, a story kept in our heads and hearts, a story of suffering and resilience, endurance and creativity … There are two special things about the Jews: that we'd endured for over 3,000 years despite everything that had been thrown at us, and that we had an extraordinarily dramatic story to tell, and that somehow these two things were connected. That we told our story to survive. We are our story.

(Schama, 2014)

The story, or the history of Judaism is important in establishing what it is today, although we have presented Judaism as beginning with Abraham, Martin Goodman (2017) has highlighted different possible beginnings. He suggests, in addition to Abraham, it possibly began with Moses, or 'Centuries later perhaps, with the establishment by Ezra of a Jewish nation focused on the worship of the same God in the Temple in Jerusalem', or even with the almost completion of the Tanakh in the second century BCE. Goodman starts his history in the first century CE in the time of Josephus 'when Judaism was described as a distinctive form of religious life' (xxix).

What is important to note is that whatever is considered the 'beginning', the belief in the relationship with the Almighty has persisted throughout the past four thousand years, the religion of Judaism has gone through various stages and developments in light of circumstances and geography. It will be of interest to note the various historical periods in the development of Judaism over the past four thousand years:

- Ancient Israel and Judah (c. 1200–586 BCE). In exploring this earliest phase of Jewish history, it has various stages beginning with the Patriarchs of the Tanakh, including Abraham, Isaac and Jacob (usually dated slightly earlier at c.2000–1700 BCE). In approximately 1700 BCE tradition suggests that Joseph is sold into slavery into Egypt, and the events of the famine means that his family joins him. A period of slavery soon follows until approximately 1300 BCE (see Chapter 6) when Moses leads the Israelites out of Egypt. The narrative in the Tanakh suggests that in approximately 1240 BCE Joshua conquers Canaan and leads the Israelites into the land. It was around this time in 1204 BCE that 'The first extra-biblical reference to "Israel"' is made and 'comes in the Victory Stele obelisk' (Joffe & Cohn-Sherbok, 2022, 34). The land of Canaan begins to be identified with the people of Israel. Around this time, the time of the Judges' ruling, Israel begins and lasts until approximately 1020 BCE when Saul becomes the first king of Israel. In 1004 BCE David becomes King of Israel, moves his capital to Jerusalem and installs the Ark of the Covenant. He is succeeded by his son, Solomon, who builds the First Temple in approximately 965–928 BCE. In 928 BCE the Kingdom splits into Judah and Israel, and the time of the prophets begins. In 586 BCE, many of the events recorded in the narrative history of the early parts of the Tanakh have taken place, and the Jews are taken into exile in Babylon. The Diaspora becomes established with a community of Jews in Elephantine, Egypt. When Cyrus, King of Persia, defeats the Babylonians, the Jews are able to return to Israel.
- Second Temple period (c. 538 BCE–70 CE). On return to Israel, the Jews rebuild the Temple, hence the Second Temple period where the Temple is the focus of Jewish identity. During this period the Torah is 'finalized', and in the fifth century BCE are the presumed events of the Book of Esther (see Chapter 6) in the Persian Diaspora. In 332 CE Alexander the Great conquers Israel but there is a degree of religious toleration for Jews. There also begins Israel's encounter with Hellenism; one of the significant elements is the Torah being translated into Greek in 285–244 BCE. This is known as the Septuagint. In the third to second centuries BCE the events of Chanukah and the retaking of Jerusalem by the Hasmoneans take place (see Chapter 6). During the second century BCE the Tanakh, outside of the Torah, was recorded. Israel or Judea is captured by the Roman Empire in the first century BCE, and the Sanhedrin becomes the ruling Jewish council. There are different rabbinic groups, such as the Pharisees

and the Sadducees who interpret Jewish law and beliefs. In 70 CE, the Second Temple in Jerusalem is destroyed by the Romans, and the Jews are scattered into the existing Diaspora. The focus of the Temple is removed.

- Rabbinic or Talmudic period (70–640). With the focus of the Temple removed, a Judaism that met the needs of Jews in the Diaspora began to develop building on some aspects of the pre-existing communities. One example is the rabbis who had begun to interpret the laws, and also the place of the synagogue 'a Greek word that means the same as the Hebrew *beit ha-knesset*, or "house of assembly." The first probably arose in Babylonian exile, but it truly developed in Second Temple Palestine, at Caesarea, Capernaum, Dor and Tiberias. Unlike temples, synagogues required no expensive priestly rites. Religious services could be held as long as the Torah and a minyan, or "quorum," of ten adult men were present. Jews throughout the Diaspora copied the model' (Joffe & Cohn-Sherbok, 2022, 77). Prayer replaced the Temple as the primary act of worship within Judaism. Judaism began to be reinterpreted without the Temple, and rabbis became the leaders and teachers of the Jewish community. It was during this time that the Oral Law, the Mishnah, began to be compiled, first by the Tanna'im in the first two centuries CE, then by Yehuda Ha-nasi in the third century (see Chapter 4). The Tanakh reached its current form in the second century, and between the third and fifth centuries the Amora'im, or rabbis of the Talmud recorded the Talmud, which was mainly completed by 485 CE (the Babylonian Talmud). In the fifth century the Jerusalem Talmud is outlined, with the various aspects being finalized in the sixth and seventh centuries in Persia by the savora'im. Although referring to the time of the pre-eminence of the rabbis in leadership, perhaps this period is considered rabbinic because of the codification of the Oral Law (see Chapter 4) and the establishment of rabbinic tradition and precedent.
- Middle Ages (640–1492). It is more correct to say that the rabbinic period continues throughout the rest of the historical periods of Judaism, as the authority of the rabbis is still in evidence. In the period from the seventh to the fifteenth century Judaism enters the Geonim and Rishonim rabbinic periods. During this time the Byzantine Empire was conquered by the Islamic Empire under Omar in 638 BCE. During this period there were times of peace and also times of migration. In the earlier period some Jews migrated from the Middle East to Europe because of the rise of Islam, but at the same time there was also what is known as the golden age of Jewish culture in Muslim-ruled Spain, from 711 CE to 1492 CE. There were also persecutions and expulsions (see Chapter 5).
- Early Modern period (1492–1750). In the late fifteenth and sixteenth centuries the Acharonim period of rabbinic Judaism begins, and the publication of Shulchan Arukh, a code of Jewish Law. The period begins with the expulsion of the Jews from Spain. Throughout this period different traditions within Judaism develop. For example, upon their expulsion from Spain Sephardi Jews spread into the Balkans, the Eastern

Mediterranean and North Africa, while Ashkenazi Jewish communities spread and develop in Eastern Europe especially in places like Prague and Poland.

- Modern period (1750–present). In the eighteenth century there was the Haskalah or Jewish Enlightenment which perhaps served as a bridge with the modern period of Judaism where modern practices were adopted, perhaps exemplified by modern over traditional dress. Elements of the primacy of the rabbis in the modern period were challenged with elements of rationality being seen to be more applicable. During this time Chassidism developed in the eighteenth century with its founder Israel be Eliezer. It was perhaps a reaction against the uncertainty of modernism and the vacuum of leadership. It was also during this time that Zionism developed and the desire for a homeland. Out of Haskalah, Reform Judaism developed in Germany, the UK and the United States in the early nineteenth century. Other events in this period include the Shoah (see Chapter 5) and the establishment of the state of Israel in 1948.

Each of these phases in the development of Judaism contributes to Jewish identity today, whether it is the narrative history of the Tanakh that provides the foundation, or the Second Temple that provides a focus in Jerusalem and wider Israel, or the rabbinic periods on which modern Judaism draws so heavily. Judaism today is thus the inheritor of this history and is not the same as that practised by Abraham, nor is it the same as the Judaism of the Second Temple. Rather it has developed into a way of life practised by millions of Jews around the world. An understanding of the history and developments throughout the past 4,000 years is important in understanding what it is to be Jewish today.

A chosen people

In outlining the place of Israel as one of the three basic concepts within Judaism Louis Jacobs (1995) suggests that 'in this context [Israel] refers to the Jewish people, known as the children of Israel … The name Israel for the State of Israel has, of course, a different connotation and was coined only when the State was established' (2). Though it is possible to suggest that in today's lexicon the two have become synonymous. As is evident from the discussion of Abraham and his descendants in the previous section Diaspora Jews see themselves as being of Israel, however that is understood. Being of Israel is linked inextricably with the covenant (see Chapter 3) and the idea of being the Almighty's chosen people. The exact meaning and interpretation of the term 'chosen people' will be explored in Chapter 3, but in relation to this introduction the phrase helps understand Judaism as the religion of the Jews. The inheritors of the traditions that have developed throughout history (see above), Judaism was first and foremost a way of understanding how to live in relation to the Almighty. There have been different foci and interpretations throughout the centuries, but the belief in absolute monotheism has remained; indeed, George Robinson (2000) highlights this transition. They were once a 'tribe, a band of nomads … But the Jews became something more. They were the bearers of a radical new concept, ethical monotheism, and the concept became the basis for a new kind of religion, Judaism. The latter was a religion marked by a new relationship between people and Deity' (7). This will be explored in much greater detail, but for now, the recognition that Judaism is primarily a religion is sufficient to note.

The Institute for Jewish Policy Research identified different traditions/groups within Judaism in the UK. They outlined:

> The proportions of Jews who self-identify as Haredi or Orthodox (19%), Reform or Progressive (18%), and non-practising (i.e. secular or cultural) (19%) are very similar; a further 27% self-identifies as 'Traditional'.
>
> (Graham & Boyd, 2024, 7)

Though in the same report, the authors use the classification of synagogues to identify different strands: Central Orthodox, Liberal, Masorti, Reform, Sephardi, Strictly Orthodox and Reform (Graham & Boyd, 2024, 117). Indeed, elsewhere I have suggested a different breakdown of traditions within Judaism (Holt, 2022):

- **Orthodox**. Orthodox is an umbrella term for traditions and influences. This 'began in the late eighteenth/early nineteenth century in Europe as a reaction against some reforming tendencies within Judaism' (306). The categorization of Orthodox on the basis of ethnicity can be misleading. Though as already indicated Ashkenazi have their roots in Eastern Europe, Sephardi have their roots in Spain and the Iberian Peninsula, and Mizrahi who are descendants of Jews who stayed in the Levant and the Middle East is one way of categorizing Orthodox Jews, but there is much more to the diversity than background.
- **Reform:** 'Reform Judaism generally teaches that the beliefs and practices of Judaism should be updated for the modern world' (Holt, 2022, 306). Again, this term is an umbrella term for many different expressions of Judaism. For some, it might be termed Progressive Judaism.
- **Conservative/Masorti Judaism**: 'Modern Conservative Judaism is mainly to be found in the USA, but there are elements and influences to be found in Britain. It has its roots in Europe in the late eighteenth century. While the modern Reform and Orthodox movements were developing, an expression of Ashkenazi Judaism arose that at a very basic level offers a middle way between them both' (Holt, 2022, 306–7).
- **Kabbalah**: 'Kabbalah is a school of Jewish mysticism that began nearly 2,000 years ago. Kabbalah was textualised in the Yalkut Re'uveni by Reuben Hoeshke in 1660, but is not restricted to an esoteric group. Aspects of Kabbalah can be seen in prayer books, popular customs and ethics in the different expressions of Judaism' (307).

Each of these expressions is in many ways an umbrella term and they will be explored in greater detail in Chapter 8. It is sufficient at this point to recognize that, as with the definition of the term 'Jew' more widely, even within the religion of Hinduism there are many differences. It might appear that there is a diversity of approach to the categorization of Jewish groups. In some ways, however, the categorization is secondary to the importance of Jewish identity. People may practise and emphasize in different ways, which will be explored throughout this book, but their identity as Jews might be seen to eradicate illusions of difference. This is perhaps too simplistic an approach, and indeed the messiness of religion and levels of observance within Judaism is evident in what is termed above as frumness. There will be groups who reject the practice of others, though important to note is that they do so in the context of their Jewishness.

Thoughts for the classroom

The diversity of Jewish experience must be recognized and emphasized when Judaism is taught. In the GCSE specifications it can sometimes be interpreted that within Judaism there are the two (almost) opposing camps of Orthodox and Reform, which is not true in and of itself with there being many more traditions than two. For those who are unfamiliar with lived Judaism this is a useful shorthand to help the pupils understand Judaism. It can almost be interpreted as Orthodox = Religious and Reform = Less religious. The falsity of such an approach was highlighted to some teachers when visiting two shuls in one day. One was Reform and one Ashkenazi Orthodox. At the end of the day, the teachers reflected that had they not been told which was which they would have assumed the opposite. All their knowledge about Judaism had been challenged in the space of a few hours. The Rabbi in the Orthodox synagogue seemed far more 'liberal' and willing to see some of challenges of Judaism. The lady in the Reform synagogue seemed far more 'hung up' on the detail and the requirements of the Law. It also challenged them when they discovered there are Bat mitzvahs within forms of Orthodox Judaism. The only thing they seemed to be able to hang onto was the separation of men and women in the shul. Following this they were able to discuss their experience and realize that all of their assumptions they based on their school experiences should be challenged, and it wasn't as clear cut as their teachers had tried to make it. The difference in Judaism seems to be less about Orthodox and Reform, and more about levels of observance or frumness. It helps teachers understand that the continuum that we have constructed of Orthodox and Reform is not as clear and delineated as is sometimes suggested.

Within Judaism there are many types of diversity. It is important to explore the diversity in the backgrounds of Jews around the world, including ethnicities, nationality, gender and sexuality. Sometimes because of the way that Judaism is taught and represented in text and images the impression can be given of stereotypes of Jews in terms of the way that they look and dress. This is across Judaism and within various traditions. One UK-based non-Jew describes learning about his Jewish friend Jeremy:

> I had known Jeremy for a few years, and I assumed he was a Reform Jew. He dressed like I did in an open shirt and trousers, or sometimes a jeans and hoodie his haircut and facial hair was not dissimilar to my own which essentially depends on mood and enthusiasm to shave. One day he commented on something, and I responded with 'But, I thought you were a Reform Jew'. His response was, 'No, I am Sephardi Orthodox'. My ignorance shone through as I asked him why he did not dress in a dark suit, etc; indeed, the only observable indicator was his kippah. His response was along the lines of, 'Because I don't follow Eastern European fashion of the nineteenth century'.

There are many things that can be unpacked from this statement; not least the assumption that Jews are a homogenous group who look and dress the same. The diversity of Judaism is thus expressed in terms of belief, ethnicity and practice. To fully represent this diversity the images and voices that are represented in the classroom must be inclusive, only then can students hope to understand the richness and diversity of Judaism as a globally lived religion.

One of the most interesting aspects in the study of religion and worldviews is the relationship between religion and culture. Speaking of a different context Christopher Gasson (2025) suggests that 'Religion and culture are deeply intertwined. For centuries it was a symbiotic relationship: religion reinforced culture and culture reinforced religion. Today it is becoming a destructive relationship' (2). The first aspect is true of Judaism: religion, culture and identity have been impossible to separate, they have formed a perfect symbiosis, and to remove one from an understanding of who a Jew is would be folly. The teacher of Judaism as a religion and worldviews must be prepared to explore all aspects of who a Jew is to fully represent Judaism today.

One other consideration when teaching Judaism is that while the understanding that each of the historical periods is contiguous with the others and an understanding of Jewish history is central to understanding Judaism today, there is an associated danger. It would be erroneous to teach historical Judaism as the way that Judaism is lived today. While that may seem an obvious point to make, it should be noted that one of the concerns in teaching Judaism in schools is the temptation for teachers to teach it through a Christian lens, which in terms of history manifests itself in the teaching of a Second Temple Judaism. Judaism has come a long way, not least 2000 years since Second Temple Judaism and it would be wrong to assume the nature of the religion and of Jewish identity has stayed the same. At various points throughout this book certain elements will be highlighted that illustrate this point. For example, in the teaching about the messiah (see Chapter 3) the 'shared' beliefs of Judaism and Christianity are not really shared at all. The teacher who tries to teach Judaism to help understand Christianity is doing the lived reality of Judaism a disservice. The problem is that for many teachers in the UK their first encounter with Judaism is through its shared stories, which are often taught within a Christian context. The teacher of Judaism must be clear that Judaism is the religion of Jews, and everything that is believed and practised is done so on their own terms.

Part 1

Key Concepts in Judaism

Chapter 1

The Nature of the Almighty

Hear, O Israel! The LORD is our God, the LORD alone. You shall love the LORD your God with all your heart and with all your soul and with all your might.

(Deuteronomy 6:4-5)

Speaking of the Almighty

The Shema outlines one of the foundational principles of Judaism, that of the uniqueness and singularity of the Almighty. The various translations of the Shema into English highlight one of the challenges that people studying and teaching Judaism may face. In the 1917 JPS translation we read that 'The LORD is One', and then in the Revised JPS (2023) 'The ETERNAL is our God, the ETERNAL alone'. How do we speak of the Almighty in a way that is both respectful and understandable? The most straightforward approach, and that taken throughout this book, is to speak of the Almighty in the way that Jews would. It should be noted that the word 'LORD' in the first recitation of the Shema above is a translation of the Hebrew YHWH, the name of the Almighty that is the Tetragrammaton (four-lettered) revealed to Moses at the burning bush. Having received his instruction to free the Israelites from the bondage in Egypt, Moses asks:

Moses said to God, 'When I come to the Israelites and say to them, "The God of your fathers has sent me to you," and they ask me, "What is His name?" what shall I say to them?' And God said to Moses, 'Ehyeh-Asher-Ehyeh.' [Meaning of Heb. uncertain; variously translated: 'I Am That I Am'; 'I Am Who I Am'; 'I Will Be What I Will Be'; etc.] He continued, 'Thus shall you say to the Israelites, "Ehyeh [Others 'I Am' or 'I Will Be.'] sent me to you'".

(Exodus 3:13-14)

Thus, the name of the Almighty is represented by the four Hebrew letters yodh, he, waw and he. The name of the Almighty is thus considered to be treated with deference as commanded in the Ten Commandments: 'You shall not [Others "take in vain".] swear falsely by-b the name of the LORD your God; for the LORD will not clear one who swears falsely by His name' (Exodus 20:7), for the Almighty's name is above all:

> O LORD, our Lord,
> How majestic is Your name throughout the earth,
> You who have covered the heavens with Your splendor!
>
> (Psalm 8:2)

The holiness of YHWH as the name of the Almighty means that while it can be written, it should never be spoken. Thus, the translation into LORD, so that when people read, they do not repeat the name.

There are, therefore, substitutions or alternative names of the Almighty are used throughout Judaism. These will be briefly mentioned here and then explored in greater detail as appropriate when discussing the characteristics of the Almighty below. These names include, but are not limited to:

- *El, Eloha, Elohim* variously translated as God possibly with the root 'el' meaning powerful.
- *El Olam* God, the everlasting
- *El Berit* God of the covenant
- *Adonai* usually translated as Lord, meaning that the Almighty is the Lord of everything.
- *Shaddai* usually translated as Almighty, sometimes El Shaddai. It is the name by which the Almighty appears to Abraham and Jacob: 'I appeared to Abraham, Isaac, and Jacob as El Shaddai, but I did not make Myself known to them by My name [LORD]' (Exodus 6:3).
- *Ha-kodash Barukh hu* 'The Holy One. Blessed be He'
- *En-Sof* The Infinite
- *Tsur Yisrael* Rock of Israel
- *Melekh Malkhe Melakhim* Supreme King of Kings

There are, however, further restrictions on the use of certain names of the Almighty. The Talmud suggests that certain names can be written but not erased, being interpreted by some to mean that they can be written but not vocalized. The Talmud suggests that these names are:

> There are names of God that may be erased and there are names of God that may not be erased due to their inherent sanctity. These are names that may not be erased: For example, several variations of the name God [Elohim]: El, Elohekha with a second person singular suffix, Elohim, Eloheikhem with a second person plural suffix; I Shall Be As I Shall Be, alef dalet, yod heh, Almighty [Shaddai], Lord of Hosts [Tzevaot], these names may not be erased … But adjectives that describe the Holy One, Blessed be He, e.g., the Great, the Mighty, the Awesome, the Prodigious, the Powerful, the Courageous, the Strong, gracious, compassionate, slow to anger, or abounding in loving-kindness; these may be erased. Apparently, gracious and compassionate are adjectives and not actual names of God.
>
> (Shevuot 35a)

There are some 'Orthodox Jews, however [who] have substituted various names such as *Elokim* for Elohim and *Ha-Shem* ("the Name") or *Adoshem* for Adonai because they believe that there are restrictions on the pronunciation of all of God's names' (Wigoder, 2002, 307). Indeed, if one watches shows such as *Shtisel*, the most common word used to refer to the Almighty is Hashem. This prohibition on certain names has also led some to use the written form G-d in translating such names into English. This is also the tendency in many classrooms and textbooks when speaking of the Almighty in Judaism. One Jew has suggested that he believes this is going too far:

> God is not the name of the Almighty. It has been translated and is therefore not a name in the same way as those prescribed in the Talmud. There is no restriction on its use.

As has been noted the approach of this book is to try and use the Almighty as a characteristic to normally refer to God, but it is against the background of this discussion. Those who use G-d do so in a way that is trying to be respectful to all Jews and also begin the discussion about the sanctity of the names of the Almighty, and how they should not be used lightly and without thought.

Absolute Monotheism

In outlining the fundamental principles of Judaism the twelfth-century rabbi and philosopher, Maimonides focused mainly on the qualities of the Creator. Indeed, the first two of his principles explored in his commentary on Mishnah Sanhedrin outline qualities of the Almighty that refer to an absolute monotheism. Outlining the second principle first, we read:

> The second principle The unity of God, may He be blessed, which is to say that we believe that He who is the cause of everything is one. And He is not like one of a pair and not like one of a group and not like one person that can be divided into many [smaller] units and not like a simple body which is numerically one [but] can be infinitely divided. Rather He – God, may He be blessed – is one in a unity that has no unity like it. And this is the second principle, [and] it is indicated by that which is stated, 'Listen Israel, the Lord is our God, the Lord is one'.
>
> (Maimonides, n.d 10:1)

This refers to the Shema and its exploration of the Almighty as one. What does this mean in the context of this first principle? Essentially, the Almighty cannot be divided and there is no other being anything like him.[1] The Almighty is singular and unique. This is the way that Jews will read the Tanakh and interpret the reference to other deities such as Baal. These

---

[1]Using the words 'he' and 'him' should not be used to gender the Almighty. Within Judaism, the Almighty is beyond such descriptions or anthropomorphic qualities, but the restriction of language and the inheritance of tradition mean that such gendered language will be used occasionally.

so-called deities are not and cannot ever be seen to be 'God' or any aspect of him. This can be seen also in the identification of the Almighty in the burning bush as Ehyeh-Asher-Ehyeh. The Almighty is 'I am', he is not to be ascribed with the appellations of humanity, the Almighty is the Almighty, nothing else is like him.

The response has suggested to some that Moses before, and perhaps after, his experience at the burning bush was a henotheist rather than a monotheist. Henotheism is the worship of one god which does not deny the possibility of the existence of other gods. In terms of the Almighty this deity is the supreme deity, and while other minor deities may exist, they are not on a par with him, and as such are not worthy of worship. For some Jews this may seem beyond the pale, as tradition and modern thinking may suggest that the traditional understanding of the Almighty was revealed all at once rather than one where the understanding of his monotheistic nature developed over time as 'superstition' and the existence of other gods was eroded from people's understanding and practice. This henotheism may have purely been the transition period as people adjusted from a belief in the existence of many gods to a belief in the one.

Elements of this are reflected in an experience found in Genesis 35 where Jacob's household, having previously accepted the God of Abraham as the god whom they worshipped, were asked to put away their idols and their foreign gods. This suggests that some, if not all of Jacob's family, were able to persist in the existence of other gods while recognizing the Almighty as pre-eminent God. Over time, this henotheism, if it ever existed, developed into monotheism that is found throughout Judaism.

The second principle of the unity and singularity of the Almighty is developed further by the first principle of Maimonides:

> The first principle To believe in the existence of the Creator, may He be blessed, and that is that there is a Being complete in all the ways of existence. He is the cause of the existence of all other things in existence. Through Him does their existence survive and from Him is their survival. And one cannot imagine the lack of His existence, since in the lack of His existence, the existence of all things dissolves and no thing's existence would survive. And if we were to imagine the lack of all other things in existence besides Him, the existence of God, may He be blessed, would not dissolve and not be diminished. Unity and Mastery only belong to God, may His name be blessed, since He suffices in His [own] existence. It is enough for Him to be by Himself and He doesn't need the existence of anything else. And everything besides Him of the angels and the bodies of the planets and what is in them and what is below them – all need Him for their existence. And this is the first principle, [and] it is indicated by the 'first commandment' – 'I am the Lord, your God' (Exodus 20:2).

> (Maimonides, n.d 10:1)

In outlining aspects of the nature of the Almighty, Maimonides again reiterates uniqueness as one of the main qualities. In reading this description, one might be tempted to liken this description to that found in the philosophy of religion of a 'necessary being'. Indeed, a being who is the cause of other all things that exist and is a 'Being complete in all ways of existence' seems to meet the criteria of 'necessary'. However, care should be taken to utilize philosophy in trying to understand the nature of the Almighty. Jonathan Sacks (2011) outlines that Maimonides, as a person of his time, was enamoured of Greek philosophy, but that we should not read these inferences into his descriptions of the Almighty. Rather than experiencing the Almighty through philosophy, Jews encounter him in relation to his creation. Sacks suggests that his search for God has been 'in people – people who in themselves seemed to point to something or someone beyond themselves' (89). With the Almighty being unique, eternal and one, Jews can find him in relationship with others, 'the belief in monotheism establishes not only that there is one God but also that mankind [*sic*] is a unity in a unified world' (Wigoder, 2002, 547):

> People within the Abrahamic monotheisms have always known that for most of us, most of the time, God, more infinite than the universe, older and younger than time, cannot be known directly. He is known mainly through his effects, and of these the most important is his effect on human lives … Over the years I have learned to find it so much more widely, in communities that care, in the kindness of strangers, in people who touch our lives, perhaps only momentarily, doing the deed or saying the word that carries us to safety across the abyss of loneliness or self-doubt.
>
> (Sacks, 2011, 92)

It could also be suggested that the Almighty, as well as being experienced in relationship with others, is also found in relationship with creation and with history. As such an exploration of the Almighty in relation to all aspects of his creation enables Jews to experience who the Almighty is, for as Clive Lawton has suggested, 'The Jewish God has a personality and will, and is never just a "life force" or inexorable power' (2016, 12). This will lead naturally to an exploration of some of the characteristics of the Almighty, which will, in some ways, be a reflection of how Jews strive to live their lives. As one Jew has suggested, the focus is not on worship of the Almighty, but on the living of the faith:

> I like the idea of a God who gives a choice between the right and wrong path. The fact that we don't see God for me puts a focus more on ourselves and what we can do to repair the damaged world, rather than adoration of a deity.

Care should be taken, however, in ascribing the characteristics of humanity to the Almighty. The Almighty is ultimately transcendent and unknowable, but humans can ascribe to the Almighty's actions qualities that can be seen to reflect human action but are much more so. The idea that the Almighty's anger is the same as humanity's would be seen to be an inadequate assertion. The Almighty's response of the making of the golden calf at Sinai is an ascribing of the actions that humans would see as anger: 'Now, let Me be, that My anger may blaze forth against them and that I may destroy them, and make of you a great nation' (Exodus 32:10). Rather the motives of the Almighty are unknown and cannot adequately be described by the narrow constraints of language. A person can see the effects and ascribe characteristics but it should also be borne in mind that these are imperfect. They 'are understood as linguistic metaphors; otherwise, it would be impossible to talk about God at all' (Kessler, 2007, 44).

The Almighty as Creator

Throughout Maimonides' Thirteen Principles the Almighty is always referred to as Creator, perhaps highlighting its centrality within Judaism. Aspects of the Almighty as Creator have been explored in the above discussion of monotheism. The prayer Adon Olam highlights the Almighty as Creator:

> Master of the Universe Who reigned
> before any creature was created.
> At the time when all was made by His will,
> then was His Name proclaimed King.
> And after all things shall cease to be
> the Awesome One will reign alone.
> He was, He is,
> and He shall be in glory.

(Davis, 1981)

Entwined with the Almighty as Creator is his nature as Eternal. The Almighty is the only being who is eternal, his characteristics are eternal, and he is the first and the last, without beginning or end.

The Almighty as Father

The ascribing of the name of the Almighty as 'Father' is central to Judaism and an outworking of the belief of him being Creator. This suggests that the focus is on individual humans as creations of the Almighty, and by extension understand this relationship as a father to a child. This is taught throughout the Tanakh, including in reference to David:

> Let me tell of the decree:
> the LORD said to me,
> 'You are My son,
> I have fathered you this day'.

(Psalm 2:7, see also Psalm 89:27)

This is further seen in *Mishnah Sotah* 9 where the same question is asked three times, with a repeated answer:

> Upon whom is there for us to rely? Only upon our Father in Heaven.

Within the fatherhood of the Almighty there are two aspects that are expressed for Jews: compassion and correction. The love and compassion that the Almighty has for his people are evident throughout the Tanakh and Jewish history. One evocative passage from Hosea illustrates this love:

> I fell in love with Israel[2]
> When he was still a child;
> And I have called [him] My son
> Ever since Egypt.
> I have pampered Ephraim,
> Taking them in My arms …
> I drew them with human ties,
> With cords of love.
>
> (11: 1, 3-4)

So much does the Almighty love his people that when they turn from him, and when they suffer, he cries:

> For if you will not give heed,
> My inmost self must weep,
> Because of your arrogance;
> My eye must stream and flow
> With copious tears,
> Because the flock of the LORD
> Is taken captive.
>
> (Jeremiah 13:17)

Some Jews use these passages to refer to the Fatherhood of the Almighty in relationship to his people, Israel, rather than to humanity as a whole:

> The fact is, however, that this formulation is modern and highly apologetical. There is much discussion on the whole question of universalism and particularism in Judaism but this particular formulation finds no support in the Jewish sources. The Bible does not speak directly anywhere of God as Father but the idea is found by implication in the verse: 'Ye are the children of the Lord your God (Deuteronomy 14:1)'. Since 'ye' are His children it follows that He is 'your' Father. But the 'ye' in the verse refers to the people of Israel. The intimate relationship described in father-children terms is reserved for God's relationship to Israel, not for mankind as a whole.
>
> (Jacobs, 1995, 164)

Whether it is communal as Israel, or with all of humanity, this relationship with the Almighty is of comfort to Jews today should they choose to focus on it. While it is a part of prayer

---

[2] It is of note that while Israel today refers to the land of Israel, it is more often used as a name for the people of Israel, and therefore all Jews throughout history and today. In this book unless the 'land of' is appended, Israel refers to the people.

many Jews will continue a focus on how to live, rather than a relationship. Understanding the personal nature of the Almighty as Father might also lead some Jews to push the boundaries of the relationship. One famous example is of Elie Wiesel, who was angry with the Almighty. In an interview in 2003, he highlighted the importance of this reciprocal relationship:

> Some people who read my first book, *Night*, they were convinced that I broke with the faith and broke with God. Not at all. I never divorced God. It is because I believed in God that I was angry at God, and still am. But my faith is tested, wounded, but it's here. So whatever I say, it's always from inside faith, even when I speak the way occasionally I do about the problems I had, questions I had. Within my traditions, you know, it is permitted to question God, even to take Him to task.

> (Tippett, 2003)

Indeed, this 'anger' and questioning of the Almighty found greater expression in a subsequent book *The Trial of God* where in response to pogroms in medieval Europe God is put on trial (Wiesel, 1995).

Alongside the Almighty's compassion and his weeping with humanity/Israel (explored further in Chapter 5) is also a father's role as disciplinarian. The Tanakh teaches the importance of boundaries that the Almighty as Father sets for his children:

> Bear in mind that the LORD your God disciplines you just as a man disciplines his son.

> (Deuteronomy 8:5)

> I will be a father to him, and he shall be a son to Me. When he does wrong, I will chastise him with the rod of men and the affliction of mortals; but I will never withdraw My favour from him.

> (II Samuel 7:14-15)

As indicated earlier, this focus on a personal relationship with the Almighty might be rejected by some Jews, either because it is out of step with thinkers such as Maimonides, or the seeming unimportance of the Divine in motivation to follow the mitzvot. Indeed, in answering the question 'Which comes closest to your view of God? God is a person with whom people can have a relationship or God is an impersonal force?' only 25% of Jews answered a personal God, with 50% an impersonal and a further 10% not believing in God (Pew Forum on Religion & Public Life, 2008, 164).

Shechinah

The focus on the Almighty as Father could be seen to reinforce a traditional view of an androcentrism. This is somewhat ameliorated by an exploration of shechinah, which is seen by some to be a manifestation of the Divine feminine. Clive Lawton (2016) has suggested that a focus on the shechinah is odd in the development of the teaching of Judaism at GCSE:

> Picking out the Shechinah as a special topic, and the one particular aspect of God for study here, is an idiosyncratic choice that does not reflect the way most Jews would articulate their religion or understanding of God. However, an academic analysis of Jewish sources might be justified in identifying the idea of the Shechinah as an important, but unconscious development in Jewish theological problem solving: 'How can God be universal, and yet be present in a manner that allows for relationship?'.
>
> (15)

This seems to be echoed in discussion of the importance of shechinah with two Jews:

> To the extent that [shechinah] reminds us that there are numerous ways of seeing God, I think it is helpful, much in the same way that any other expression of the divine (e.g. Avinu Malkenu or Ein Sof) can achieve the same thing. But I am not sure that it is important compared to, say, the teachings on ethics. [I'm] mystified why it's on the curriculum. I never heard it growing up at all.

Believing in the Almighty, Jews balance the seeming contradiction of immanence and transcendence. How is the Almighty intimately present in every person's life? It is through the Divine Presence; this is developed further in the concept of Malkuth with Kabbalah (see below). Jews would be able to point to various events that evidence this intimate involvement such as the covenant with Abraham (see Chapter 3), the freeing of the Israelites from Egypt and the subsequent Exodus (see Chapter 6), and the events of Purim (see Chapter 6). The Divine Presence is often represented by a pillar of fire seen in the burning bush, or the guiding of the Israelites in the Exodus, and in the menorah of the Temple, and the ner Tamid in the synagogue.

There are many ways in which the shechinah can be found in a person's life. The Talmud teaches of different occasions when a person can experience the Divine Presence, such as studying Torah:

> Rabbi Halafta of Kefar Hanania said: when ten sit together and occupy themselves with Torah, the Shechinah abides among them, as it is said: 'God stands in the congregation of God' (Psalm 82:1). How do we know that the same is true even of five? As it is said: 'This band of His He has established on earth' (Amos 9:6). How do we know that the same is true even of three? As it is said: 'In the midst of the judges He judges' (Psalm 82:1) How do we know that the same is true even of two? As it is said: 'Then they that fear the Lord spoke one with another, and the Lord hearkened, and heard' (Malachi 3:16). How do we know that the same is true even of one? As it is said: 'In every place where I cause my name to be mentioned I will come unto you and bless you' (Exodus 20:21).
>
> (Pirkei Avot 3:6)

Or praying:

> The Divine Presence dwells in any place where there are ten adult male Jews.
>
> (Talmud Sanhedrin 39a)

In a Beth Din:

> Three who sit in judgment, the Divine Presence is with them.
>
> (Talmud Berachot 6a)

In many other places and circumstances:

> The Divine Presence is above the head of the sick person, as it is stated: 'God will support him on the bed of illness'.
>
> (Talmud Shabbat 12b)

> Come and see how beloved the Jewish people are before the Holy One, Blessed be He. As every place they were exiled, the Divine Presence went with them.
>
> (Talmud Megillah 29a)

> The praise of joy mentioned here is to teach you that the Divine Presence rests upon an individual neither from an atmosphere of sadness, nor from an atmosphere of laziness, nor from an atmosphere of laughter, nor from an atmosphere of frivolity, nor from an atmosphere of idle conversation, nor from an atmosphere of idle chatter, but rather from an atmosphere imbued with the joy of a mitzva.
>
> (Tractate Shabbat 30b)

Essentially there is no place where the Almighty is not. This gives Jews strength to know that no matter how low a person gets there is always hope.

The Almighty as Merciful

El Malei Rachamim (Merciful God or God, full of mercy) is a prayer that is offered at the burial of a person and highlights the centrality of the mercy and compassion as characteristics of the Almighty within Judaism. Bradley Artson (2002) outlines the motherly nature of the Almighty suggesting that rachamim is:

> a kind of love that comes from the word rechem, a womb. It is a mothering love, and we even affirm that mother-love is so important that the Talmud refers to God as Rachamana, the womb-like one who births new worlds.

It has been argued that this aspect of the Almighty – his love – is often overlooked by observers of Judaism, and even by some Jews themselves.

> I often hear people say that Judaism is a religion of law but not of love. They claim that it is more about fearing God and feeling guilty rather than loving God and feeling joy. They

conclude that it leads us to a life of weakness and submission ... Judaism is quite the opposite of these misconceptions. Judaism is the true religion of love. It is founded upon love and its purpose is love.

(Aaron, 2015, 3–4)

Indeed, it is the religion of love because 'the mysterious oneness of God is love' (Aaron, 2015, 11). This love, compassion and mercy are central to understanding the nature of the Almighty in Judaism. It is why throughout history and the Tanakh a loving relationship can be found. It is no coincidence that the story of Hosea, whether true or metaphorical, highlights the compassion, mercy and loyalty of the Almighty to his people, as a husband to an unfaithful wife as explored in a discussion of the Almighty as Father, with the conclusion

> But I seemed to them as one
> Who imposed a yoke on their jaws,
> Though I was offering them food ...
> I will heal their affliction,
> Generously will I take them back in love.

(Hosea 11:1, 4; 14:5)

Much more of the compassion and love of the Almighty will be explored in Chapters 2 and 3, but it is important to note that this love and compassion are intertwined with every other characteristic of the Almighty. The Fatherhood of the Almighty is an expression of his love, as is his role of Creator, and other aspects explored in this chapter. This love also helps humanity understand their relationship to, and standing before, the Almighty.

The Almighty as Lawgiver

In some ways, exploring the role of the Almighty as Lawgiver immediately following the assertion that the Almighty is love highlights the complementary nature of the Almighty as Father. On the one hand, the Father is compassionate and on the other he gives the law. These two aspects of the Almighty are present within the Abrahamic covenant; on the one hand there are the conditions of the covenant (brit) and on the other the infinite love of the Almighty (chesed) (see Chapter 3). If one aspect is emphasized it leads to a skewed view of the Almighty, and of the Covenant. Too far one way and a legalistic view of the Almighty is adopted, while too far the other way and love means that a person can do what they want. While, as suggested above the role of the Almighty as Lawgiver might be overemphasized by observers, or even by Jews themselves, it is nevertheless the case that he is the source of the Law, and as such has set boundaries for the ways Jews live, and the positive and negative consequences of such.

> For the LORD is our Judge, The LORD is our Lawgiver, The LORD is our King; He will save us.

(Isaiah 33:22 JPS 1917)

Through creation the Almighty 'establishes principles, laws, boundaries and borders' (Aaron, 2015, 19). This Law and these laws were revealed at Sinai to Moses (see Chapter 4). As such, he is of the source of the Written Law found in the Torah, and also the Oral Law which, it is believed by many, were both given to Moses at Sinai, the Written is recorded in the Torah, while the Oral Law was passed on by word of mouth and was eventually recorded in the Mishnah and Gemara, together forming the Talmud (see Chapter 4). Recalling the Introduction to this book, one of the pillars of Judaism is seen to be the Law/Torah. These laws revealed by the Almighty have persisted throughout the ages and form the basis of Jewish living in today's world. Thus, the importance of the Almighty as lawgiver is central to understanding the lived reality of Judaism today, in concert with the other characteristics and roles of the Almighty.

A corollary to this belief is the role of the Almighty as Judge; as the source of the Law he exercises judgement according to that same Law. In assigning him this role it perhaps conjures up the image of a harsh schoolmaster and a punitive judge. Though there is value within Judaism to this perspective, and if a binary afterlife is a thing (see Chapter 2) then the Almighty will separate people and assign them to their place of reward or punishment, this view of the Almighty as Judge can miss some of the nuance of the Almighty as Judge for Jews today. Considering The Almighty's judgement on Rosh Hashanah, David Aaron (2006) suggests that his role as judge is corrective and more focused on this life:

> [I]t is a compassionate evaluation of what we have done and how we have used our potential that year. From this, He determines what measures must be taken to get us back on track to fulfil our potential. If God makes a judgment at all, He makes it with tremendous respect and love for us; with enormous sensitivity and consideration for the challenges He has given us.

There may seem to be a contradiction between the Almighty as Judge and as Merciful in the sense that they seem incompatible. Indeed, in the *Bereshit Rabbah*, Abraham questions the Almighty:

> Rabbi Levi said: 'Shall the Judge of all the earth not practice justice?' (Genesis 18:25) – [Abraham argued] 'If You wish to have a world, there can be no strict justice, and if you wish strict justice, there can be no world. But you seek to hold the rope at both ends; You wish [to have] a world and You wish [to have] strict justice. Choose one of them. And if You do not ease up a bit, the world will be unable to endure.' The Holy One blessed be He said to Abraham: 'You love righteousness and abhor wickedness'.

> (39:6)

This has perhaps led to the focus on one at the expense of the other. Jews, however, believe both of the Almighty, and his role in terms of both mercy and justice lie at the heart of a relationship with the Almighty.

In tandem with the Almighty's role as Lawgiver and as Judge is the belief that he is Just. Psalms 89:15 teaches:

Righteousness and justice are the base of Your throne; steadfast love and faithfulness stand before You.

Again, in Deuteronomy:

Yea, all His ways are just; A faithful God, never false, True and upright is He.

(Deuteronomy 32:4)

Although a person can look at the world and see apparent injustice in legal systems, and even perhaps in the struggles and triumphs that people have, for Jews the constant is the belief that the Almighty is Just, and that all apparent injustice is temporary or in the eyes of the beholder. Jews believe that justice is not something that just happens, or something that is external to the Almighty. Rather justice is just the way that the Almighty is; it is an inherent part of him. As such a Jew can have hope that all the actions of the Almighty are just. They are reminded of this during the weekday Amidah where he is addressed as the 'king Who loves charity and Justice'.

The Almighty as the Rock of Israel

Psalms teaches of the Almighty as the Rock of Israel:

May the words of my mouth and the prayer of my heart be acceptable to You, O LORD, my rock and my redeemer.

(Psalm 19:15)

Further imagery of the Almighty as the rock is attributed to David in 2 Samuel 22:2–4:

O LORD, my crag, my fastness, my deliverer! O God, the rock wherein I take shelter: My shield, my mighty champion, my fortress and refuge! My saviour, You who rescue me from violence! All praise! I called on the LORD, And I was delivered from my enemies.

There are different images that the title of 'Rock' can conjure in a person's mind. In 2 Samuel a rock is a source of shelter, a shield, a fortress and a refuge. All of which describe a person's relationship with the Almighty perfectly. A person can seek refuge in the Almighty because of his power, his love and his immutability – the Almighty does not change. This is taught by Moses in his farewell:

For the name of the LORD I proclaim; Give glory to our God! The Rock!—whose deeds are perfect, Yea, all His ways are just; A faithful God, never false, True and upright is He.

(Deuteronomy 32:4)

As such, a person can have complete faith and confidence in the immovable rock and redeemer who is the Almighty. Its importance in the belief and life of a Jew is highlighted in the fact that just before the Amidah is begun on the morning of Shabbat, the phrase 'Tzur Yisrael' is repeated which means 'Rock of Israel'.

The title was mired in controversy at the establishment of the State of Israel in 1948. The Declaration of the Establishment of the State of Israel includes the phrase 'Rock of Israel':

> Religious Zionists insisted God's name was a necessary component of the document establishing the state of Israel. Zisling, leading the secularist Zionists, was committed to a separation of religion and state and would not sign a political document which rested on allusions to the supernatural. He maintained that the inclusion of God's name imposed an expression of belief on non-believers … Forging a compromise, Ben-Gurion used the phrase 'the Rock of Israel' to satisfy both parties but left out the theological component, 'and its Redeemer', contained within the Bible … People with knowledge of the Torah hear the phrase Tzur Yisrael in its biblical and sacred context. For atheists, the phrase Tzur Yisrael connotes a more literal reference to the Jewish people's connection to the military, the Land of Israel or Jewish cultural and historical traditions.

(Kolodny, 2018)

Indeed, although the focus here is on the theological interpretation of the phrase 'Rock of Israel', it is an important aspect of Judaism already noted that Judaism is a big tent that has space for secular and religious approaches. As such, Rock of Israel becomes a statement of faith and of identity. The rock provides hope, strength and refuge, along with a hope of redemption.

Ein Sof (En Sof)

The *Zohar* teaches:

> Therefore THE HOLY ONE, BLESSED BE HE, says to them, 'Even though I am like you in your forms', MEANING IN VISION AND LIKENESS, still in all: 'To whom then will you liken Me, that I should be his equal'. Before the Holy One, blessed be He, created an image in the world and BEFORE He formed a form, the Holy One, blessed be He, was alone in the world, without a form or likeness. For one who conceives Him before the grade of Briyah, WHICH IS BINAH when He is without any form, must not make any form or image in the world – neither with the letter Hei nor with the letter Yud, or even to call Him by the Holy Name or any letter or dot. This is why the Torah says, 'For you saw no manner of form', MEANING you did not see anything with a form or likeness … After He made that image of the Chariot of supernal man, He descended AND WAS ATTIRED there. In him, He is named by the form of THE FOUR LETTERS Yud Hei Vav Hei, NAMELY THE TEN SFIROT – KETER, CHOCHMAH, BINAH, TIFERET AND MALCHUT-so people could grasp Him by way of His attributes, WHICH ARE THE SFIROT in each and every attribute. He was

called El, Elohim, Shadai, Tzva'ot, Eheyeh, in order that they could recognize Him in each and every attribute, and how He rules the world with Chesed and Judgment according to the actions of the people.

(Bo: 217)

The description of the Almighty as Ein Sof links with other aspects of the characteristics outlined above. It is mainly found within Kabbalah (see Chapter 8), and explains the Almighty as nameless and formless, and often as 'without end' or Infinite (Kurzweil, 2007, 337). In essence, the Almighty can sometimes be described as a 'Holy Nothingness' where:

God is the ocean and we the waves. Each wave has its moment when it is identifiable as a somewhat separate entity. Nevertheless, no wave is entirely distinct from the ocean, which is its substantial ground. Furthermore, because the waves are surface manifestations of the ocean, our knowledge of the ocean is largely dependent upon the way the ocean manifests itself in the waves.

(Rubenstein, 1992, 299)

This is the concept of the Almighty that lies behind the expression of the Almighty when 'he descended and was attired', meaning that he was given name and, to some extent, 'form' in the conceptualization of humanity. This true identity of the Divine is often described in early Kabbalistic literature as 'the transcendental "hidden God"' (Wigoder, 2002, 240).

Though the belief in the Almighty's transcendence and immutability will be found throughout Judaism, the concept of Ein Sof is of particular relevance and importance within Kabbalistic understandings. As a result of the inability to know the Almighty fully, it is possible to begin to know of him following creation, the first act of which is known as Tzimtzum ('contraction' or 'constriction'). In Tzimtzum the Almighty is seen to be the Almighty contracting so that creation can take place:

With this divine gesture, God restricts himself in zimzum, clearing the empty space that is necessary for creation. The emanation and the creation of the world are then able to occur in the center of God following this act of zimzum. In this process, God limits his omnipotence, so that a finite world can exist within finite contours. Without zimzum, there would be no creation.

(Schulte, 2023, 1)

This explains the belief that the Almighty is both transcendent and immanent. Rabbi Schneur Zalman of Liadi (n.d.) in his work Lessons in Tanya explores the inter-relatedness of the Creator and creation. The suggestion is that the Almighty is not like a silversmith who is separate from his creation:

Rather, the activating force of the Creator must continuously be present in the thing created to give it life and ongoing existence.

(Shaar Hayichud Vehaemunah, Chapter 2)

Lest any attempt is made to suggest a pantheism within Judaism Kabbalists are at pains to point out the difference between pantheism and panentheism: 'Whereas pantheism equates god with the world, panentheism means that God is in all the worlds. A Kabbalist would say that everything resides in God' (Kurzweil, 2007, 274).

As indicated in the passage from the Zohar above the Almighty is named by the form of the ten sefirot 'so people could grasp Him by way of his attributes'. These are known as 'emanations' or sometimes 'channels'. George Robinson (2000) highlights that:

> It may help to think of the sefirot as the 'channels' that allow us to focus on and hear the 'radio signals' of the All Powerful mixed in among the static of everyday life. The emanations, then are the ways in which God is able to interact with the sensual world, the world we inhabit.

> (274)

The ten sefirot are:

1 *Keter (Crown). This represents the thought that takes place before any action is performed. In terms of the Almighty this has reference to 'first stirrings of Will'. It may also be termed 'Ayin' (nothingness) for creation by the Almighty sprang from nothing, an infinite void.*
2 *Chokmah* (Wisdom). This represents the first thought that led to creation; the inspiration that leads to thought.
3 *Binah* (Understanding). This represents the concretization of that inspiration into thought. As the Almighty is without gender, Chokmah and Binah often go together, as the male and the female. The sperm of the idea that finds its fulfilment in conscious thought.
4 *Chesed* (Loving Kindness or Mercy). This represents the loving nature of the Almighty (see above).
5 *Gevurah* (Power or Judgement). This represents the power and judgement of the Almighty; this is often focused on to the detriment of love. Both should be counterbalanced.
6 *Tiferet* (Beauty or Compassion). This represents the quality that balances love and judgement. It also unites the first nine of the sefirot as can be seen in Figure 1.1.
7 *Netzach* (Triumph or Endurance). Netzach works in harmony with Hod and represents the grace of the Almighty that is found within the world.
8 *Hod* (Majesty or Splendour). This represents the way that the judgement of the Almighty is found within the world.
9 *Yesod* (Foundation). This represents Tiferet and Malkuth are connected – Tiferet being the male aspect of the Almighty, while Melkuth (or Shechinah) is seen to be the female aspect. This enables creativity and fertility to be found throughout the world.
10 *Malkuth* (Sovereignty). This represents the Divine Presence and is often translated as shechinah (see above).

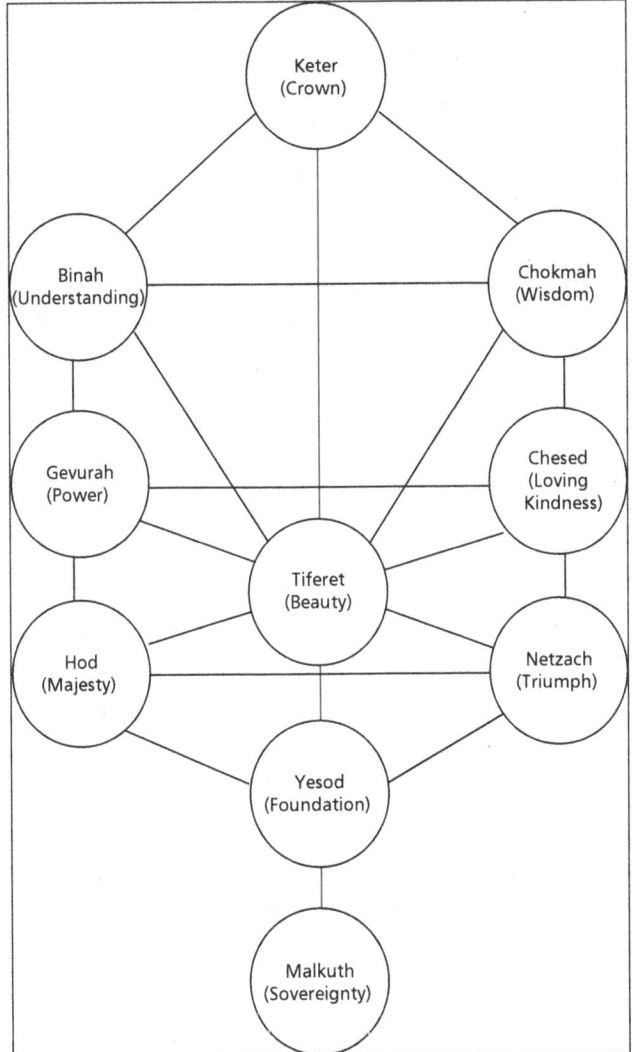

Figure 1.1 The Tree of Life of the Ten Sefirot.

They are often, in Kabbalistic writings, referred to as the 'Tree of Life' (see Figure 1.1) and are a manifestation of aspects of the Divine. They are a way that the love of the Almighty (the right-hand side of the diagram) and the judgement of the Almighty (the left-hand side) are balanced and evidenced from and towards the Almighty. Kurzweil (2007) explains this reciprocal and intertwined impact of the belief in Ein Sof and the sefirot within Kabbalah, and perhaps in wider Judaism:

> Kabbalists conceive of the universe as a downpour of divine plenty from above that constantly creates and sustains the world. This downpour comes in the form of the ten sefirot, which manifest out of the pure divine light that shines from above. God contracts

and forms each of the sefirot and their combinations, and this action results in the continuous creation of the world.

Regarding the sefirot, however, Kabbalists teach that the relationship goes both ways between God and humans. Not only is there a downpour of divine light in the form of the ten sefirot, but also there's a response from humans who use the ten sefirot and show God their thoughts, deeds, and actions, which are really the ten sefirot in various combinations. This is the basis of the idea of reward and punishment. Humans use or abuse the world and experience the consequences of their deeds. Kabbalists conceive of a universe in which God is aware of every minute detail of what is going on, so God knows how each person uses the ten sefirot, either for the repair of the world or for its destruction.

(72)

Although not focused on by some Jews, the idea of Ein Sof and the balancing of judgement and love can be seen to permeate the Jewish idea of the Almighty as we have explored in the various characteristics in this chapter.

Thoughts for the classroom

There is much in the above discussion about the Almighty in Judaism that could find expression in the classroom. A recognition of the diversity of approaches and emphases within Judaism towards the importance of the Almighty is an important starting point whatever the age of the students that are being taught. For younger children it would include the adoption of qualifying phrases such as 'many Jews believe' or 'for most Jews'. This is indicating a diversity of approach within Judaism without having the children becoming tied up in knots as they struggle to understand the basic concepts of belief in practice. As the students in the classroom get older, teachers can begin to include discussion of the nature of the Almighty and also questions about his existence within Judaism. Perhaps more evident within Judaism is the possibility that the Almighty is not thought of regularly in a person's life; consider the following from a Jew living in the UK today:

> I am not sure what I believe [about the Almighty] and what I do not. It changes from day-to-day. In any event, I don't think 'belief' is a very important consideration in Judaism. What is more important is what we do.

The way that religions and worldviews are often taught in the classroom, and a way that I have advocated (Holt, 2022) explores the beliefs which underpin the practices. This can be taught in two ways, either beginning with beliefs and seeing their outworkings in the practices of believers or looking at the practices and seeing how they link to the beliefs. The two, I argue, should not be taught independently because the practices do not make sense without the belief. Judaism perhaps more than any other religion challenges this approach. It is possible for a person to live their faith without thinking too much about the underpinning beliefs (see Chapters 6 and 7).

However, having said that, and as indicated in the Introduction, the belief in the Almighty is one of the central identifiers of Judaism, and a person's and community's relationship with the Almighty has lain at the heart of Judaism since the beginning. Thus, it should be an important part of an exploration of Judaism within the classroom.

The idea of the name of the Almighty is an important consideration in Judaism, and within the classroom. Speaking in a different context, Wendy Doniger (1991) argues that 'Naming is always a matter of the convenience of the namers, and all categories are constructed' (36). As such, when a person suggests and uses a name, this is perhaps an indicator of a relationship, one which could suggest a power dynamic. Within Judaism, it is not people who name God, rather it is the Almighty who has provided the name; and in so doing, it could be suggested as Salman Rushdie (1991) has, that 'To give a thing a name, a label, a handle; to rescue it from anonymity … in short to identify it – well, that's a way of bringing the said thing into being' (63). This may be a Jewish approach, and is certainly a Kabbalistic idea, that the Almighty is brought into the mind and conception of humanity through his grace, and the manifestation of himself through the names and characteristics by which he is known.

One of the most important discussions before beginning to teach about the Jewish belief in the Almighty is how 'he' should be spoken of. There are different points that should be explored with students. On the one hand, the name of the Almighty is so sacred for Jews that it cannot be spoken or written. In many classrooms this will lead to the use of G-d in text. In others, it will be the replacement of the word 'God' with the Almighty, as in the approach taken within the book. Other terms such as Hashem, Adonai or the Lord are also possibilities. This is a theme explored at the beginning of this chapter, but it is important for the teacher to consider their approach that is most representative of, and sensitive to, the Jewish community. Consistency will also be the key, and the idea that the name of the Almighty should not be used lightly. One of the other points in the use of language related to the Divine is the use of gendered terms. The Almighty is neither male nor female, but the English language and tradition have ascribed male terms such as 'he' and 'him' to the Almighty. Sometimes the avoidance of any such language leads to convoluted sentences, and this may be felt appropriate. If gendered language will be used, and I have found in the writing of this book, that it is almost impossible to avoid such, then a recognition of the limitations of the language used should be discussed with children.

Although an exploration of Kabbalah is perhaps inappropriate for many classrooms due to complexity and age, there is an important aspect that can help frame the discussion of the Almighty in Judaism. As children within the classroom usually understand Judaism from outside the tradition, and usually from a Christian perspective as explored in this chapter, this has led to an over-focus on the legalistic aspects of the nature of the Divine. As is evident from the names and characteristics of the Almighty, there is a balance between the masculine and the feminine, between the 'legalistic' and the 'loving'. It is imperative that both aspects of the Almighty are explored within the classroom; this reflects the reality of the Almighty in a person's life and prepares for an exploration of the Abrahamic Covenant and what this means for Jews today. The Tree of Life within Kabbalah highlights this balance clearly, and while it may not be used it can be used to help clarify this understanding of the Almighty in a teacher's mind.

Chapter 2

The Nature of Humanity

In exploring the nature of the Almighty in Chapter 1 we were able to observe the importance of his various characteristics, as such how humanity stands in relationship to the Almighty is found in the names that are used. For example, understanding the Almighty as Creator helps Jews understand that they are creations, similarly using the name of Father conjures up a paternal relationship. None of these are perfect descriptions, either of the Almighty or of humanity's relationship to him, but they are a beginning. Throughout this chapter we will explore the nature of existence, the nature of humanity, the purpose of life, and concepts of life after death as taught across Judaism. As with all aspects of Judaism there will be unifying concepts but also differences of interpretation and expression.

The nature of existence

As is evident from the discussion in the previous chapter surrounding the Almighty as Creator, he is the source of everything. When the Almighty created it was out of nothing, and from nothing; the Tanakh describes it as a 'void' (Genesis 1:2). This belief, perhaps in dialogue with the Roman world and then with Christianity, has become known as *creation ex nihilo*, a phrase that is now used within Judaism. 2 Maccabees describes the evident nature of this:

> I beg you, my child, to look at the heaven and the earth and see everything that is in them, and recognise that God did not make them out of things that existed. And in the same way the human race came into being.
>
> (7:28)

There is some discussion that prior to this point, and even in some readings of Maccabees the creation out of nothing may be a later interpretation and the consensus before Judaism's encounter with Greece and Christianity was creation using pre-existing matter:

> The God of the Rabbis, like that of Philo, appears to have created the earth from some kind of primordial stuff. The biblical account itself seems to suggest such an idea. Seladyah's God does not mess around with stuff.
>
> (Satlow, 2006, 203)

In this approach, when the Tanakh speaks of creation it might identify this pre-existing matter:

> ... the earth being unformed and void, with darkness over the surface of the deep and a wind from God sweeping over the water.
>
> (Genesis 1:2)

A point that is made in the Midrash:

> A certain philosopher once asked Rabban Gamliel, saying to him: 'Your God is a great artist, however he found many excellent raw materials that helped him: Emptiness, disorder, darkness, wind, water, and depths'.
>
> (Bereshit Rabbah 1:9)

Further, Satlow (2006) suggests that it was Seadyah in the tenth century CE who introduced 'the notion of creatio ex nihilo ("creation from nothing") into Jewish readings of the Hebrew Bible. For Se'adyah, God creates with will – God wills it and it is. God built the world and all in it from nothing at all' (203). Though for many people Philo of Alexandria (first century CE) introduced some of these ideas. While many Jews today accept and teach the principle of creation ex nihilo (linked with Ein Sof), there is space for creation out of pre-existing matter. In many ways, for Jews the mechanics of creation is unimportant, it is more important that the who and purpose of creation are considered. A point made in the Talmud:

> Rebbi Jonah in the name of Rebbi Levi: The world was created with Bet. Since Bet is closed from all sides but open from one side, you have no right to investigate what is above, what is below, what is before, and what is after, except starting with the day the world was created and onwards. One asks the Bet, who created you? It points out to them its point and says, this One above. And what is His Name? It points out to them its back point and says, the Eternal is His Name.
>
> (*Jerusalem Talmud Chagigah* 2:1.84)

Linking with the belief in Ein Sof (see Chapter 1), this highlights the will of the Almighty in creation. The Almighty created the world, and this shows his power and his love. Power is shown in the act of creation, and love through the beneficence of the Almighty who created the world for humanity (see below). Everything is dependent on the Almighty, nothing would exist without his will or his power.

The account of creation helps Jews understand the nature of the Almighty, the nature of the created world including humanity, and the purpose of life. It can thus, whether accepted literally or metaphorically, help introduce many of these concepts. It is important to understand that the two different, and many would see as complementary, versions of creation found in Genesis 1 and 2. In Genesis 1 and the beginning of chapter 2 the seven days of creation are narrated:

1 The Almighty creates Light, Night and Day
2 Sky is created

3 Land, sea and vegetation are created
4 The celestial bodies of the sun, moon and stars are created
5 Sea animals and birds are created
6 Land animals and humanity are created
7 The Almighty rests.

At the conclusion of the seven-day creation narrative a slightly different focus is adopted in chapter 2 from verse 4 onwards. The focus of this narrative is very much around the place and creation of humanity:

> When the LORD God made earth and heaven – when no shrub of the field was yet on earth and no grasses of the field had yet sprouted, because the LORD God had not sent rain upon the earth and there was no man to till the soil, but a flow would well up from the ground and water the whole surface of the earth – the LORD God formed man from the dust of the earth. He blew into his nostrils the breath of life, and man became a living being. The LORD God planted a garden in Eden, in the east, and placed there the man whom He had formed. And from the ground the LORD God caused to grow every tree that was pleasing to the sight and good for food, with the tree of life in the middle of the garden, and the tree of knowledge of good and bad.
>
> (Genesis 2:4–9)

The second account becomes more important when discussing the nature of humanity; it does not add much to the discussion of the nature of existence but does begin to explore the place of humanity within it. It is of note to suggest that the two taken together highlight the justice and love of the Almighty. On the one hand the world can be seen according to the laws set out (Genesis 1), whereas the Almighty's compassion for humanity is exemplified in the second account. Thus, they can be read together. Rashi suggests this reading:

> GOD [AS JUDGE] CREATED – It does not state The Lord (the Merciful One) created, because at first God Intended to create it (the world) to be placed under the attribute (rule) of strict justice, but He realised that the world could not thus endure and therefore gave precedence to Divine Mercy allying it with Divine Justice. It is to this that what is written in (Genesis 2:4) alludes – 'In the day that the Lord God made earth and heaven'.
>
> (*Rashi on Genesis* 1:1)

The love that is shown through creation is based on the Almighty, who is in control and is the source of all creation. Many times, in the exploration of the 'Creation story' it is possible that the order of the events and its literal nature can be focused upon. For Jews, this may miss the point of the story; in creation the Almighty is manifest, and in being so humanity becomes 'God's partner, completing the creative act, and thus initiating redemption' (Wigoder, 2002, 195). In so doing the Creator and the created are in a relationship which makes sense of life. More of this relationship will be explored in the next two sections and will draw on the writings of Martin Buber (1970).

When considering the nature of existence, its importance is also not just of creation in the past, but also the ongoing creation and presence of the Almighty in the world today. The Morning prayer often includes the words:

Who in goodness renews each day continuously the act of creation.

The Almighty is not someone who has created the world and left it to its own devices, rather for Jews the Almighty is intimately involved in creation every day. One Jew suggests that this phrase means three things:

- The Almighty is continually speaking the universe into being
- Each morning people wake to a world that is (or can be) entirely new
- No matter the events of the day, a new day is a chance to begin again (Barenblat, 2015).

This means that 'As humans made in the Divine image, we are invited into the ongoing process of creation. As we start the Torah cycle over again this week, may we be reminded of the power and potential of the creative process to renew us and our Judaism' (Allen, 2018).

The nature of humanity and the purpose of life

As explored in the previous section on the nature of existence, 2 Maccabees suggests that humanity was created out of nothing. This, again, is subject to different views, especially as the stories of creation emphasize slightly different aspects of the creation of Adam and Eve. In Genesis 1 it says:

And God said, 'Let us make man in our image, after our likeness. They shall rule the fish of the sea, the birds of the sky, the cattle, the whole earth, and all the creeping things that creep on earth'. And God created man in His image, in the image of God He created him; male and female He created them.

(26–7)

Suggesting an intention followed by the creation. Whereas in Genesis 2:

... the LORD God formed man from the dust of the earth. He blew into his nostrils the breath of life, and man became a living being.

(7)

The suggestion here is that humanity was formed from the dust of the earth; this may be semantics as creation ex nihilo would suggest that the dust was formed first and then humanity. What is important about the creation of Adam and Eve drawing on both narratives in Genesis is that:

1 Humans are created in the image of the Almighty.
2 Humans are given responsibility and stewardship over the earth and everything within it.

A third element could be added based on the creation narrative:

3 Fill the earth (with offspring).

The belief that humans are created in the image of the Almighty places them at the heart of the story of the universe. It makes the nature of existence for Jews to be a relationship between the Almighty and a person. Martin Buber (1970) highlights the importance of this relationship as the ultimate expression of what he terms I-Thou:

> That you need God more than anything, you know at all times in your heart. But don't you know also that God needs you – in the fullness of his eternity, you? How would man exist if God did not need him, and how would you exist? You need God in order to be, and God needs you – for that which is the meaning of your life … That there are world, man, the human person, you and I, has divine meaning. Creation – happens to us, burns into us, changes us, we tremble and swoon, we submit. Creation – we participate in it, we encounter the creator, offer ourselves to him, helpers and companions.
>
> (130)

This reciprocal relationship is unique to humans and means that of all creation 'Beloved is man for he was created in the image [of God]. Especially beloved is he for it was made known to him that he had been created in the image [of God]' (*Pirkei Avot* 3:14). It is in the discussion of the two types of relationships 'I-It' and 'I-Thou' that Buber highlights the importance of not just the relationship with the Almighty but also with other people. If a person is focused on 'It' they are not in a relationship but place themselves at the centre. Buber (1970) argues that 'The world as experience belongs to the basic word I-It. The basic word I-You establishes the world of relation', suggesting that I-Thou is more desirable because in this a person 'establishes the world as relation' (56–7). In this relationship the most important is the relation with the Almighty, but also in relation to 'life in nature' and life with other people (56–7). Others are not experienced as objects, rather 'He is no longer He or She, limited by other Hes and Shes, a dot in the world grid of space and time, nor a condition that can be experienced and described, a loose bundle of named qualities. Neighbourless and seamless, he is You and fills the firmament' (Buber, 1970, 59). Through this approach to life a person can encounter the world in all its goodness and find their place therein.

This relationship with all life on the earth is an important part of the responsibility and stewardship that humanity is given. In being created, humans are born neutral with inclinations to do good (*yetzer tov*) and an evil or selfish impulse (*yetzer ra*). The nature of humanity and the purpose of life are to follow the path of good, and to improve the world around them. This is highlighted in the concept of *tikkun olam*, or the responsibility to repair the world. This is highlighted in the *Talmud*:

> Rav Naḥman bar Rav Ḥisda interpreted homiletically: What is the meaning of that which is written: 'Then the Lord God formed [vayyitzer] man' (Genesis 2:7), with a double yod?

> This double yod alludes to that fact that the Holy One, Blessed be He, created two inclinations; one a good inclination and one an evil inclination … This alludes to the difficulty of human life; woe unto me from my Creator [yotzri] and woe unto me from my inclination [yitzri]. If one opts to follow either his Creator or his inclination, woe unto him from the other.
>
> (Berakhot 61a: 3–4)

When speaking of what they felt is the purpose of life, a number of British Jews highlighted this as the main focus:

> We don't know and we can't know [the purpose of life]. We are here without our consent but have an obligation to improve the world for others.
> To do the right things every day and to try most days to do small or large acts of kindness to others.
> To do good deeds in the time we are alive and try to improve the world and bring joy when you can.

This responsibility is played out in many ways in the life of a Jew; in the way that the mitzvot are followed (see Chapter 4) which are of two types – between people and the Almighty, and those between people, in the way that they care for the world and seek justice (see Chapter 7), in the way that they relate to the Almighty, and in the way that they relate to others. In this, the two aspects of the Almighty are seen; on the one hand there is a responsibility to be held to account, as indicated in *Pirkei Avot*:

> Akabyah ben Mahalalel said: mark well three things and you will not come into the power of sin: know from where you come, and where you are going, and before whom you are destined to give an account and reckoning. From where do you come? From a putrid drop. Where are you going? To a place of dust, of worm and of maggot. Before whom you are destined to give an account and reckoning? Before the King of the kings of kings, the Holy One, blessed be He.
>
> (3:1)

While the Shema focuses the love of humans on the Almighty:

> You shall love the LORD your God with all your heart and with all your soul and with all your might.
>
> (Deuteronomy 6:5)

This verse and the associated verses are so important for Jews that they are taught to their children, they are worn by some Jews during prayer as they 'Bind them as a sign on your hand and let them serve as a symbol on your forehead' (Deuteronomy 6:8). Along with other texts they are contained in the phylacteries or tefillin (see Figure 2.1).

They are also placed 'on the doorposts of your house and on your gates' (Deuteronomy 6:9), found on all of the doorposts (apart from the bathroom) of the homes of many Jews in the form of a mezuzah (see Figure 2.2).

Figure 2.1 Tefillin/Phylacteries.

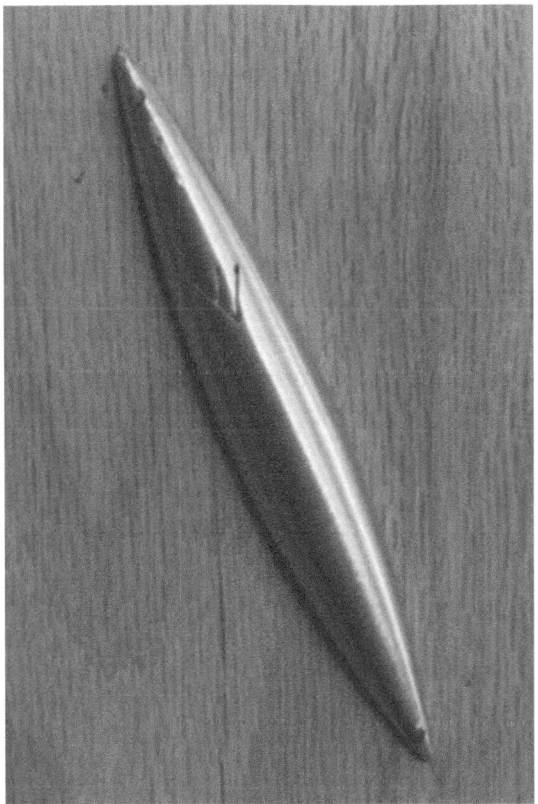

Figure 2.2 A modern mezuzah affixed to a door post.

The love that is expected of humans is also focussed on others. The Torah teaches:

> Love your fellow [neighbour] as yourself: I am the LORD.

> (Leviticus 19:18)

While a person may not be able to know their specific purpose on earth, they are able to live it as they seek good and live in relationship with the Divine and with others, as they live in love.

This relationship is further exemplified when Jews consider the first command (for some the first blessing) given to Adam and Eve:

> God blessed them and God said to them, 'Be fertile and increase, fill the earth and master it'.

> (Genesis 1:28)

The world was created to serve as a habitation for humanity, and it is to be filled and subdued so that it is a place fit for habitation:

> For thus said the LORD, The Creator of heaven who alone is God, Who formed the earth and made it, Who alone established it – He did not create it a waste, But formed it for habitation: I am the LORD, and there is none else.

> (Isaiah 45:18)

There is much discussion about the applicability of this command or blessing today. For many Jews, especially in certain forms of Orthodox Judaism, they believe it is incumbent upon them to have many children. While some Jews would perhaps adapt themselves to the modern world and have a small number of children; interestingly, there is Talmudic authority that suggest that two children is a sensible number which some Orthodox Jews will also adhere to. In a one-sentence commentary on Genesis 1:28 Richard Friedman (2001) suggested succinctly that 'This commandment has now been fulfilled' (12). This interpretation may quite easily be reached by some Jews as they look at the population of the world and perhaps may feel that their responsibility is to repair the world or to subdue it in a way that it becomes habitable for people and for the Divine. Although this may be a small interpretation, the command thus has different expressions within the Jewish community.

Life after death

Picking up on the conversation alluded to in the Introduction, in response to the question 'What do you believe about life after death?', one elderly Jewish lady responded:

> Do you know, I don't know. I've never really thought about that. I'll need to ask the Rabbi.

The questioner was from a Christian background and was confused by the response. How could a lifelong Jew, a religiously observant lady, never have thought about life after death? From their perspective the afterlife was a motivating factor in living a good life. Why did this lady keep the laws of kashrut? Why did she observe Shabbat? This is a useful introduction to the beliefs about life after death in Judaism, in contrast to many other religions, for many Jews it is a question that may not hold much relevance. This is also reflected in the myriad of different beliefs that can be found across Judaism. Amy-Jill Levine suggests:

> Jewish beliefs in the afterlife are as diverse as Judaism itself, from the traditional view expecting the unity of flesh and spirit in a resurrected body, to the idea that we live on in our children and grandchildren, to a sense of heaven (perhaps with lox and bagels rather than harps and haloes). Belief in an afterlife typically correlates with our theology. If we believe in a just and compassionate living G-d, faithful to the promises made to Israel, we may well also believe in resurrection in the Messianic age, when justice and compassion will prevail over sin, evil and death.
>
> (Schwartz A., 2011)

This does not even mention the belief that life after death may entail reincarnation rather than resurrection, or the continuation of memory as a form of afterlife.

This diversity is perhaps because of the seeming vagueness of the Torah, and more widely the Tanakh when speaking about life after death. Some may point to the use of the term *sheol* as an indicator that there is a life after death. For example, following the apparent death of Joseph:

> Jacob rent his clothes, put sackcloth on his loins, and observed mourning for his son many days. All his sons and daughters sought to comfort him; but he refused to be comforted, saying, 'No, I will go down mourning to my son in Sheol'. Thus his father bewailed him.
>
> (Genesis 37:35-36)

The suggestion here could be that sheol is emblematic of the final resting place of the body, maybe even just referring to the grave. Whereas other passages might indicate it as a destiny, or place from which people are resurrected; consider 1 Samuel 2:6:

> The LORD deals death and gives life, Casts down into Sheol and raises up.

It could be both a place of rest and punishment, Isaiah describes the underworld:

> Sheol below was astir To greet your coming … Your pomp is brought down to Sheol … Once you thought in your heart, "I will climb to the sky; Higher than the stars of God I will set my throne. I will sit in the mount of assembly, On the summit of Zaphon: I will mount the back of a cloud— I will match the Most High." Instead, you are brought down to Sheol, To the bottom of the Pit.
>
> (Isaiah 14: 9, 11, 13-15)

The Torah also describes it as a place where the anger of the Almighty burns:

> For a fire has flared in My wrath And burned to the bottom of Sheol, Has consumed the earth and its increase, Eaten down to the base of the hills.

(Deuteronomy 32:22)

Although there are references to what could be considered a continuation of life after death, it is generally agreed that ideas that built firm beliefs about the nature of the after-life developed after the Babylonian exile 'probably through external influences' (Wigoder, 2002, 36). This is not to suggest that Judaism 'borrowed' from other traditions, rather that in encountering other beliefs such as Greek or Persian, a theology that addressed such questions was felt to be needed.

Resurrection and olam ha-ba

The idea of a resurrection can be found in Daniel, but is developed further in the post Tanakh periods. Daniel records:

> At that time, the great prince, Michael, who stands beside the sons of your people, will appear. It will be a time of trouble, the like of which has never been since the nation came into being. At that time, your people will be rescued, all who are found inscribed in the book. Many of those that sleep in the dust of the earth will awake, some to eternal life, others to reproaches, to everlasting abhorrence.

(12:1–2)

While in 2 Maccabees we read of the assumption of a resurrection:

> And when he was at his last breath, he said, 'You accursed wretch, you dismiss us from this present life, but the King of the universe will raise us up to an everlasting renewal of life, because we have died for his laws'.

(7:9)

This passage has been described as 'one of the first explicit allusions in Jewish literature' to the resurrection of the body (Klawans & Wills, 2020, 268). During the Second Temple Period there was disagreement between different jews on the reality of the resurrection; groups such as the Saducees rejected the belief, while Pharisees and other fully accepted it.

The suggestion here is of a resurrection to 'eternal life' and 'everlasting abhorrence' that were subsequently developed in the idea of *olam ha-ba* (the world to come) and the division of *Gan Eden* and *Gehinnom*. As highlighted in the discussion of the nature of humanity (see above) where humanity has the choice of following a good inclination or one an evil inclina-tion this is reflected in the possibility destiny of humanity. Within the Talmud, Yochanan ben Zakkai, in the first century, speaks of the dualistic nature of the world to come:

> I have two paths before me, one of the Garden of Eden and one of Gehenna.

(Berakhot 28b)

Gan Eden is described as a land of milk, honey, balsam and wine. Yakult Shimoni describes it as a place with 800,000 different types of trees, 500,000 types of fruit; and 'In each corner stand 600,000 angels singing in the praise of God' and the Almighty 'sits in the Garden of Eden, explaining the Torah to the righteous of all ages' (Wigoder, 2002, 225). On the other hand, the Talmud describes Gehinnom as a hot and fiery place of judgement:

> The Gemara elaborates: Our fire is one-sixtieth of the fire of Gehenna.
>
> (Berakhot 57b)

For some, the 'destination' of Gan Eden is to be found within the messianic age (see below). The overall message is, however, that a person should live according to the mitzvot; though even this suggests a centrality to Jewish living that would not really be accepted by most Jews. A Jew is observant because that is what the Almighty asks, the sense of reward or punishment is not really thought about or explored. There is a Day of Judgement, and belief in this is exemplified in the observance of Rosh Hashanah and Yom Kippur (see Chapter 6). While Gehinnom is seemingly a place to fear, it may not have much of a place in the minds of Jews, a place of punishment is rejected by some:

> The souls of those who are found wanting will not 'live forever in the presence of God', but no particular punishment is identified. Perhaps missing out on the reward is punishment enough, or perhaps by then all souls will have come right.
>
> (Lawton, 2016, 30)

While in this description one might envisage two separate places, as identified earlier olam ha-ba may be more identified with the messianic age (see below).

There has also been, for many Jews, a move away from a belief in the physical resurrection and the binary of Gan Eden and Gehinnom. While there is a belief in the immortality of the soul 'it is dissociated from traditional notions of messianic redemption and divine judgment' (Cohn-Sherbok, 1997, 175). Chief Rabbi, J. H. Hertz suggested:

> Many and various are the folk beliefs and poetical fancies in the rabbinical writings concerning Heaven, Gan Eden, and Hell, Gehinnom. Our most authoritative religious guides, however, proclaim that no eye hath seen, nor can mortal fathom, what awaiteth us in the Hereafter; but that even the tarnished soul will not forever be denied spiritual bliss.
>
> (Jacobs, 1988, 415)

Point seven of the *Pittsburgh Platform* (1885) highlights for Reform Jews 'that the soul is immortal, grounding this belief on the Divine nature of the human spirit, which forever finds bliss in righteousness and misery in wickedness. We reject as ideas not rooted in Judaism the belief in bodily resurrection and in Gehenna and Eden (Hell and Paradise) as abodes for eternal punishment or reward.' This, again, highlights the difficulty of saying anything concrete about Jewish beliefs about the afterlife.

Messianic Age

One view within Judaism is that the resurrection will take place when the *mascheach* or messiah comes, during the messianic age. Responding to worries of people that they would miss out on olam ha-ba, this time of peace (see below) there is the belief that 'When mascheach comes, every person who ever lived will be literally physically resurrected and will return to Jerusalem to be present at the moment when the perfection of the world is announced' (Dosick, 1995, 46).

The *Mishneh Torah* describes the messianic age, the olam ha-ba or world to come in a utopian way:

> In that era, there will be neither famine or war, envy or competition for good will flow in abundance and all the delights will be freely available as dust. The occupation of the entire world will be solely to know God. Therefore, the Jews will be great sages and know the hidden matters, grasping the knowledge of their Creator according to the full extent of human potential, as Isaiah 11:9 states: 'The world will be filled with the knowledge of God as the waters cover the ocean bed'.
>
> (Kings and Wars 12:5)

Echoing further writings found in Isaiah:

> Thus He will judge among the nations And arbitrate for the many peoples, And they shall beat their swords into ploughshares And their spears into pruning hooks: Nation shall not take up Sword against nation; They shall never again know war.
>
> (Isaiah 2:4)

> The wolf shall dwell with the lamb, The leopard lie down with the kid; The calf, the beast of prey, and the fatling together, With a little boy to herd them. The cow and the bear shall graze, Their young shall lie down together; And the lion, like the ox, shall eat straw. A babe shall play Over a viper's hole, And an infant pass his hand Over an adder's den. In all of My sacred mount Nothing evil or vile shall be done; For the land shall be filled with devotion to the LORD As water covers the sea.
>
> (Isaiah 11:6–9)

This will be an age of peace, an age where the messiah will reign. In this understanding, for many Jews this life is a time to prepare the world for the messiah's arrival. For some Orthodox Jews this is a time of preparation, the time where the building towards the messianic age began with the destruction of the Second Temple in 70 CE. This does not mean that there was not a hope and expectation before this time; the promise there would be a messiah from the line of David; 'The Psalms of Solomon extol [this] messianic king who will rebuild the land and draw all nations to Zion. Such a conception served as the basis for subsequent rabbinic reflection about messianic redemption, the ingathering of the exiles, and salvation in the world to come' (Cohn-Sherbok, 2017, 464).

For some other Jews the idea of the messiah has less importance because it is not found in the Torah, and the prophecies of Isaiah and others may refer to a specific context during the prophets' own lifetimes. This would suggest that the destruction of the Second Temple gave rise to a greater focus on a future deliverance; and while there might be mention of a future messianic age, the person of the messiah is less important. There are different interpretations of the messianic age across Judaism:

- Many Orthodox Jews believe in a messiah who will come, gather all of his people to the land of Israel, and the resurrection of the dead. In light of this it is not unusual for the coming of the messiah to be prayed for each day.
- Within Masorti/ Conservative Judaism there is a hope for the messianic age; but the idea and ideal are of more importance. In the Statement of Principles of Conservative Judaism:

> For our people, we dream of the ingathering of all Jews to Zion where we can again be masters of our destiny and express our distinctive genius in every area of our national life …. We affirm Isaiah's prophecy (2:3) that ' … Torah shall come forth from Zion, the word of the Lord from Jerusalem' … We do not know when the Messiah will come, nor whether he will be a charismatic human figure or is a symbol of the redemption of humankind from the evils of the world. Through the doctrine of a messianic figure, Judaism teaches us that every individual human being must live as if he or she, individually, has the responsibility to bring about the messianic age. Beyond that, we echo the words of Maimonides based on the prophet Habakkuk (2:3) that though he may tarry, yet do we wait for him each day.
>
> (The Jewish Theological Seminary of America et al. 1988, 25–7)

- Within Reform Judaism, the idea of a specific messiah is not generally focused on, and maybe even rejected and 'they have sought to transform the messianic idea into a notion of progress towards a state of intellectual and moral human perfection' (Wigoder, 2002, 523–4). The goal is of a transformed world. In the Amidah, the prayer for a redeemer is replaced with a prayer for redemption. The individual is replaced by the community.

Clive Lawton (2016) suggests that the idea of a messiah and the messianic age can be focused on too much in learning about Judaism. He suggests that 'for most Jews the idea of the messiah is simply used as a means to spur them on to try to make the world a better place, or to provide them with hope when they are subject to cruelty and persecution'. Further that 'they focus on the idea of the messianic age as a goal and ideal' (21). Though it is interesting to note that the celebration of Shabbat and other elements of Jewish celebration of festivals, such as the blowing of the shofar, point towards olam ha-ba, the messianic age, suggesting a greater centrality.

Whichever view of the messiah and the messianic age a Jew accepts, as Lawton suggests their responsibility is both to prepare themselves, and the world for this time.

Examples of how the actions of Jews can usher in the time of the messianic age are suggested in the Talmud:

> Rabbi Yoḥanan said in the name of Rabbi Shimon ben Yoḥai: If only the Jewish people would keep two Shabbatot in accordance with their halakhot, they would be immediately redeemed.

> (Shabbat 118b)

The immediate redemption meaning the beginning of the messianic age. Jews should do all they can to live their faith in a way that means the messiah will come. For some, however, the time will not be quickened through their actions, but that is part of their faith in the Almighty:

> We are aware that it, too, has its inherent dangers: inertia, quietism and a generalized sense that since God will send the Messiah in His good time, what we human beings do has little significance. We strive, therefore, to remind ourselves of the classical Jewish teaching that God and humanity are partners, not only in creation and revelation, but in redemption as well.

> (The Jewish Theological Seminary of America et al. 1988, 27)

The way that this occurs will be explored further in a discussion of tikkun olam/repair of the world in Chapter 7.

Memory

There are other interpretations of existence after death within Judaism. One is the idea that a person lives on in the memory of others; for some Jews this is the only existence that continues. This life and the impact that a person has during it are what matters, and the only thing that exists. Dara Horn suggested this when reflecting on what she believes, as a Jew, about life after death:

> I saw this as a way of saying our genes are expressed in our lives, that every ancestor is alive within us. At the end of my novel, when this child is about to be born, he is told that this 'world to come' is just a fake – the real 'world to come' is his life, the world he's being born into. And in one sense it's just a rational fact: The dead live in us genetically; we are carrying the dead into the future, even if their names are not remembered.

> (Schwartz, 2011)

The suggestion is that the Mourner's Kaddish might support such a view, as it does not mention the afterlife, only creation anew:

> 'May His great Name be magnified and sanctified in the world that He will create anew etc.', after which they detach earth and pluck grass [out of the ground] and cast it behind their back and wash their hands with water.

For some Jews who believe 'this life is it', this is not a negative view of life and its purpose. Rather, in living in obedience to the Almighty a person changes and strengthens the world and then passes on the world that is being redeemed to the next generation, hopefully to live on in memory, but mostly in genetics.

Reincarnation

In tandem with the immortality of the soul, a small number of Jews believe in reincarnation, which may also be termed *Gilgul Ha-nefesh* (rolling of the soul). This is mainly found in traditions such as Kabbalah (see Chapter 8), but it is argued by followers of Kabbalah that 'the greatest of the Jewish sages believed, wrote and taught about reincarnation' (Kurzweil, 2007, 101). In the *Sefer HaBahir* ('The Book of Brightness'), popular in the thirteenth century, the following conversation is recorded:

Why is there a righteous person who has good, and [another] righteous person who has evil?

This is because the [second] righteous person was wicked previously, and is now being punished.

Is one then punished for his childhood deeds? Did not Rabbi Simon say that in the Tribunal on high, no punishment is meted out until one is twenty years or older.

He said: I am not speaking of his present lifetime. I am speaking about what he has already been, previously.

It continues with the example of a person planting a vineyard to grow grapes; at each attempt he would fail, and he would start again. The question is asked 'How many times' should he plant? 'He said to them: For a thousand generations. It is thus written (Psalm 105:8)' (haKana, n.d., 195). While there may be occurrences of the creation of new souls, for most people on earth, in this Jewish understanding they have lived before. The example is used of the sixteenth-century Jewish mystic, Isaac Luria. It is said that by peering into a person's face he was able to discover the nature of the past lives of the soul, and as a result was able to advise what aspects of life and spirituality they should focus on in their current incarnation.

Karma is an integral part of the reincarnation process. Although there are some who describe the process in a positive way, in the sense that the soul is given many different opportunities to fulfil its work, and therefore death is a 'graduation' (Kurzweil, 2007, 107) there is still the idea that reincarnation can be both positive and negative. Mari Silva (2021) approaches it describing the same beliefs, but from a different perspective:

Gilgul is seen as a punishment and a very harsh one indeed for the one who must go through it. Simultaneously, it shows the mercy of God, as no one is cast-off to nothingness from him for always. Even those who deserve to have their souls extinguished or go extinct (keritut) are given a chance to do better through gilgul. Some put a lot of emphasis on the justice that comes with transmigration, some focus more on mercy. It serves one purpose: To purify the soul and give the chance to start afresh and do better.

(83)

There is the possibility of reincarnation into animals. The process is outlined in the following way:

- The soul is created by the Almighty.
- The soul exists before being placed into the body ('He blew into his nostrils the breath of life, and man became a living being' (Genesis 2:7).
- The soul seeks for its purpose in life.
- The soul seeks to fulfil its purpose through enjoying life and repairing the world.
- If the soul has not fulfilled its purpose, it is reincarnated.

Within the process there are varying suggestions as to how many reincarnations there are; some say three while others suggest that there could be thousands considering the Sefer HaBahir above. If a soul does damage to the world in a way that the soul is damaged, then it is possible that the soul ceases to exist. Outside of that, the question can be asked about the ultimate destination of the soul within the cycle of reincarnation. Kurzweil (2007) suggests that:

After death, the soul returns to God and once again basks in God's divine light. Souls that need to return to finish their work go back into the world. Souls that have finished their work return to God and wait for the perfection of the world as a whole.

(106)

Thoughts for the classroom

The natures of existence and of humanity are indelibly tied up with Jewish beliefs about the Almighty. Creation, whether that of the universe, or of humanity and their natures are expressions of the characteristics of the Almighty. The universe is created as habitation for humanity, as an expression of the love of the Almighty. The idea elucidated above that a person needs 'God in order to be, and God needs you' highlights the reciprocal relationship that a Jew should have with the Almighty. The world is also a place for a person to do good, to follow their positive inclinations and to live in the way that the Almighty has prescribed. There is a temptation for a teacher to group the 'Abrahamic' faiths in a way that creation and the purpose of life may seem synonymous. There are unique and important differences that Judaism holds in relation to Christianity and Islam. A way to explore this comparison may be through a similar and different exercise (see Figure 2.3).

It is not necessary to draw links, though the teacher may wish to, what is important is for uniqueness of Jewish beliefs to be explored along with their impact on the lived reality of Judaism for Jews today.

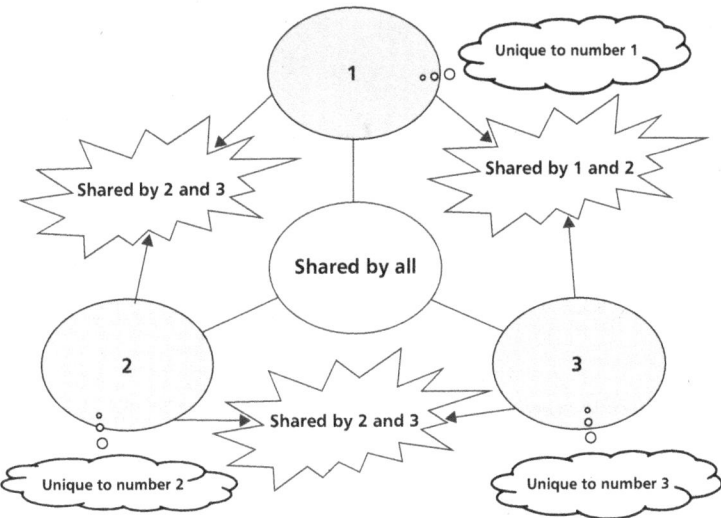

Figure 2.3 Similar and Different.

As is suggested above, sometimes in the classroom the over-focus on the days of creation means that the importance of creation for Jews is missed. The ongoing nature of creation, where the Almighty is not a distant deity but someone who is the ongoing cause of each new day, each new life and of everything is an important aspect of Jewish belief that should not be overlooked. The Almighty continues to speak the universe into existence every day, not just in the first seven. Again, these beliefs of the initial and ongoing creation should be included in any exploration of the nature of existence and creation. At this point, humanity's relationship with creation as stewards has been alluded to in this chapter but will be explored in much more detail in Chapter 7 as we explore the importance of tikkun olam and the responsibility to repair the world.

One of the most distinctive aspects of Jewish belief is the vagueness and seeming unimportance of life after death for Jews. Whichever interpretation of life and death is accepted by Jews it is incidental to the way that they live their lives. It is almost tempting to not really explore Jewish beliefs about life after death within the classroom, but the accepted wisdom of the classroom and the exam specifications suggest that this is not possible. The teacher should be clear that the way a person lives is important but not in a way that makes a future inheritance dependent on it.

Chapter 3

A Covenant People

For you are a people consecrated to the LORD your God: of all the peoples on earth the LORD your God chose you to be His treasured people. It is not because you are the most numerous of peoples that the LORD set His heart on you and chose you – indeed, you are the smallest of peoples; but it was because the LORD favoured you and kept the oath He made to your fathers that the LORD freed you with a mighty hand and rescued you from the house of bondage, from the power of Pharaoh king of Egypt. Know, therefore, that only the LORD your God is God, the steadfast God who keeps His covenant faithfully to the thousandth generation of those who love Him and keep His commandments, but who instantly requites with destruction those who reject Him – never slow with those who reject Him, but requiting them instantly.

(Deuteronomy 7:6-7)

The belief that Jews are a covenant people of the Almighty lies at the heart of Judaism and of Jewish identity. Wigoder (2002) suggests that if the Exodus is 'traditionally perceived as the central motif of Judaism, the covenant was viewed as the central mechanism' (188). The Almighty has chosen the people of Israel, the Jews to be his people, as they, in turn, have accepted the Almighty as the only God. What this means will be explored in this chapter and it will also build on elements of the preceding three chapters.

When Jews as a covenant people are spoken of, it usually refers to the Abrahamic Covenant, also known as the Covenant of the Pieces; subsequently developed by the Sinaitic Covenant, which is seen as a 'renewal and expansion of Abraham's covenant' (Wigoder, 2002, 187). There are, however, in the Tanakh a series of covenants made with Adam, Noah, Abraham, Jacob, Moses and David. Although the main focus of this chapter, and of Jewish identity is Abraham, it is possible to see the Adamic, the Noahic Covenants as being preludes to the covenant made with Abraham; similarly, those made with Moses and David are important expressions or developments of the Abrahamic Covenant. Each of these covenants reflects a Jewish understanding of their identity in relation to the Almighty, and the nature of the Almighty. This chapter will explore each of these covenants and how they contribute to Jewish identity and belief; in so doing it will narrate the various covenants with little commentary. At the end of this narration, a more in-depth exploration of the importance of the covenant in the lives of Jews today will be undertaken. This approach is adopted as it may be seen that all form part of one great whole and are different facets of the Almighty's reciprocal relationship with humanity, and Jews more specifically.

Adamic Covenant

The first covenant appears to be universal in nature and applicable to all of humanity as Adam and Eve are the progenitors of humanity or may be seen to be emblematic of each person. In the Genesis narrative, Adam and Eve are given stewardship and dominion over all of creation; the Almighty also fixes the laws of nature as a symbol of the covenant:

> Thus said the LORD: As surely as I have established My covenant with day and night –
> the laws of heaven and earth.
>
> (Jeremiah 23:25)

These highlight the belief that the Almighty is both the Creator and that he has chosen humanity for a specific role and purpose (see Chapter 2). Upon eating of the fruit of the Tree of Knowledge of Good and Evil, the Almighty casts Adam and Eve out of the Garden of Eden and establishes 'a new covenant – "be fruitful and multiply and subdue the earth"' (Robinson, 2000, 261). This command re-emphasizes humanity's role in the world in being asked to 'subdue' it, and also to fill it. The suggestion is also that these commands continue with each subsequent generation.

Noahic Covenant

The second covenant is similarly universal in nature, and in many ways reaffirms the covenant made with Adam. Indeed, Genesis 9 begins with the commands given in Eden:

> God blessed Noah and his sons, and said to them, 'Be fertile and increase, and till the
> earth. The fear and the dread of you shall be upon all the beasts of the earth and upon
> all the birds of the sky – everything with which the earth is astir – and upon all the fish of
> the sea; they are given into your hand'.
>
> (Genesis 9:1–2)

Though it is important to note that the language of the covenant is used for the first time here. In the Adamic Covenant, the covenantal aspects are inferred, whereas in the conversation with Noah, we read:

> And God said to Noah and to his sons with him, 'I now establish My covenant with you
> and your offspring to come, and with every living thing that is with you – birds, cattle, and
> every wild beast as well – all that have come out of the ark, every living thing on earth'.
>
> (Genesis 9:8–10)

The promise of the Almighty that forms part of the covenant is that:

> I will maintain My covenant with you: never again shall all flesh be cut off by the waters of
> a flood, and never again shall there be a flood to destroy the earth.
>
> (Genesis 9:11)

The covenant is confirmed with an *ot* (token or symbol). In this case, a rainbow:

> God further said, 'This is the sign that I set for the covenant between Me and you, and
> every living creature with you, for all ages to come. I have set My bow in the clouds, and
> it shall serve as a sign of the covenant between Me and the earth. When I bring clouds
> over the earth, and the bow appears in the clouds, I will remember My covenant between
> Me and you and every living creature among all flesh, so that the waters shall never
> again become a flood to destroy all flesh'.
>
> (Genesis 9:12–15)

It would appear in this summary that the only responsibility placed upon humanity is the command to fill the earth. However, the Talmud offers a further exegesis of Genesis 9 and identifies what are traditionally known as the Noachide Laws (though it is commonly believed that they were first given to Adam) that are incumbent on all of humanity. Based on Tosfeta Avodah Zarah 9, the seven laws are:

> The sons of Noah were given seven commandments: courts, idolatry, [blasphemy,]
> forbidden sexual relations, bloodshed, theft, and [consuming] the limb of a living
> animal.

A similar list is found in Sanhedrin 56a:

> The mitzva of establishing courts of judgment; and the prohibition against blessing,
> i.e., cursing, the name of God; and the prohibition of idol worship; and the prohibition
> against forbidden sexual relations; and the prohibition of bloodshed; and the prohibition
> of robbery; and the prohibition against eating a limb from a living animal.

The laws are those on which all people will ultimately be judged, and in the Jewish interpretation form the basis of laws. The importance of these has been highlighted in the modern day by a modern Noahide Movement known variously as The Bnei Noah (Children of Noah) or Noahidism. Feldman (2017) notes the importance within such an approach of the sharing of these seven laws, and their basis as a just society:

> In the 1980s, the Lubavitcher Rebbe of the Chabad Hasidic movement, Menchem
> Mendel Schneerson, promoted the idea that gentiles had a place in the covenant with
> God through observance of the Seven Noahide Laws. For the Rebbe, spreading aware-
> ness of the seven laws was part of his vision for a global tikkun (rectification) that would
> unify mankind under a common moral code in preparation for messianic times ... For

the Rebbe, only a universal social contract, grounded in faith in one God, could prevent human atrocities like genocide. To this day, Chabad maintains an ongoing campaign to present diplomatic leaders with the Noahide Laws, encouraging political leaders to proclaim the universality of the laws as a moral code for all of humanity.

Although a small movement, it highlights the importance of the laws for all of humanity in the Jewish worldview.

Abrahamic Covenant

With the Abrahamic Covenant, the Almighty formalizes a more concentrated relationship with what will become known as the House of Israel. Elements of the story of Abraham have been explored in the Introduction, but their further contextualization in the context of the covenant will be developed here.

In many ways, it is straightforward to outline the two sides of the Abrahamic Covenant according to the account in Genesis:

> The LORD said to Abram, 'Go forth from your native land and from your father's house to the land that I will show you. I will make of you a great nation, And I will bless you; I will make your name great, And you shall be a blessing. I will bless those who bless you And curse him that curses you; And all the families of the earth Shall bless themselves by you'.
>
> (Genesis 12:1–3)

The headlines of the Covenant of the Almighty with Abraham is that he will be a great nation and that all the world will be blessed because of Abraham and his descendants. The precise elements of the covenant are explained further in chapters 15 and 17 of Genesis. Genesis 15 begins with a vision for Abram who is worried that he is childless, and that his heir would be his servant Eliezer. In response to Abram's concern the Almighty reassures him that Eliezer would not be his heir, and that his 'very own issue shall be your heir' (Genesis 15:4). To further confirm this:

> He took him outside and said, 'Look toward heaven and count the stars, if you are able to count them.' And He added, 'So shall your offspring be.' And because he put his trust in the LORD, He reckoned it to his merit.
>
> (Genesis 15:5–6)

Abram is promised again that he will be a great nation, and that his seed would be as numerous as the stars. The Almighty changed Abram's name to Abraham, meaning 'father of multitudes' because he will be made 'the father of a multitude of nations' (Genesis 17:5).

As the second part of the Almighty's Covenant explored in Genesis 15, Abraham and his descendants are promised a land:

> Then He said to him, 'I am the LORD who brought you out from Ur of the Chaldeans to assign this land to you as a possession'. ... On that day the LORD made a covenant with Abram, saying, 'To your offspring I assign this land, from the river of Egypt to the great river, the river Euphrates ... '.

(Genesis 15:7, 18)

This 'Promised Land' later became known as Israel (its first use as attached to the land is found in 1 Samuel 13:19), named after Abraham's grandson, Jacob (later Israel). The exact location is described at various points in the Tanakh, not always consistently, it is identified with the land of Canaan (Genesis 17:8; Numbers 34:2); the land demarcated by the Red Sea, the Mediterranean and the Euphrates (Exodus 23), alongside other interpretations.

This covenant is confirmed with the offering of a 'a three-year-old heifer, a three-year-old she-goat, a three-year-old ram, a turtledove, and a young bird' (Genesis 15:9) which Abraham brought before the Almighty and 'cut them in two, placing each half opposite the other; but he did not cut up the bird' (Genesis 15:10). For this reason, the covenant is sometimes called *Brit Bein HaBetarim* or Covenant of the Pieces. The covenant is further confirmed by the sign or symbol of the covenant, *brit milah* or circumcision:

> Such shall be the covenant between Me and you and your offspring to follow which you shall keep: every male among you shall be circumcised. You shall circumcise the flesh of your foreskin, and that shall be the sign of the covenant between Me and you. And throughout the generations, every male among you shall be circumcised at the age of eight days. As for the homeborn slave and the one bought from an outsider who is not of your offspring, they must be circumcised, homeborn and purchased alike. Thus shall My covenant be marked in your flesh as an everlasting pact. And if any male who is uncircumcised fails to circumcise the flesh of his foreskin, that person shall be cut off from his kin; he has broken My covenant.

(Genesis 17:10-14)

Thus, the terms of the covenant on the part of Abraham and his descendants are circumcision (see Chapter 6) and to worship the Almighty and by implication follow his commands (see below: the Sinaitic Covenant). Although not evident in the passages outlined above, the suggestion is that in the subsequent command to sacrifice Isaac and Abraham's willingness to do so, results in blessings and the terms of the covenant being confirmed. The Almighty says:

> Because you have done this and have not withheld your son, your favoured one, I will bestow My blessing upon you.

(Genesis 22:16–17)

Further confirmed in Genesis 26:

> I will make your heirs as numerous as the stars of heaven, and assign to your heirs all
> these lands, so that all the nations of the earth shall bless themselves by your heirs—
> inasmuch as Abraham obeyed Me and kept My charge: My commandments, My laws,
> and My teachings.
>
> (4–5)

This is later confirmed in the covenant at Sinai, but for many Jews is inherent in the Genesis narrative. The Prophet Jeremiah hearkens back to the confirmation of the covenant and its conditional nature when he writes:

> I will make the men who violated My covenant, who did not fulfil the terms of the cove-
> nant which they made before Me, [like] the calf which they cut in two so as to pass
> between the halves.
>
> (Jeremiah 34:18)

This covenant is important for Jews throughout history and today as it confirms the identity of the Jews as a people and more specifically the chosen people of the Lord. This concept needs greater unpicking (see below) but at this point, it is important to note how Wayne Dosick (1995) explains this concept:

> Throughout the centuries, detractors of Jews and Judaism have pointed to the concept
> of chosenness as an attempt by Jews to flaunt supposed superiority and great-ness.
> In reality, just the opposite is true. The concept of chosen people means not that Jews
> were chosen for special privilege, but for sacred responsibility: to be … a 'light unto the
> nations' (after Isaiah 42:6, 496), a faith community reflecting God's light of love and law.
> The sacred Jewish responsibility is to receive, learn, live, and teach God's word and
> will. Receiving and transmitting the 'yoke of the Kingdom of God' is no easy tasks it is a
> heavy burden, but one that is willingly and even joyously, but always humbly, accepted.
>
> (19)

Echoed by two Jews living in Britain today:

> [The covenant] highlights the expectation that we are subject to a higher ethical stand-
> ard, being a light to the nations.
>   I think we have a sense of righteousness and justice and always trying to do the right
> thing.

The Abrahamic Covenant establishes for Jews an important aspect of their relationship with the Divine. Weinfeld (1970) argues that the covenant is an example of a suzerain-vassal treaty being 'an obligation of the vassal to his master, the suzerain, the "grant" consti-tutes an obligation of the master to his servant' (185). The covenant is therefore 'a reward for loyalty and good deeds already performed' and 'an inducement for future loyalty' (Weinfeld, 1970, 185). This establishes, in light of Chapter 1 and the discussion of the characteristics of the Almighty, the belief in his omnipotence and the complete dependence of humanity on the Almighty. This is developed further in the Covenant at Sinai.

Sinaitic Covenant

The Sinaitic Covenant (or Mosaic Covenant) was an expansion and renewal of the Abrahamic Covenant; it has to be seen in that light. It is not a new covenant, rather it is a development of the Covenant with Abraham that seems to make the terms more conditional in nature, described by Weinfeld as 'an obligatory type' of covenant (1970, 184).

The covenant can be described as an 'if-then' covenant confirming its conditional nature, exemplified in Exodus 19:

> Now then, if you will obey Me faithfully and keep My covenant, you shall be My treasured possession among all the peoples. Indeed, all the earth is Mine.
>
> (6)

It was not just for that moment, we read in Deuteronomy:

> I make this covenant, with its sanctions, not with you alone, but both with those who are standing here with us this day before the LORD our God and with those who are not with us here this day.
>
> (19:13–14)

Those who were not 'with us' is interpreted to mean that 'the covenant is made not just with those who were present at Sinai, but it is renewed with every Jew in every generation. According to one Jewish legend, the souls of all Jews who would ever live were present at Sinai' (Dosick, 1995, 18). Moses received the covenant and its associated law at Sinai and read it to the people in the wilderness:

> Moses went and repeated to the people all the commands of the LORD and all the rules; and all the people answered with one voice, saying, 'All the things that the LORD has commanded we will do!' Moses then wrote down all the commands of the LORD.
>
> (Exodus 24:3–4)

The covenant was sealed with burnt offerings and the sacrifice of bulls. At the conclusion of the sacrifice Moses again 'took the record of the covenant and read it aloud to the people. And they said, "All that the LORD has spoken we will faithfully do!"' (Exodus 24:7). The promises of the Abrahamic Covenant continue, and the Almighty's promises are reiterated:

> I will abide among the Israelites, and I will be their God. And they shall know that I the LORD am their God, who brought them out from the land of Egypt that I might abide among them, I the LORD their God.
>
> (Exodus 29:45–6)

The promise that the Almighty would abide with them links very much with the concept of shechinah (explored in Chapter 1), which is symbolized in the Exodus story with the pillar of fire/smoke; but is also represented in the Tabernacle which the Almighty commanded Moses to make. This served as a portable dwelling place for the Almighty and served as the focal point for worship and sacrifice; and continued in use until it was replaced by the Temple built by Solomon as a dwelling place for the Almighty.

Tradition suggests that the record that Moses made because the written Torah (see Chapter 4) containing the 613 mitzvot or commandments of the Lord. The number of 613, while widely accepted, is built on tradition rather than a precise number. The initial identification of 613 is ascribed to Simlai in the third century; in the Talmud it is recorded:

> Rabbi Simlai taught: There were 613 mitzvot stated to Moses in the Torah, consisting of 365 prohibitions corresponding to the number of days in the solar year, and 248 positive mitzvot corresponding to the number of a person's limbs.
>
> (Makkot 23b: 18)

The beauty of this tradition is the suggestion that the mitzvot should be followed every day of the year, and by the entirety of a person. As to the exact number Ibn Ezra in *Yesod Moreh* suggests that there are many ways of counting the mitzvot, but in reality, there are many more than 613, though they may not all be listed:

> And in the pursuit of truth, there is no end to the number of commandments, as the poet said, 'I have seen an end to all perfection; Your commandment is exceedingly broad'. (Psalms 119:96) And if we were to count the principles, the general rules, and the enduring commandments, the commandments would exceed six hundred and thirteen.
>
> (2)

At the same time there are 'less than 613 [that] are relevant today', some of which are impossible because they surround worship in the Temple. The 'most acceptable' list of the 613 is believed to be those enumerated by Maimonides, but they are not without their critics (Drazin, 2009, 206).

It is these, and further rabbinic mitzvot, that have led to the identification of Jews as a People of the Law. These laws govern every aspect of a person's life; and for many Jews are the basis for how they live today. There are different categories of mitzvot that are found in the Torah; in the *Sefer HaChinukh* (a thirteenth-century rabbinic text) the following categories and types are mentioned by the author in his introduction:

- Positive commandments (*mitzvot aseh*), 'those that it commanded us to do add up to two hundred and forty-eight.'
- Negative commandments (*mitzvot lo ta'aseh*), meaning the things that it is commanded 'to not do, three hundred and sixty-five.'

- Some are commanded for all of the Jews 'including males and females – at all times and in every place. And some of them are [those] that only Israelites are obligated in every place and at all times, but not priests and Levites.'
- Those mitzvot for which 'only priests alone are obligated – in every place and at all times.'
- Some to which 'only a king of Israel is obligated.'
- 'Some that an individual is not obligated by himself, but rather only the entire community.'
- Some are commanded for all Jews but only 'in a certain place and at a certain time – that being the Land of Israel when most of the Jewish people are dwelling there.'
- Some commands are given to men and women separately.
- Some of these commandments are that 'that a person is obligated to do constantly', which are suggested to be: to know the Almighty as Creator, to not to have any other gods besides the Almighty, to know the Almighty's Oneness, to fear the Almighty, to love the Almighty, to not follow the passions of the heart.
- 'Some that he is obligated to do at a specific time and not before then – such as the commandment of sukkah (dwelling in a hut), lulav, resting on the holidays, recitation of Shema and all that is similar to them – that have a set time to do them in the year or in the day.'
- 'And there are some of them that a person is never obligated to do unless he is caused by a matter that comes to his hand that requires that commandment that is fitting for that matter.'

Other suggestions of categories include mitzvot between the Almighty and people, and then mitzvot between people. Over the years the Written Law of the Torah, and the Oral Law passed on since Moses has been collected into *Halakhah* (the way to behave), and this has guided the rituals, and also the behaviour of Jews throughout the centuries. In addition to the Written and Oral Torahs, there are also rabbinic rulings. Jews today hold different views about the authority of Halakhah; while for some Orthodox Jews it cannot be changed except in very minor circumstances, others such as many Reform and Masorti Jews might consider continued halakhic discussion to allow for reinterpretation. Elements of the mitzvot and their interpretation will be developed in the subsequent chapters of this book.

The purpose of the Covenant at Sinai is to confirm the relationship between the Almighty and his people. While to an outside observer, following the mitzvot may seem onerous, for many Jews it is as simple as breathing as it is what they have always done. The Covenant establishes that a Jew is focused less on what they believe, rather what they do:

> For while it is rooted in faith, in creed, Judaism is not a religion dependent on profession of belief. It is, far more, a religion of action, of deed, of mitzvot – at each and every moment, at each and every opportunity – waiting to be done.
>
> (Dosick, 1995, 35)

As suggested earlier, the covenant is to be lived every day and with a person's whole self. In the subsequent chapters that explore religious expressions and ethical approaches within Judaism (Chapters 6 and 7), much greater outlining of some of the mitzvot will be developed. In this chapter, we have laid the basis of why the covenant is the basis for the actions of Jews, and the importance of Judaism as a religion of action and of practice.

Davidic Covenant

There are two passages in the Tanakh that are believed by some Jews to establish what is known as the Davidic Covenant or the Covenant with David. In 2 Samuel 7, it says:

> I will give you great renown like that of the greatest men on earth. I will establish a home for My people Israel and will plant them firm, so that they shall dwell secure and shall tremble no more. Evil men shall not oppress them any more as in the past, ever since I appointed chieftains over My people Israel. I will give you safety from all your enemies. 'The LORD declares to you that He, the LORD, will establish a house for you. When your days are done and you lie with your fathers, I will raise up your offspring after you, one of your own issue, and I will establish his kingship … I will establish his royal throne forever. I will be a father to him, and he shall be a son to Me … Your house and your kingship shall ever be secure before you; your throne shall be established forever'.
>
> (9–14, 16)

And in Psalms 89:

> I will sing of the LORD's steadfast love forever;
> to all generations I will proclaim Your faithfulness with my mouth.
> I declare, 'Your steadfast love is confirmed forever;
> there in the heavens You establish Your faithfulness'.
> 'I have made a covenant with My chosen one;
> I have sworn to My servant David:
> I will establish your offspring forever,
> I will confirm your throne for all generations.' Selah.
> Your wonders, O LORD, are praised by the heavens,
> Your faithfulness, too, in the assembly of holy beings.
>
> (2–6)

There are different aspects to the covenant that could be seen to be continuing the covenant originally made with Abraham. In establishing a home for his people, the Almighty is confirming the inheritance of the land of Canaan. In the exploration in 2 Samuel that 'I will be a father to him, and he shall be a son to Me' it seems that this:

> … is an adoption formula and actually serves as the judicial basis for the gift of the eternal dynasty. This comes to the fore in Ps. II where we read: 'he (=God) said to me:

'you are my son, this day have I begotten you. Ask me and I will give you nations for your patrimony and the ends of the earth for your possession'

(vv. 7–8) (Weinfeld, 1970, 190)

This again confirms the Abrahamic Covenant that through Abraham's seed would all the nations of the earth be blessed, and this would be in part through the establishment of the throne of David forever, and in tandem with Jeremiah 33:17–21 a king of the line of David would fulfil the role of prophet, priest and king. As indicated in Chapter 2, for many Jews this indicated that the messiah would be a great king through the line of David. As was also noted, this belief has dissipated for many, in favour of a messianic age, if of anything.

Brit/Chesed

As indicated within Chapter 1, there are two complimentary views of the Almighty exemplified in his characteristics and in the Kabbalistic Tree of Life. These two aspects find expression within the covenantal relationship between Jews and the Almighty. On the one hand, the Almighty is Lawgiver and Judge; on the other he is Father, merciful and expressed in shechinah. These two aspects are reflected in the two aspects of the covenants and the Hebrew words associated with them: brit and chesed. On the one hand, covenants place a responsibility on Jews throughout the ages. Dosick (1995) suggests that 'the if-then nature of the brit is disturbing, for it seems that the personal relationship between God and His people should be unconditional, not dependent on behaviour' (18). In this sense, an over focus on the demands of justice and of the law leads to an impression of the Almighty, and the covenants, as restrictive and also punitive. Whereas a focus on 'the concept of chesed … [meaning] "covenantal love"' gives Jews the hope that the Almighty's 'unconditional love, the providential care, the ultimate forgiveness, the grace' gives a person hope that they will always be loved, no matter how many mistakes they make (Dosick, 1995, 18).

> The conduct of those bound in a covenant was characterized by loyal mutual service, and Yahweh could be expected to render kindness and succour, and even punishment where punishment could be conceived of as the instrument to restore covenant relationships.
>
> (Glueck, 1967, 6)

This is evident throughout the Tanakh in various examples, where the love of the Almighty is expressed despite the rebelliousness of Israel. One example already alluded to in a discussion of the Almighty as Father (see Chapter 1) focuses on the metaphorical nature of the story of Hosea and his adulterous wife, Gomer, whose relationship is symbolic of the Almighty and Israel. Indeed, chapter 3 of Hosea provides a microcosm of both relationships:

> The LORD said to me further, 'Go, befriend a woman who, while befriended by a companion, consorts with others, just as the LORD befriends the Israelites, but they turn to other

gods and love the cups of the grape.' Then I hired her for fifteen [shekels of] silver, a homer of barley, and a lethech of barley; and I stipulated with her, 'In return, you are to go a long time without either fornicating or marrying; even I [shall not cohabit] with you'. For the Israelites shall go a long time without king and without officials, without sacrifice and without cult pillars, and without ephod and teraphim. Afterward, the Israelites will turn back and will seek the LORD their God and David their king – and they will thrill over the LORD and over His bounty in the days to come.

Israel is forgiven, and brought into a relationship; there is a period of penance, but eventually Israel will be reconciled with the Almighty. A further example is found in the making of the golden calf at Sinai, on descending the mount and discovering many Israelites worshipping a golden calf as the 'god, O Israel, who brought you out of the land of Egypt!' (Exodus 32:4). The Exodus account describes that the Almighty was angry and wished to destroy them, but Moses reminded him of the covenant he had made with Abraham, Isaac and Jacob, and the punishment was abated because of the love inherent in the covenant and the Almighty. The prophet Nehemiah remembers the reaction of the Almighty to this event as an expression of his compassion:

You, in Your abundant compassion, did not abandon them in the wilderness. The pillar of cloud did not depart from them to lead them on the way by day, nor the pillar of fire by night to give them light in the way they were to go. You endowed them with Your good spirit to instruct them. You did not withhold Your manna from their mouth; You gave them water when they were thirsty. Forty years You sustained them in the wilderness so that they lacked nothing; their clothes did not wear out, and their feet did not swell.

(Nehemiah 9:19–21)

When speaking of the covenant, it is important for Jews to remember that both brit and chesed 'create the unique covenantal distinction of the Jewish People as God's selected nation' (Dosick, 1995, 19).

Thoughts for the classroom

In many ways, just as the nature of the Almighty serves as the context within which Jews live their lives and express their faith, so too are the covenants that have been made with the Almighty. Many elements of their promises and responsibility find expression in the daily lives of Jews, and while the outworkings may be spoken of or observed, they may be a silent context and background. This reiterates the view that should be explored in the classroom, that it is the actions of Jews that are most important and that beliefs may not be the most talked about aspects of Jewish life. Having said that, however, the covenant with Abraham and its subsequent clarifications in the Mosaic and Davidic covenants, lie at the heart of Jewish identity. When considering who is Jewish (see Introduction) the exploration of lineage, a nation and as the chosen people are all directly related to the

Abrahamic Covenant. One cannot understand the importance of the Almighty, the importance of the Law, or the importance of Israel (identified as the three pillars of Judaism above) without reference to the covenant.

The specific covenants of Abraham and Moses are identified for study in all GCSE specifications, and suggest an importance that Clive Lawton (2012) suggests is disproportionate to the lived reality today, and that 'for most Jews, ideas of the Covenant are nowhere near as important as the idea of the giving of the Torah, which is one of the central points of ideological dispute between diverse Jewish denominations. When most Jews think about the giving of the Torah, they do not single out the Ten Commandments from the other mitzvot' (17). This is an important focus to understand when teaching the importance of the mitzvot, perhaps because of the Christian lens through which most teachers teach and curriculum writers develop their curriculum, there may be an over-focus on aspects such as the Ten Commandments, or on elements that people assume are 'the most important'. Indeed, some GCSE questions surround which is the most important covenant for Jews, which is obviously nonsense.

One way that teachers could approach the importance of the covenants in the classroom with students of any age is through the stories of Adam, Noah, Abraham and Moses. The importance of storytelling is explored in Chapters 5 and 6, but at this point, it is important for a teacher to realize that a story is not just a story; it is a way to communicate the beliefs and practices of a religion. It is impossible to understand Jewish identity today without an exploration of the stories of the prophets. While it is appropriate to focus on Abraham and Moses as the 'founders' of Judaism, whatever that means, an exploration of Adam and Noah can help students understand far more than how the world was created and the fact that the Almighty loves animals. They establish the Almighty as not just God for Jews, but in a Jewish worldview, the god of the whole world.

Chapter 4

Sacred Writings

In this chapter, we will explore the various aspects of text within the context of the sacred writings of Judaism, and how they are used by Jews today. While Jews are sometimes described as a 'People of the Law' meaning the Torah, there are other sacred texts of Judaism which sit alongside the Torah. Indeed, the Tanakh (also spelled, the Tenakh) is the compilation of the Torah (Law), Nevi'im (Prophets) and the Ketuvim (the Writings). While the exploration of the Tanakh will form the first part of this chapter, text and literature is important in all aspects of Judaism, and there are other writings such as the Talmud that many see as important as the Torah, with the Torah being the Written Law and the Talmud, the Oral Law, and this will also be explored. In addition, texts such as the Apocrypha (*HaSefarim haChitzoniyim*) and Midrash will also be touched upon as forms of Jewish writing, and sources for how a Jew might live their lives.

The Tanakh

As suggested above, the fundamental text of Judaism is the Torah; one British Jew has suggested:

> The Torah is the foundation of Judaism on which we can place several millennia of development and new insights to understand what we obliged to do today. I find the Torah portions each Shabbat very interesting and especially when links are made between then and now. I see myself as a star in a universe and part of the whole Jewish world. Together with the *Nevi'im* (Prophets) and the *Ketuvim* (the Writings) they form the Tanakh.

(see Table 4.1)

The Tanakh was not produced all at once; the timeline of its compilation is usually seen to follow various stages. It is suggested that most of the texts were passed on orally for different lengths of time and at different times. It is suggested that the concretization of any timeline of the compilation of a written library of texts is 'largely a matter of conjecture'

Table 4.1 The Sections and Books of the Tanakh

Torah (Five Books of Moses, Pentateuch, or Khumash)		Bereishit/ Genesis Shemot/ Exodus Vayikra/ Leviticus Bamidbar/ Numbers Devarim/ Deuteronomy
Nevi'im (Prophets)	Nevi'im Rishonim (Former Prophets)	Yehoshua/ Joshua Shoftim Shmuel Aleph/ 1 Samuel Shmuel Bet/ 2 Samuel Melakhim Aleph/ 1 Kings Melakhim Bet/ 2 Samuel
	Nevi'im Aharonim (The Latter Prophets)	Yish'yahu/ Isaiah Yirmiyahu/ Jeremiah Yehezkel/ Ezekiel
	Trei Asar (The Twelve Minor Prophets)	Hoshea/ Hosea Yoel/ Joel Amos/ Amos Obadayah/ Obadiah Yonah/ Jonah Mikah/ Micah Nakhum /Nahum Habakuk/ Habakkuk Zefanyah/ Zephaniah Haggai/ Haggai Zekaryah/ Zechariah Malakhai/ Malachi
Ketuvim (Writings)	Sifrei Emet (Poetic Books)	Tehillim/ Psalms Mishleh/ Proverbs Iyob/ Job
	Megillot (Scrolls)	Shir ha-Shirim/ Song of Songs Ruth/ Ruth Eikhah/ Lamentations Kohelet/ Lamentations Ester/Esther Danyel/ Daniel Ezra/ Ezra Nehemyah/ Nehemiah Dibrei Hayamim Aleph/ 1 Chronicles Dibreu Hayamim Bet/ 2 Chronicles

(Wigoder, 2002, 122). The first mention of a written text of the book of the Torah is in approximately 622CE when King Josiah ruled. This is alluded to in *2 Kings*:

> The king went up to the House of the LORD, together with all the men of Judah and all the inhabitants of Jerusalem, and the priests and prophets – all the people, young and old. And he read to them the entire text of the covenant scroll which had been found in the House of the LORD. The king stood by the pillar-a and solemnized the covenant before the LORD: that they would follow the LORD and observe His commandments, His injunctions, and His laws with all their heart and soul; that they would fulfil all the terms of this covenant as inscribed upon the scroll. And all the people entered into-b the covenant.
>
> (23:2–3)

Whether this refers to the entirety or a portion of what is now known as the Torah is unknown. In Nehemiah, written in approximately the fifth century BCE people ask for the book of the Torah of Moses to be read. This has led many to assume that the book was complete before the Israelites were taken into exile in Babylon.

The remainder of the texts in the Tanakh are believed to have been written in the Second Temple Period (see Introduction). The suggestion is that these books were collected into a normative collection in the first and second centuries CE, and it wasn't 'until the middle of the second century CE [that] there [was] unshaken agreement as to the scope of the Hagiographa' (Wigoder, 2002, 123).

The Torah is traditionally seen by Jews to be revealed by the Almighty at Sinai:

> 'All the things that the LORD has commanded we will do!' Moses then wrote down all the commands of the LORD.
>
> (Exodus 24:3–4)

Drawing on this passage in his *Commentary on Mishnah Sanhedrin*, Maimonides outlined this view:

> The Torah is from Heaven and that is that we believe that this Torah that is given to us through Moshe, our teacher – peace be upon him – is completely from the mouth of the Almighty; which is to say that it all came to him from God, may He be blessed, in a manner that is metaphorically called speech. And no one knows how it came to him except Moshe himself, peace be upon him – since it came to him. And [we believe] that he was like a scribe who is dictated to and writes down all of the events, the stories and the commandments. And therefore, [Moshe] is called the engraver.
>
> (10.1.25)

When the Torah scrolls are raised before the congregation in the synagogue, the following might be recited:

> VeZot haTorah – This is the Torah that Moses set before the people Israel–by the mouth of God, through the hand of Moses.

Apart from the final few verses of Deuteronomy, which narrate the final days of Moses, many Jews believe that the entirety of the Torah was written by Moses, with the words directly revealed or dictated as *Menachot* 30a suggests: 'The Holy One, Blessed be He, dictated and Moses wrote the text and repeated after Him' (8). As the verse in Exodus 24 was given at Sinai, there is also the tradition that Moses continued to write in the same way as instructed by the Almighty until the Torah was complete, perhaps as many as forty years later.

There are varying attitudes among Jews as to the status of the Torah as the word of the Almighty. In 2022, survey found among British Jews that:

- 12% believe that the Torah is the actual word of the Almighty (Orthodox 58%, Charedi 98%, Traditional 13%).
- 38% believe that it is the inspired word of the Almighty but should not be taken literally (Orthodox 36%, Charedi 5%, Traditional 53%).
- 50% believe it is a book of history written by people (Orthodox 7%, Charedi 1%, Traditional 34%) (see Boyd, 2023a).

This approach to the authority of the Torah is important when considering the interpretation of halakhah (law) and the possible changing of such (see Chapter 7).

The Torah outlines the history of the world from Adam to Noah, and from Noah to Abraham, and then the history of the Jews from that point until their re-entry into Canaan with Joshua following the disappearance of Moses. These narratives, whether historically accurate or not, are important for Jews in understanding the nature of the Almighty, the place of humanity, and the importance of the covenantal relationship (see Chapters 1–3). Many of the other aspects of Torah surround laws surrounding how Jews should live.

The Torah is the centre of study for Jews. The blessing of studying the Torah is equal to all other mitzvot:

> These are the matters that a person does them and enjoys their profits in this world, and nevertheless the principal exists for him for the World-to-Come, and they are: Honouring one's father and mother, and acts of loving kindness, and bringing peace between a person and another, and Torah study is equal to all of them.
>
> (Shabbat 127a:15)

The Torah can be studied individually, where a person studies in dialogue with the text; in community either part of prayer services where the Torah is read (see Chapter 6), or as part of a *beit midrash*, a house of study. The other texts outlined in this chapter are used to support the study of Torah. So important is the study of Torah that in Charedi forms of Orthodox Judaism, many men study Torah full-time and do not engage in other occupations.

Other sections of the Tanakh form part of the study of the Torah, and for some are included in the shorthand reference 'the Torah'. The other two sections of Nevi'im and

Ketuvim are seen by many of the Jews to be inspired but not in the same way as the Torah may be seen to be the direct word of the Almighty.

Sections of the Nevi'im (prophets) will be read in worship services and as part of devotion. Within the Nevi'im the history of Israel as a nation is recorded, from the time of Joshua to the return after the Babylonian exile, throughout which Israel seems to go through a cycle of prosperity and opposition. Israel is sometimes in the ascendancy, but sometimes in subjugation. As such the messages of the prophets seek to reorient Israel towards their covenants with the Almighty, and by so doing they come back into relationship with him and the land. In a sign of the reciprocal relationship between people and the Almighty, the prophets often interceded with the Almighty on behalf of the people. In a world where the people of Israel may be oppressed, the narrative of the prophets gives Jews hope and guidance.

The Ketuvim (Writings) is a collection of religious writings in the form of poetry, wisdom, story, prayer and is described as 'the canonical collection from the post-prophetic age' (My Jewish Learning, n.d.a). The various texts are used throughout Jewish worship, and again they help Jews understand the nature of their covenant with the Almighty. The most often used are the Psalms which can be found being used in individual and communal prayers. In Chapter 3 we explored the example of Hosea and how his relationship with Gomer was an allegory of the Almighty's relationship with Israel. Similarly, Job may not be intended to be taken literally but could be seen to be a midrash (see below) on the themes of evil and suffering. Five of the texts: Ecclesiastes, Esther, Song of Songs, Ruth and Lamentations are known collectively as the Hamesh Megillot (Five Scrolls) and read in the various festivals of Sukkot, Purim, Passover, Sahvuot and Tisha B'Av.

There are many commentaries on the Tanakh, not least the Talmud (see below) and its exposition of the Torah. Some of the more famous commentaries were written by Rashi (1040–1105), Abraham Ibn Ezra (1092–1167), David Kimkhi (1160–1235) and Nakhmanides (1194–1270). The source of all Tanakh and Talmud quotations in this book are taken from sefaria.org, which is a great resource in bringing all of the resources to help study the Tanakh into one place. As a reader opens a verse from the Tanakh, on the right a menu opens which gives the option of associated readings for the verse in commentaries, the Talmud, Halakhah, the Tanakh and more. More recently commentaries such as *The Torah: A Women's Commentary* explore the voices of women in understanding the Torah (Eskenazi & Weiss, 2008), this too is freely available on Sefaria.

The Talmud

The Torah is the Law – the Talmud is the way – for example, if we imagine Moses on Mount Sinai being told 'keep the sabbath day holy'; Moses asked the Lord what does this mean?. The Lord says 'Don't write this down, but these are the things permissible and impermissible'.

The above comment from a Jewish person can be seen to encapsulate the view of many Jews when it comes to a discussion of the law (see Chapters 1 and 3) and the importance of texts within Judaism. A more common way to express the relationship between the two is to speak of the Torah as the Written Law, and the Talmud as the Oral Law. Matt Greene (2020) has described the Talmud in the following way:

> Our most sacred text isn't the Torah, the purported word of Hashem, but the Talmud, a multi-volume companion text that interprets, expands and comments. Essentially the Talmud is marginalia, a conversation. A beneath-the-line comments section. What Judaism essentially amounts to is a four-thousand-year-old argument.
>
> (16)

This, in many ways, is perhaps the inverse of what may be taught or observed, indeed for many Jews to draw distinctions between the authority of the Torah and the Talmud is not desirable. As suggested, the Talmud is seen as the recording of the Oral Law that was given on Sinai to Moses and passed on through the generations. In terms of Jewish practice, the Talmud has perhaps had, and continues to have, the most influence on the daily lives of Jews. Safrai (1976) suggests this with reference to the Middle Ages:

> It became the basic – and in many places almost the exclusive – asset of Jewish tradition, the foundation of all Jewish thought and aspirations and the guide for the daily life of the Jew. Other components of national culture were made known only in so far as they were embedded in the Talmud. In almost every period and community until the modern age, the Talmud was the main object of Jewish study and education; all the external conditions and events of life seemed to be but passing incidents, and the only true, permanent reality was that of the Talmud.
>
> (376)

The Talmud was a composition of rabbinic Judaism. In the first centuries of the Common Era, following the destruction of the Second Temple in 70 CE centuries, a great number of judgements and opinions passed by Jewish teachers built up. They were all to do with the way that the Jews were expected to behave. These important pieces of information were passed down by word of mouth and were later recorded in the Mishnah ('study by repetition'). The first record of a written Mishnah, or the Oral Torah is in the late second to early third centuries 200 CE, they were collected together into one book – the Mishnah by Judah ha-Nasi in an attempt to 'systematize the *halakhah*' (Wigoder, 2002, 542). As this developed it became 'a compilation of legal rulings based on biblical law, actual practice, and spiritual vision' (Greenspahn, 2009, 3). The worry was that the collection of rulings and traditions might be forgotten.

The structure of the Mishnah is that it is split into six sederim (orders):

- *Zerim* (seeds) which explores prayers, blessings, tithes and agricultural laws (this is split into eleven masechot or tractates).

- *Moed* (festival) which explores the laws associated with Shabbat and the celebration of other festivals (this is split into twelve masechot).
- *Nashim* (women) mainly focusing on laws concerning marriage and divorce (this is split into seven masechot).
- *Nezekin* (damages) focuses on aspects of courts, and civil and criminal law (this is split into ten masechot).
- *Kodashim* (holy things) explores Temple and sacrifice rituals, also the laws of kashrut (this is split into eleven masechot).
- *Tohorot* (purities) explores laws concerning purity and impurity (this is split into twelve masechot).

The teachings of the Mishnah usually organize the received traditions by presenting cases that had been brought to judgement and are then developed by the debate that surrounded the issue, concluded by the judgement given which, as has been suggested, is based on the halakhah in the Torah, actual practice and the spiritual vision, or spirit of the law. This enabled the mitzvot to be interpreted and codified and to be remembered.

Following the establishment of the Mishnah, the rulings began to be discussed. Soon, there was more material taking the form of debate and discussion that developed in subsequent centuries, usually seen to be until the beginning of the sixth century. These writings are known as the *Gemara*: 'the starting point of the Gemara discussions is the Mishnah text, the end point is the decision as to what is accepted as law' (Wigoder, 2002, 748). There is a much broader range of material in the Gemara than the Mishnah as it includes discussions, debates, Midrash, stories about rabbis and many more types of narrative material; these are then used to build rulings on various issues.

The Mishnah and the Gemara were brought together to form the Talmud, the first version of which is found in the fifth century. It was not the case that the Talmud contained the Mishnah and then the Gemara, rather it contains a Mishnah and then the associated discussions and commentary follow. In online editions, these immediately follow, whereas in Hebrew texts, they often surround the Mishnah text and may include later commentaries. It still has a great effect on the way that Jewish people live. Jewish people sometimes refer to it to try to work out how they should behave in certain situations.

There are seen to be two editions of the Talmud that developed simultaneously in different areas; perhaps reflecting the concerns of the different communities: The Jerusalem Talmud and the Babylonian Talmud. Both contain the Mishnah of Judah ha-Nasi. The Jerusalem Talmud was compiled in the fourth and fifth centuries in the rabbinical academies of Caesarea, Sepphoris and Tiberias, leading some to name it the Palestinian Talmud, while the Babylonian Talmud was compiled in rabbinical academies of Mesopotamia including Nehardea, Nusaybin, Mahoza, Pumbedita and the Sura Academy. While neither includes commentary on every Mishnah, the Babylonian Talmud has Gemara for thirty-seven out of the sixty-three masechot, while the Jerusalem Talmud has Gemara for thirty-nine. Despite this, the Jerusalem Talmud is about a third of the size of the Babylonian Talmud as the Jerusalem Talmud is more succinct, while the Babylonian is more discursive in nature including stories, midrash (see below) and even jokes.

As to their authority; traditionally the Babylonian Talmud:

> has been considered the more authoritative of the two Talmuds. This privileging of the Bavli [Babylonian] reflects the fact that Babylonia was the dominant centre of Jewish life from talmudic times through the beginning of the medieval period. The first codifiers of halakhah (Jewish law), based in Baghdad in the eighth through 10th centuries, used the Bavli as the basis of their legal writings. Reflecting the prevalent attitude toward the Yerushalmi [Jerusalem], the Machzor Vitri, written in France in the 11th or 12th century, comments, 'When the Talmud Yerushalmi disagrees with our Talmud, we disregard the Yerushalmi'.
>
> (Jacobs, n.d.)

Though this is not the whole tale; the Jerusalem Talmud was used alongside the Babylonian Talmud by Maimonides, and many Jews will continue to refer to both. There are more copies of the Babylonian Talmud printed than the Jerusalem Talmud, perhaps suggesting its primacy.

It is indisputable that both versions of the Talmuds are 'treasure trove[s] of Jewish thought, history, Bible, exegesis, folklore and much more. Ultimately, the Talmud shaped the very nature of Judaism and Jewishness and its laws transformed Jewishness and its laws transformed Judaism into an all-encompassing way of life' (Wigoder, 2002, 750). It serves as the link between the Torah and Jewish practices today. There are, however, differing approaches to the authority of the Talmud within Judaism. For many Orthodox Jews the Talmud is seen to be authoritative as an addition to and clarification of the Torah. The belief that the Talmud is based on the Oral Law given to Moses at Sinai persists within Orthodox Jewish communities. As such, the Talmud is immutable and should be consulted and followed.

For other Jews, the Talmud is foundational and an important aspect of Jewish life today, though its origin at Sinai may be questioned. It may also be considered that just as rabbis throughout the ages have considered the implications of *halakhah* and their Talmudic interpretations for Jewish life, this can and should continue in the modern world. Some scholars have observed that Judaism and its practices have developed in dialogue with its surrounding community (Greenspahn, 2009) and that in light of this, it is possible to see the responsibility to continue that discussion and interpretation today. The Past President of the World Union for Progressive Jews has suggested:

> [The Talmud's part of] how Reform Judaism looks at rabbinic law ... We see ourselves as successors reclaiming the core Torah text. The rabbis of today and of yesteryear are of equal authority. The amoraim [rabbinic sages quoted in the Talmud] do not get special consideration. Contemporary commentary is equally as interesting and holy, if you will.
>
> (Heilman, 2012)

Indeed, it is possible to see that while 'the Talmud is the original and most extensive body of Oral Torah, the Oral Torah is properly comprised of every piece of discussion and tradition in all of the texts that have been developed and are still developing around the challenge of how to understand and apply the mitzvot of the Torah to contemporary life' (Lawton, 2012, 66). There are a small number of Jews known as Karaite who reject rabbinic Judaism and the concept of Oral law. They believe that halakhah can only be found in the Torah, and the wider Tanakh.

The Talmud forms the application of the mitzvot in Jewish life today, they also find expression in the daily prayers offered by Jews, and are discussed in Yeshivas and study groups. It is less likely that they are studied alone, or mined for guidance. Daf Yomi is a practice established in Poland in 1923 by Rav Meir Shapiro of studying a page of the Talmud each day; to complete the 2,711 pages of the Babylonian Talmud takes approximately seven and a half years. These studies might take place at home, in shul or online in groups or through podcasts and social media pages. The development of wider study opportunities means that while in the past the study of Talmud may been the preserve of men, it is no longer so. For example, Hadran is an organization dedicated to advancing the study of the Talmud by women bringing together the page from the Talmud (the DAF) and partnering it with podcasts and other resources (Hadran, 2025).

The Talmud is the background to the life and practice of many Jews today. It may not, however, be front and centre in their consciousness. In an exploration of the belief in the Almighty in Chapter 1, we found that the Almighty is implicit in everything that a Jew does, in many ways, this can also be said of the Talmud. A Jew will know how to behave and live a Jewish life, but not necessarily the debates and discussions that have led to this point. In many ways, it is at this point that the relevance of the song *Tradition* from *Fiddler on the Roof* can be seen. When asked why men and women do not dance together, or why many other things are done in certain ways accompanied with the question 'Where is it written?', the response is 'Tradition'. This is not a throwaway term that seeks to be disingenuous, it is a background for many practices within the Jewish community. Even the overall message of the film – the idea that tradition can and should be challenged in light of the 'modern' world and its developments – reflects the different approaches to the Talmud by Jews in the modern world. One British Jew today has suggested that:

> The Torah is not that important for me. I follow certain practices more so because of tradition rather than what's written in the Torah.

As indicated earlier, the encounter between Judaism and the modern world, as it has throughout history, has potential to change the practices and expressions of Judaism. Greenspahn (2009) suggests one area where this has developed is in the area of the role of women (see Chapter 7) where, as in the past, 'forces from outside of the Jewish community will be as influential as any from within in determining the roles of women in ... Judaism' (11).

The Apocrypha

In addition to the Tanakh and the Talmud, there is also the Jewish Apocrypha (*HaSefarim haChitzoniyim*, 'the outer books'), whose composition is referred to in one of its books, *2 Esdras*:

> So during the forty days ninety-four books were written. And when the forty days were ended, the Most High spoke to me, saying, 'Make public the twenty-four books that you wrote first and let the worthy and the unworthy read them; but keep the seventy that were written last, in order to give them to the wise among your people. For in them is the spring of understanding, the fountain of wisdom, and the river of knowledge'.
>
> (14:44–47)

These are books that were written within the Jewish community and as such are of interest here. George Robinson notes that 'Since Talmudic scholars did not accept them in the canon, these books were preserved only in Christian churches or in the libraries of the Dead Sea sect ... Because they are part of the Catholic and Greek Orthodox canon, the number of books in the Apocrypha is frozen' (2000, 260). The writings, such as the books of the Maccabees, Esdras, Judith, Baruch and the Wisdom of Solomon, were most likely written in the Second Temple Period, more specifically between 300 BCE and 100 CE. Some of the books are examples of history (such as Maccabees), and reflect the time which produced them, while others are writings of the filling in of existing texts in the Tanakh (such as Esdras and Baruch). While interesting for Jews and reflective of elements of history, they were rejected in the rabbinic period, Rabbi Akiva in the Mishnah Sanhedrin suggested that:

> All of the Jewish people, even sinners and those who are liable to be executed with a court-imposed death penalty, have a share in the World-to-Come ... And these are the exceptions, the people who have no share in the World-to-Come, even when they fulfilled many mitzvot: ... one who reads external literature.
>
> (10:1)

Julian Sinclair (2008) suggests that 'Today, only 1 Maccabees is of enduring relevance, with the other works of the Apocrypha the preoccupation of academics alone' (further discussion of the Maccabees can be found in Chapter 6). Therefore, while they may be of interest, in exploring the lived reality of Judaism, these are not a major focus except in the celebration of Chanukkah.

Midrash

Midrash (meaning study or interpretation of text) is a literary form that is found throughout the Talmud (especially the Babylonian Talmud) and within Jewish culture and tradition. They are imaginative or inspired readings of narratives that reimagine the story. A midrash essentially begins with a text and then works out from there to offer commentary, story and interpretation. Gary Porton (1985) highlights the different types of midrash:

> The meaning of 'midrash' is much less well-known than the meaning of 'rabbinic'. Even to those familiar with Hebrew terminology, the word 'midrash' has a variety of connotations. It has been used to describe biblical interpretations or exegesis, sermons, and haggadic (nonlegal) discussions … 'Midrash' refers to statements, comments, or remarks that are juxtaposed to the accepted authoritative Jewish Scriptures.
>
> (4)

Porton (1985) suggests that rabbinic midrash deserves 'the same attention that has been paid to Mishnah, Tosefta, the Talmuds, the liturgical statements and the mystical texts of Judaism of late antiquity' (12). That may go beyond what many Jews would suggest, but it does highlight their popularity in helping understand the text of the Tanakh. Midrash is often understood as an activity centred on the Almighty and therefore can serve a useful purpose as Jews try to understand and live their faith better. Neusner (2014) highlights three different midrashic processes:

- Paraphrase: in this 'the exegete will state in other words the self-evident and ordinary sense of the Hebrew'.
- Prophecy: where 'the exegete will read Scripture as an account of things that are now happening or are going to happen'.
- Parable or allegory: here 'the exegete will read Scripture as an account of what the words say but with deeper meanings' (1–2).

When used in the way of a story, Wilda Gafney (2017) describes their nature:

> They reimagine dominant narratival readings while crafting new ones to stand alongside – not replace – former readings. Midrash also asks questions of the text; sometimes it provides answers, sometimes it leaves the reader to answer the questions.
>
> (3)

Indeed, in Knox's book, she creates a womanist midrash, which gives voice to and 'attends to marginalized characters in biblical narratives' (3), although writing from a Christian perspective, she is mindful to continue in the mode of rabbinic midrash in contemporary and historical times. She retells the stories of people like Rivqah (Rebekah), Miryam (Miriam) and the Women of Midian.

Within Judaism there is Halakhic midrash which focuses on midrash surrounding the Torah, and especially the Law. There is also Aggadic midrash which focuses on the parts of the Tanach that are not to do with law. There are many classic examples within Judaism that will be referred to, including:

- Rabbi Akiva's Alphabet where Akiva offers midrash on the letters of the Hebrew alphabet.

- Midrash Esther
- Midrash Shmuel (on the books of Samuel)
- Midrash Rabba (a collection of ten commentaries on Genesis, Exodus, Leviticus, Numbers, Deuteronomy, Song of Songs, Ruth, Lamentation, Ecclesiastes and Esther).

Modern Jewish midrash include examples such as:

- *Dirshuni: Israeli Women Writing Midrash* (2022) edited by Tamar Biala (2022).
- *Storahtelling*, a New York-based charity that through storytelling and theatre 'Mavens transform Scripture into scripts, making ancient stories and traditions accessible for new generations, advancing Judaic literacy and raising modern social consciousness with meaningful conversations' (Labshul, 2018).
- Matt Bar, a modern Jewish rapper, who reinterprets tradition in his lyrics and music.

These texts provide interesting and engaging dialogue and discussion with the text that appeals to many Jews, and the idea of storytelling (see below) perhaps forms a central part of Jewish identity.

Thoughts for the classroom

Within an exploration of the sources for the narratives within the Tanakh and within wider rabbinic literature, there are a range of possibilities that arise for their use in the classroom. The stories are opportunities for critical reading. At no point does this mean that the teacher or pupils seek to criticize the stories. It is possible to explore the texts in terms of understanding the lives and experiences of the individuals within the texts and the communities which produced them.

Within the classroom, there has been a development in the use of hermeneutics in terms of reading sacred texts. As historical texts that are used within the Jewish community, it is possible to see that the Tanakh and the Talmud can be used in the same way. As we understand a hermeneutic approach to be about 'the art or science of interpretation, concerned with meaning and significance' (Bowie et al., 2020, 3), it is possible to move beyond sacred text to read the narratives to see how they are imbued with meaning and significance.

This type of approach should include the reading of the text (most likely in English) to explore the things we learn about Judaism and the Almighty from the narrative; what we learn about the community that produced it; what links there are to wider Judaism; the possible historicity claims that can be made; and how the text links with, and is used, by Jews today. Pupils in schools are used to having narrative curated or mediated for them, and engagement with the source material helps pupils engage with the narrative in a much more effective and authentic way.

There are many stories told within Judaism. There have been volumes filled with stories from throughout history, and there is only the opportunity to draw on brief examples. It should also be noted that throughout this book there have been, and will be, examples from the texts that are used to underpin or illustrate teachings as given expression in Judaism.

Storytelling lies at the heart of understanding Judaism. It has to be utilized correctly and enthusiastically by the teacher. The stories of the prophets and others can be used to frame morality, teachings and also the boundaries of Judaism. Trevor Cooling suggests that stories are 'big ideas sometimes referred to as a metanarrative, which express our whole understanding of the whole world and help people to make sense of their lives' (2002, 45). This is just so with Judaism. As we reflect on some of the stories, they can help us understand the important aspects of Judaism. We can understand the nature of existence, the Almighty and more, through a utilization of stories of Judaism in the classroom.

Robin Mello (2001) explains that learning can be deepened with the use of story. Stories also have many levels of understanding that need to be analysed and studied for academic understanding. The stories that are told help us understand what is important for Jews then, and today. Miller Mair suggests that this is so: 'All our stories are expressions of ourselves even when they purport to be accounts of aspects of the world. We are deeply implicated in the very grounds of our story telling' (1989, 257). Judaism can thus be experienced through its stories. Whatever age of student we are working with, using the stories can help them understand more deeply not just the events of the narrative but also the teachings of Judaism and their importance to Jews today.

One of the interesting aspects in the use of these texts in the teaching of Judaism within the classroom is the identification of 'Sources of Wisdom and Authority' in the exam specifications. The vast majority of the texts referred to can be found within the Tanakh, and very few are to be found in the Talmud, suggesting a primacy of the Tanakh that might not be reflective of the reality of Jewish life. When Jews are seeking answers to how they should behave, most often they refer to their rabbis, or to other rabbis, who draw on tradition and on the mitzvot and Talmud. To create an authentic view of Judaism elements of the Talmud, rather than just the Tanakh should be explored.

Chapter 5

Antisemitism

It may seem strange to have a chapter on antisemitism[1] in a book about Judaism, but the persecution that Jews have faced and continue to face is seen by many Jews as a part of their identity. In *Jews in the UK today: Key findings from the JPR National Jewish Identity Survey* in exploring the level of importance given to different aspects of Jewish identity, 95 per cent responded that 'Remembering the Holocaust' was either fairly important (24%) or very important (71%); and the third most favourable answer was 'Combatting antisemitism' with 92 per cent (fairly important 28%; very important 64%) responding positively (Graham & Boyd, 2024, 31). Antisemitism is not a new phenomenon; it is something that seems to have found expression throughout history and has not been limited to times or places. In the next chapter we will explore Jewish festivals which will include Pesach/ Passover, Chanukah and Purim. In each of these celebrations the targeting of Jews or the people of Israel is a central part of the narrative, and the deliverance of the people from such heinous intentions and actions is what is celebrated.

History

It is impossible to capture the history and experience of antisemitism in a book. An author can only try and highlight the various events that form the Jewish experience and lead to a reconciliation of 'such misery [resulting from antisemitism] with God's ways'

---

[1]There are various spellings of Antisemitism, including hyphenation and capitalization. In April 2015, the International Holocaust Remembrance Alliance's (IHRA) Committee on Antisemitism and Holocaust Denial issued a letter in which they suggested that the preferred spelling is 'antisemitism'. They argued that 'the hyphenated spelling allows for the possibility of something called "Semitism", which not only legitimizes a form of pseudo-scientific racial classification that was thoroughly discredited by association with Nazi ideology, but also divides the term, stripping it from its meaning of opposition and hatred toward Jews'. Originally a misnomer coined by Moritz Steinschneider and Wilhelm Marr who were describing hatred of Jews, rather than those who were racially Semitic. The IHRA (2015) outlined that 'The unhyphenated spelling is favoured by many scholars and institutions in order to dispel the idea that there is an entity "Semitism" which "anti-Semitism" opposes. Antisemitism should be read as a unified term so that the meaning of the generic term for modern Jew-hatred is clear'. This book utilizes this convention throughout except when an author in a quoted text uses a different approach.

(Cohn-Sherbrook, 1989, Preface). Using a simple timeline of Jewish history, it is possible to highlight events that are examples of the persecution of Jews, and what would be known today as antisemitism. Care should be taken in using this list as it is illustrative only, there are many other examples and experiences that could be included, both known and unknown. In looking at history to provide examples, a person is reminded that generally only the experiences of the victors, and the larger events are remembered. In summarizing these events, Edward Flannery (1985) argued:

> Antisemitism is not, despite a common opinion, as old as the Jews. While occupying a homeland of their own, Jews encountered the normal hostility of rival powers but nothing that could strictly be called antisemitism. This development was reserved for the Diaspora, the dispersion, and it was not until the third century B.C.E. that its presence there could be clearly discerned.
>
> (7)

He does, however, concede that 'Israel's Exodus from Egypt in the thirteenth pre-Christian century has been called the "first pogrom", and some historians concede it an antisemitic character. And antisemitic it was if, and only if, one unduly stretches the meaning of the word' (Flannery, 1985, 7). There is a concern with Flannery's suggestion that attempts are sometimes made to stretch the meaning of antisemitism. His argument is that strictly speaking it is 'hatred or contempt and a stereotyping of the Jewish people' (1985, 4). Defining it is as such seems sensible, but then if an an alternative explanation is suggested then it removes the hatred of Jews as a motivation and therefore may be used to explain it away. This is a fine line to navigate, but an explanation of the actions of the Pharaoh as a worried monarch with security concerns, and not a fear of or hatred of the Israelites would be concerning. Similarly, attributing the actions of Mordecai to a concerned national leader, does not explain the desire to restrict the practice of Jews and ultimately put them to death.

Examples of what could be termed antisemitism since the times recorded in the Tanakh include, but are not limited to:

- Third century BCE Hecataeus of Abdera wrote a history of Jewish origins and in so doing described Judaism as 'misanthropic and inhospitable way of life' (Flannery, 1985, 12). This was developed by Manetho in the same century; an Egyptian historian and priest he wrote scathingly of Jews. This approach is similarly found in the later writings of Chaeremon, Lysimachus, Poseidonius, Apollonius Molon, Apion and Tacitus.
- Second century BCE The capture and desecration of the Temple by the Seleucids (see Chapter 6).
- Second century BCE Jews are expelled from the City of Rome.
- 19 CE Jews are again expelled from the city of Rome, this time by the Emperor Tiberius.
- 38 CE The Alexandrian pogrom, or Alexandrian riots. In these events, Greek Alexandrians did not want Jews to receive the same rights of citizenship, and therefore attacked, scourged and murdered Jews. Jews were restricted to one quarter of the city.

- 70 CE The Roman capture of Jerusalem and the destruction of the Second Temple.
- 94 CE Apion of Alexandria attacks Jews in his writings. In *Against Apion Book 2* Josephus refutes the rewriting of history by Apion, and describes him as 'the common slanderer of men' (1999, 963). Apion narrates several pernicious falsehoods about Jews, and one that Josephus narrates suggests that they 'bear no good will to any foreigner' (1999, 967), leading to the suggestion that Jews had sacrificed Greeks within their Temple.
- 100 CE Tacitus writes a polemic against Jews, describing them in the most denigrating terms, and repeating the claim that they set themselves apart, regarding 'the rest of mankind with all the hatred of enemies' (*The History*, Book V, Chapter 5). The trope of Jewish wealth is also introduced in this book.
- 119 CE Circumcision is banned by the Roman Emperor, Hadrian. In 131 CE (other sources 136 CE) Hadrian renames Jerusalem Aelia Capitolina and forbids Jews from entering.
- 167 CE Melito of Sardis writes *On the Passover*, which is the first recorded instance of Christians holding all Jews responsible for the death of Jesus, their Messiah.
- 305/306 CE The Council of Elvira forbids socializing, marriage and sexual intercourse between Christians and Jews.
- 339 CE Marriage between Christians and Jews is forbidden in the Roman Empire on pain of death.
- 353 CE Christians who convert to Judaism will have their property confiscated.
- 408 CE The burning of Haman during the festival of Purim is forbidden in the Roman Empire. Opponents believe they are making fun of Christianity.
- 415 CE A ban issued in the Roman Empire banned the building of synagogues.
- 418 CE Severus of Menorca forces 540 Jews to convert to Christianity.
- Sixth century CE Jews are excluded from citizenship in the Byzantine Empire, and their rights are severely restricted. The use of Hebrew in worship is forbidden, and the declaration of the Shema is banned.
- 589 CE The third Council of Toledo bans Jews from holding positions of authority and reiterates the ban on inter-marriage.
- 608 CE Across the Byzantine Empire Jews are massacred and pogroms established.
- Seventh century CE Judaism is prohibited in Hispania and Septimania.
- 629 CE Byzantines enter Jerusalem and kill many Jews.
- 640 CE Umar expels Jews from Arabia.
- 681 CE The Twelfth Council of Toledo pass laws that require the burning of the Talmud and other Jewish writings.
- 692 CE Christians are forbidden from bathing with Jews or face excommunication.
- 720 CE Omar II forbids Jews from worshipping on the Temple Mount, the site of the Dome of the Rock, a mosque built on the site of the Temples.
- 807 CE Jews in the Abbasid Empire are required to wear a yellow belt.
- 850 CE Jews in the Abbasid Empire are required to wear specific clothing and patches on their clothes to distinguish them from Muslims.

- 888 CE The patch is redesigned with the image of an ape.
- 985 CE Jews are expelled from Sparta in an effort to rid the city of a plague.
- 1008 CE Jews in the Abbasid Empire are forced to wear a wooden golden calf.
- Eleventh century CE Jews in Mainz, Kairouan, Limoges and other towns are expelled.
- Eleventh–twelfth centuries CE The First Crusades mean that many Jews are killed, and their rights severely restricted.
- 1144 CE The death of William of Norwich in which Jews are wrongly blamed in the first example of blood libel in Europe. The Peterborough Chronicle records of the event: 'the Jews of Norwich bought a Christian child before Easter and tortured him with all the same tortures with which our Lord was tortured, and on Long-Friday hanged him on a cross for love of our Lord' (Swanton, 1997, 265).
- Twelfth century Over 200,000 Jews are killed in the Almohad Empire.
- 1171 CE Thirty-one Jews are burned at the Stake in Blois, France for blood libel.
- Twelfth century Philip II of France imprisons all Jews and demands a ransom, and annuls all loans to Christians by Jews, expels Jews from Paris, and confiscates all Jewish property.
- 1189 CE Pogroms in London which then spread around England
- 1190 CE All Jews in Norwich killed in their homes
- 1190 CE Fifty-seven Jews are killed in St. Edmunds, 500 Jews are massacred in York.
- Thirteenth–nineteenth century Obscene images of Jews become 'popular' in wider society.
- 1204 CE The Pope requires Jews to wear clothing to separate themselves from Christians.
- 1205 CE Jews are expelled from towns in Spain.
- 1210 CE King John imprisons most of England's Jewish population, demanding 66,000 marks for their release.
- 1222 CE Jews are forbidden from building new synagogues in England.
- 1240 CE Jews are expelled from Brittany
- 1255 CE The Statute of Jewry, a series of anti-Jewish laws are introduced in England.
- 1267 CE In addition to a yellow star, Jews in Vienna are forced to wear a cone shaped headdress.
- 1275 CE Jews in England are forced to wear a yellow badge.
- 1282 CE All synagogues in London are closed.
- 1290 CE The heads of Jewish families are arrested; a ransom of £12,000 is demanded by the King of England, Edward I.
- 1289 CE Jews are expelled from Anjou and Gascony.
- 1290 CE The Edict of Expulsion. All Jews are expelled from England, taking only what they could carry. The expulsion is generally believed to have lasted until the mid-1650s.
- 1291 CE Jews are forbidden from settling in France.
- Fourteenth–fifteenth century CE In many areas of Europe Jews are blamed for the Black Death, resulting in violence, massacres and expulsions.
- Fifteenth century CE Expulsions across Europe continue.

- Fifteenth century Martin Luther writes against the Jews, suggesting that harsh treatment should be adopted against them.
- Fifteenth century Ivan the Terrible forbids Jews from entering Russia.
- 1555 CE Pope Paul IV reemphasizes anti-Jewish laws, including the wearing of a yellow hat or scarf.
- Seventeenth–eighteenth century CE Pamphlets, expulsions, attacks, and massacres continue.
- Nineteenth century CE Pamphlets, expulsions, attacks, massacres continue.

Many of the same attacks and tropes continued into the twentieth century. The above timeline makes sober reading, and some of the events are glossed over. For example, when events of a century are summarized, this is usually because there were so many events in the century. In listing the events, the specific tropes and accusations have been avoided as not to appear to give them attention. In general, antisemitic tropes that have been uttered by people and in writings generally surround various dangerous, hurtful and false assumptions. Jeffrey Goldberg (2015) summarizes them in this way:

> Europe has blamed the Jews for an encyclopedia of sins. The Church blamed the Jews for killing Jesus; Voltaire blamed the Jews for inventing Christianity. In the febrile minds of anti-Semites, Jews were usurers and well-poisoners and spreaders of disease. Jews were the creators of both communism and capitalism; they were clannish but also cosmopolitan; cowardly and warmongering; self-righteous moralists and defilers of culture. Ideologues and demagogues of many permutations have understood the Jews to be a singularly malevolent force standing between the world and its perfection.

The Shoah/ Holocaust

The *Holocaust* or the *Shoah* is the most extreme event of antisemitism that has occurred in the history of the world. To begin to explore the Shoah in the classroom is daunting but important. Before progressing, it is important to note the importance of language in the teaching of these events:

> For many people the term 'Holocaust' is problematic. A composite of two Greek words, 'Holocaust' suggests the offering of a sacrifice by burning. The term can mistakenly imply that the mass murder of the Jews was a form of martyrdom rather than the result of genocide. For this reason, many prefer to use the Hebrew word 'Shoah' which means 'catastrophe'.
> (International Holocaust Remembrance Alliance, 2019, 25)

It is not wrong to use the word 'Holocaust'. It is the term that is used throughout the world and there are many organizations dedicated to teaching and remembering about these events that use it in the name. Indeed, there is an Holocaust Remembrance Day. It is, however, important to use language in a way that leaves no question that the harsh treatment and killing of Jews was an evil, and was not purposeful or meaningful in any way, no matter what lessons people have tried to take from it. It was a depraved act, however, it is important to help students understand that those who perpetrated the Shoah cannot be explained away 'as inhuman monsters' (International Holocaust Remembrance Alliance, 2019, 29). To do so would be to discount them as an aberration, and write off any possible explanation of these inhuman acts. Indeed psychological experiments by people like Milgram (1974) and Zimbardo (2007) explored issues post war about human nature, compliance to authority, and other issues. Each of these experiments showed that it was not people who were diagnosed sadists who performed these acts, but the capacity was within people more generally.

Possibly the most oft shared description of the Holocaust is that within it six million Jews died at the hands of the Nazis. This is horrendous, and decimated the Jewish population of the world, and as suggested earlier is the largest single example of antisemitism and hatred in the history of the world. In many ways this is an unfathomable number. The experiences of these six million Jews, and the millions of others who were persecuted should never disappear, and should always be remembered. The remembrance of the victims of the Holocaust is central to Jewish identity in the world today. In explaining the importance of a memorial in the shul (see Figure 5.1), the Rabbi explained:

It is placed above the door so that we can never forget. It is one of the pillars of our communal identity today.

Figure 5.1 A door plaque in Heaton Park Shul, Manchester dedicated to the martyrs of the Holocaust.

The focus of this book and the space available means that all of the events of the Holocaust will not be outlined here. In many ways the exploration of the events is better suited to the history classroom. The religion and worldviews classroom is better equipped to explore other elements that arise out of the Holocaust. In all of its teaching, the voices of the individual should never be forgotten:

> Repeated references to 'the six million' risk subsuming communities and individuals into a faceless mass and attempts to envision the enormity of numbers can further depersonalize and dehumanize. Instead, wherever possible use case studies, survivor testimony, and letters and diaries from the period to show human experience. Learners should be able to give examples of how each 'statistic' was a real person, with a life before the Holocaust, existing in a context of family, friends and community. Emphasize the dignity and humanity of the victims at all times.
>
> (International Holocaust Remembrance Alliance, 2019, 28)

The skirting over the number and the lack of description of the events is not to diminish them in any way; it is important for them to be taught, and in many ways the religion and worldviews classroom cannot teach what it needs to without an understanding of these events and their context.

Also important are the other aspects of the Holocaust, including the steps that led to the murders including the discrimination and persecution, alongside the growing acceptability of antisemitism within society. Although many aspects such as Kristellnacht will find coverage within history it can provide context, along with the wearing of the Star of David, the burning of books, the confiscation of property, the stereotyping, the blaming, and the othering of Jews. In establishing the Jews as 'other', i.e. not part of the German 'we', it enabled the development of more violent restrictions.

Thoughts for the classroom

Exploring any form of antisemitism in the classroom is fraught with problems (see below) and this is amplified when speaking about one of the most heinous genocides to have been perpetrated by humanity. How can the teacher hope to do it justice, and have students learn from its events? In many ways the focus in the religion and worldviews classroom should be different to approaches found in History and English Literature classrooms. It is easy to default to a treatment of the events of the Holocaust or the Shoah from a purely historical perspective. This is an important lens through which to explore the motivations, events and consequences; but hopefully many of these will have been explored in History. The Shoah is perhaps best taught as a cross-curricular topic. In this way, the history of it is taught as a background to the learning within the religion and worldviews classroom. What then should be the focus of the teaching of the Shoah in this context? The questions that the Shoah raises for Judaism and for individual Jews about the nature of the Almighty and the problem of suffering are areas with which Jews have wrestled over the years? The Holocaust Education Trust (n.d.) highlights the reasons for such an approach:

> Adopting a cross-curricular approach therefore allows teachers of different subjects to pool their skills and expertise in order to encourage students to look at the same event from different perspectives. Students can thereby apply the knowledge and skills learned in one subject to another, all the while deepening their understanding of the Holocaust. There are also pragmatic arguments in favour of cross-curricular provision. The scale and complexity of the Holocaust mean that it is doubtful whether it can ever be effectively taught in just a handful of lessons.
>
> (6)

Caution should be made of the encouragement to 'look at the same event from different perspectives'. This means through the lenses of different subjects, rather than from the different perspectives of those involved such as Nazis. While this is something that most if not all teachers would not countenance, it can be inadvertently done. Take for example the use of *The Boy in the Striped Pyjamas*; the UCL Centre for Holocaust Education found that this book of fiction was used in over a third of English schools. The Director of the Centre Ruth-Anne Lenga cautioned against its use without careful consideration:

> As a work of fiction and drama this book and associated film may have some worth, but as a resource for teaching this important history it is flawed. Even if used solely to identify the errors and mistruth inherent within it, students would need to already have established sound historical, evidence-based knowledge to be able to do that. With time for teaching this subject being a major challenge in schools across the country, this would, in many cases, simply not work. The potential for giving young people the impression that ordinary Germans were in some way 'victims' of the Holocaust is insensitive and dangerous. With the rise in antisemitism, such as it is in this country, and that so often manifests through trivialisation, distortion and denial of the Holocaust, this book could potentially do more harm than good.
>
> (UCL Centre for Holocaust Education, 6)

The Holocaust Educational Trust (n.d) suggests many texts can be used to teach the 'reality' of the Shoah, including:

- Art Spiegelman (1987), *Maus*
- Loïc Dauvillier (2014), *Hidden*
- Hans Peter Richter (1987), *Friedrich*
- Morris Gleitzman (2006), *Once* and the subsequent novels in the series.

There are many ways to explore Jewish responses to the Shoah, but the most important way is through the voices of those who lived through it, and the voices of those who died within it. For everyone else while they can try and intellectualise it, and reflect on the lessons that can be learned, it is those with the experience to whom the world must listen.

As time passes the opportunity to meet Holocaust survivors is diminishing, but we can listen to their words either through recordings or through their written testimonies. Rabbi Israel Spira spoke movingly of the experience of these testimonies:

> Every day, every child, after studying the daily lessons prescribed by our sages, should learn about the Holocaust, for it says in our holy Torah: 'Then it shall come to pass, when many evils and troubles are come upon them, that this song shall testify before them as a witness' (Deuteronomy 31:21). *The suffering and the testimonies, when told by Holocaust survivors, are a song, a hymn of praise, a testimony to the eternity of the Jewish people and the greatness of their spirit.*
>
> (Eliach, 1982, 2, emphasis added)

There are many authors who provide a richness of approach to the events of the Shoah from a Jewish perspective. One such author is Viktor Frankl and his book *Man's Search for Meaning* (2004). Indeed, Frankl's first paragraph reminds the reader of his purpose, which aligns well with the purpose of learning about the Shoah in the religion and world-view classroom:

> This book does not claim to be an account of facts and events but of personal experiences, experiences which millions of prisoners have suffered time and again. It is the inside story of a concentration camp, told by one of its survivors. This tale is not concerned with the great horrors, which have already been described often enough (though less often believed), but with the multitude of small torments. In other words, it will try to answer this question: How was everyday life in a concentration camp reflected in the mind of the average prisoner?.
>
> (17)

To try and summarize Frankl's work simply is a fool's errand, but engagement with his work is fruitful when a person is trying to understand a Jewish response to the Shoah. He identifies the 'striving to find a meaning in one's life is the primary motivational force in man' (2004, 103). This can be found in the approach that a person takes to life; in many ways a person has no control over the conditions within which they find themselves: 'It is not freedom from conditions, but it is freedom to take a stand toward the conditions' (2004, 132). He explains this further in suggesting that 'It is not freedom from conditions, but it is freedom to take a stand toward the conditions' (2004, 75). In this way meaning can be found in suffering: 'In some ways suffering ceases to be suffering at the moment it finds a meaning, such as the meaning of a sacrifice' (2004, 117). In discovering the purpose of life and viewing the future optimistically a person can mentally survive. Frankl summarizes three ways in which humans can find meaning:

> We can discover this meaning in life in three different ways: (1) by creating a work or doing a deed; (2) by experiencing something or encountering someone; and (3) by the attitude we take toward unavoidable suffering.
>
> (2004, 115)

It could also be summarized in finding a work to do, showing and experiencing love, and by changing our perspective. He uses an example of a person reacting negatively to suffering in seeking vengeance, this may become all-consuming and be part of a downward spiral. He recognizes there are concerns with his approach but was at pains to emphasize 'that in no way is suffering necessary to find meaning. I only insist that meaning is possible even in spite of suffering – provided, certainly, that the suffering is unavoidable' (2004, 117).

Through all of this he kept his faith in the Almighty and used him as an inspiration to keep going. He suggests using the knowledge of the Divine, or of a loved one as an inspiration in how to face suffering:

They must not lose hope but should keep their courage in the certainty that the hopelessness of our struggle did not detract from its dignity and its meaning. I said that someone looks down on each us in difficult hours – a friend, a wife, somebody alive or dead, or a God – and he would not expect us to disappoint him. He would hope to find us suffering proudly – not miserably – knowing how to die.

(2004, 90–1)

Knowing that we are in a relationship and are loved inspires a person to endure suffering positive and not to disappoint them. This suggests that when faced with any degree of suffering, purpose can be found in the attitude that is adopted. This approach to 'surviving' the camps has been criticized by some:

Despite Frankl's qualifying statements, the tenor of his book implied that volition, religious conviction, and a positive attitude could increase one's chance of survival. He suggests that those who fought hard enough to survive could do so; the corollary is that those who perished did not fight.

(Middleton-Kaplan, 2014, 9)

The implication that Middleton-Kaplan takes from this is that it could lead to victim blaming; he is not suggesting that Frankl says this but that it could be used to imply that a person's attitude could determine their fate. It is undeniable that in the Shoah 'attitude mattered little for survival' (Pytell, 2003, 379), but Frankl's work suggests that it could affect the way a person lived and how they faced that suffering.

Elie Wiesel is also a writer who explores his own experience in the Nazi concentration camps of Auschwitz and Buchenwald. Particularly poignant are the descriptions of his family life prior to the camps, and then the deaths of his mother and sister at the hands of the Nazis; that is then followed by his father's death in Buchenwald. A major theme of the book is Elie Wiesel's struggle with his faith in the face of all that is happening to him. This is illustrated in the evocative description of this challenge:

Never shall I forget those flames that consumed my faith for- ever.
Never shall I forget the nocturnal silence that deprived me for all eternity of the desire
    to live.

Never shall I forget those moments that murdered my God and my soul and turned
   my dreams to ashes.
Never shall I forget those things, even were I condemned to live as long as God
   Himself.
Never.

(Wiesel, 2006, 34)

Further:

Some of the men spoke of God: His mysterious ways, the sins of the Jewish people, and
the redemption to come. As for me, I had ceased to pray. I concurred with Job! I was not
denying His existence, but I doubted His absolute justice.

(Wiesel, 2006, 45)

Despite this diminution of faith within Auschwitz he was led to reflect afterwards:

I would be within my rights to give up faith in God, and I could invoke six million reasons
to justify such a decision. But I am incapable of straying from the path charted by my
forefathers, who felt duty-bound to live for God. Without the faith of my ancestors, my
own faith in humanity would be diminished. So my wounded faith endures.

(Hirt-Manheimer, 2021)

Wiesel illustrates the very Jewish approach that having received the faith of his ancestors,
it is that tradition that enables him to cling onto his faith despite everything. He does not
lessen the challenge that the Shoah is and was, but he highlights how despite the reality
of everything faith can endure. (Wiesel, Night, 2006). This is further illustrated in his play,
The Trial of God that is deeply informed by his experience in Auschwitz and is based on
events he witnessed there. The play places the Almighty on trial in Shamgorod, Ukraine
in 1649 after a pogrom has killed many Jews. Speaking of the actual trial that Wiesel
attended in Auschwitz it is recorded by Robert McAfee Brown:

The trial lasted several nights. Witnesses were heard, evidence was gathered, conclu-
sions were drawn, all of which issued finally in a unanimous verdict: the Lord God
Almighty, Creator of Heaven and Earth, was found guilty of crimes against creation and
humankind. And then, after what Wiesel describes as an 'infinity of silence', the Talmudic
scholar looked at the sky and said 'It's time for evening prayers', and the members of the
tribunal recited Maariv, the evening service.

(Wiesel, 1995, vii)

This highlights the juxtaposition of the recognition of the evil that was the Shoah, but at
the same time a recognition of the Almighty's guilt did not take away the faith of the Jews.
   There are many other writers who engage with the themes, some are survivors
including:

- *If This Is a Man / The Truce (A Survivor's Journey Home from Auschwitz)* by Primo Levi
  (1996).

- *A Soul Beneath the Earth: A Holocaust Memoir of Faith and Resilience* by Freda Perelmuter Schipper and Sandy Schipper Wolberg (2022).

Other writers, in what is now termed Holocaust Theology, have tried to reconcile the reality of the Shoah with the existence of the Almighty. In such a way, exploration of the lessons learned from the Shoah can also be a focus of learning. The questions of faith that it raises can also be explored philosophically, though they should never be removed from the events that took place, this is not a theoretical event. One example of a Jewish writer who tried to make sense of, or learn from, these events was Emil Fackenheim (1969) who recognized the Almighty's presence during the Shoah, and afterwards. There was, however, in his estimation no 'redeeming Voice' heard but there was a 'commanding Voice'. This voice proclaimed a 614th mitzvot: 'the authentic Jew of today is forbidden to hand Hitler yet another victory!' He further explained the meaning of this:

> We are, first, commanded to survive as Jews, lest the Jewish people perish. We are commanded, second, to remember in our guts and bones the martyrs of the Holocaust, lest their memory perish. We are forbidden, thirdly, to deny or despair of God, however much we may have to contend with Him or with belief in Him, lest Judaism perish. We are forbidden, finally, to despair of the world as the place which is to become the kingdom of God lest we help make it a meaningless place in which God is dead or irrelevant and everything is permitted. To abandon any of these imperatives, in response to Hitler's victory at Auschwitz, would be to hand him yet other posthumous victories.
>
> (1969, 150)

Fackenheim in not without his critics. Some suggest that the command for Jews to survive does not need stating; however, the most important aspect of this remembrance is to mend or repair the world, not least the seeming rupture with the Almighty in contrast to the world pre-Shoah:

> Historical continuity is shattered because 'at Auschwitz not only man died, but also the idea of man'; because our 'estrangement from God' has become so 'cruel' that, even if He were to speak to us, we have no way of understanding how to 'recognize Him'.
>
> (1982, 250)

The task is, therefore, to respond, and Fackenheim suggests that is through 'Tikkun Olam, to mend the world' (1982, 350). Only then can the seeming separation from shechinah be mended; it is the world and relationship that needs mending. This approach has had an impact on the thinking of Jews since the Holocaust both in terms of memory (see Figure 5.1) and of action.

One of the sayings that is oft repeated when remembering those who were killed, is 'Never again'. One Jew spoke to me and suggested that this phrase was laughable in the twenty-first century. His argument was that as we look at the history of the world since 1945, albeit on smaller scales there have been many genocides. Therefore, helping students understand not just the evil that is genocide, but also the slippery slope that leads to such events is an important part of Holocaust education.

The aims of teaching about the Holocaust put forward by the International Holocaust Remembrance Alliance (2019) are ambitious, daunting and important:

1 *Develop knowledge of the Holocaust, ensuring accuracy in individual understanding and knowledge and raising awareness about the possible consequences of antisemitism;*
2 Create engaging teaching environments for learning about the Holocaust;
3 Promote critical and reflective thinking about the Holocaust including the ability to counter Holocaust denial and distortion;
4 Contribute to Human Rights and genocide prevention education (4).

Teachers of religion and worldviews should consider how best they can design a curriculum that will meet these aims. The discussion undertaken above about exploring challenges to faith, the survival of faith, and the importance of the individual voice are key; and there should always be an exploration of the lessons that can be learned, indicated in the above aims as contributing to Human Rights and genocide prevention education.

The work of the Holocaust Educational Trust in the UK is invaluable to those who teach about the Holocaust. It provides physical and online resources, as well as Continuing Professional Development opportunities for teachers. A lot of its materials are immediately useable within the classroom. It has also developed a cross-curricular approach that helps see how the religion and worldviews classroom can work with other subjects such as history, art, drama and English. This cross-curricular resource highlights the distinctive role that religion and worldviews teaching can play in the exploration of the Holocaust. It suggests that the following can be taught:

• The connections between beliefs – both religious and secular – and actions.
• Moral dilemmas and choices, and the factors which can influence them.
• Responses to 'fundamental' questions such as the nature and causes of suffering and 'evil', and – ultimately – what it means to be human.
• The interaction, and sometimes conflict, between different faiths and/or belief systems.

> Individual and collective identity. In addition, the study of pre-war Jewish life and culture with which the scheme of work begins may be seen as a means of deepening understanding of Judaism. However, this comes with the caveats that Judaism should not be defined by the Holocaust and that European Jewish culture was not exclusively or, in some communities and for some individuals, mainly connected with religion.
>
> (Holocaust Educational Trust, n.d.a 5)

Perhaps one of the most important aspects of teaching the Holocaust in the religion and worldviews classroom, as mentioned, is to avoid the temptation to teach it as a history lesson. The history must be taught, but its challenge, impact and lessons remain the focus when exploring the issues of faith that it raises.

Today

If we then fast forward to today, it is undeniable that antisemitism is still a plague that Jews experience around the world. David Baddiel, writing in 2021, gives a litany of events in the previous year:

> In Paris, a student was beaten unconscious on the subway for speaking Hebrew on his phone. During the Yellow Vest protests in the city a writer and philosopher was set upon by crowds shouting 'dirty Jew' … In Berlin, a teenager was strangled by three men shouting anti-Semitic abuse at him. On Yom Kippur, a gun-wielding man tried unsuccessfully to enter a synagogue where approximately eighty congregants were worshipping. After the failed attempt, the gunman shot at nearby individuals, killing two and wounding two others, none of whom was affiliated with the synagogue. In London, a rabbi was hospitalised after being attacked by two teenagers yelling 'Kill Jews'. Near where I live, in Belsize Park, shops were daubed with Stars of David and the legend 9–11. In Melbourne, a Jewish boy was forced to kiss a classmate's shoe. In Poland, a Jewish cemetery was vandalised with the words 'Jews eat children'. In Amsterdam, on Bevrijdingsdag, the national holiday commemorating liberation from the Nazis, a Jewish man was assaulted by revellers singing songs about gassing Jews. In Moscow, a yeshiva was set on fire. In Istanbul, a synagogue was firebombed. In Ukraine, rocks were thrown at the windows of synagogues. As the year came to an end, five people were shot and killed in a kosher grocery store in Jersey City, New York. This – a handful of the total incidents – is why Jews don't feel white, if by white you mean safe.
>
> (111–3)

Indeed, in 2018 an EU report entitled *Experiences and perceptions of antisemitism* explored Jewish experiences of hate crime, discrimination and Antisemitism in Austria, Belgium, Denmark, France, Germany, Hungary, Italy, the Netherlands, Poland, Spain, Sweden and the United Kingdom. These countries were chosen because collectively they form 96 per cent of the Jewish population in the EU. The key findings were reported as:

- Antisemitism pervades everyday life
- Pervasive antisemitism undermines Jews' feelings of safety and security
- Antisemitic harassment is so common that it becomes normalized
- Antisemitic discrimination in key areas of life remains invisible (European Union Agency for Fundamental Rights, 2018).

The report highlighted specific examples of antisemitism based on the experiences of individual Jews. In their summary of 'manifestations of antisemitism against [the] Jewish community as a problem' the report highlighted the percentages of Jews who reported experiencing different aspects of antisemitism. In the UK (and as an average across the twelve reporting nations), respondents reported having experienced: antisemitism on the internet, including social media 84 per cent (89%); expressions of hostility towards Jews in the street or other public places 52 per cent (73%); antisemitism in the media 61 per cent (71%); antisemitism in political life 84 per cent (70%); vandalism of Jewish buildings or institutions 45 per cent (66%); antisemitic graffiti 45 per cent (64%); and desecration of Jewish cemeteries 45 per cent (63%) (European Union Agency for Fundamental Rights, 2018, 22).

As explored in the Introduction, antisemitism focuses on both the religious and secular aspects of Judaism. Exploring his lived experience, and the experience of Jews during the Second World War, David Baddiel (2021) has explained:

> Except Antisemitism has very little to do with religion. As I have often said, I'm an atheist and yet the Gestapo would shoot me tomorrow. Racists who don't like Jews never ask the Jew they are abusing how often they go to synagogue. They just see the Jewish name and they know. Which is why it's racism. One's Jewishness, just like one's skin colour, is an accident of birth, and as far as the racists are concerned – and they, sadly, are the people that matter as far as racism goes – you can never lose either.
>
> (41)

This means that Jews in the modern world are victims of religious and ethnic forms of prejudice. However, while the discussion of race seems to have been moved past, those racial stereotypes and hatreds seem to persist; with the othering of Jews, the basis for further restrictions and discrimination is laid. Modern antisemitism is the inheritor of the antisemitism that is found throughout history, using the same tropes and tactics. David Baddiel stated:

> Jews are stereotyped, by the racists, in all the same ways that other minorities are – as lying, thieving, dirty, vile, stinking – but also as moneyed, privileged, powerful and secretly in control of the world. Jews are somehow both sub-human and humanity's secret masters. And it's this racist mythology that's in the air when the left pause before putting Jews into their sacred circle. Because all the people in the sacred circle are oppressed. And if you believe, even a little bit, that Jews are moneyed, privileged, powerful and secretly in control of the world … well, you can't put them into the sacred circle of the oppressed. Some might even say they belong in the damned circle of the oppressors.
>
> (Baddiel, 2021, 19)

In many ways the spread of antisemitism has increased in recent years. Speaking of antisemitic abuse of the actress Maureen Lipman, Julia Neuberger (2019) suggests:

> The anonymity and ease of tweeting and posting on Facebook seems to lead to all sorts of racist, misogynistic comments and the vicious trolling of a variety of people.
>
> (112)

Social media and the amplification and anonymity that the internet provides has provided a whole new way of spreading hate in a way that it reaches millions of people around the world. The qualifications of a person to whom people listen may be seen to be how engaging or how loud they are. Tom Nichols (2017), writing to an American audience, suggests that there has been the death of the intellectual, in real terms meaning that those who have most knowledge of a topic are often rejected or not listened to. He uses his own experience as an expert in 'arms control and foreign policy' as an example. He reports being 'astonished at the way people who did not have the first clue about those subjects would confidently direct me on how best to make peace between Moscow and Washington' (xi). The world of 'alternative facts' and the right to express opinion regardless of consequence, and behind a veil of anonymity means that things that would not have entered the public discourse in the recent past are seen to be fair game. This is true of antisemitism and antisemitic tropes. As such, the experience of Julie Neuberger in the 1950s and 60s who was able to be shielded from much antisemitism (2019) would be impossible today unless a person was able to disconnect completely from the world around them.

There is also an additional aspect of antisemitism that should be mentioned. It is an area that is problematic and raises issues both for Jews themselves, and for non-Jews. This is the idea of self-deprecating Jewish humour that sometimes leans into the stereotypes and tropes that are common in antisemitism. Consider this excerpt from a stand up routine by the Jewish comedian, Eric Neumann (2024):

> My Orthodox friend recently got married and didn't invite my girlfriend to his wedding because he doesn't approve of me dating a non-Jew. Why don't you say it's because you are Jewish and don't want to pay for an extra plate.

This is a difficult area to explore; on the one hand, a person is free to poke fun of themselves, or even to use language that would not be acceptable of an 'outsider'; but on the other hand, could its use be given as a justification by others that 'Well, if person x can say it, why can't I?' This is a nuance to the discussion on antisemitism that does not have an easy answer. It would be simple to say that anything that perpetuates antisemitic tropes should not be used. The question in response to that is about who has the authority to make such a proclamation?

The establishment, and continued existence, of the State of Israel is important to many Jews today (see Figure 5.2). This has led to a further expression of antisemitism, when it is conflated with anti-Zionism. One Jew has suggested that the main challenge of living in Britain is:

> Antisemitism and growing explicit hatred towards all Jews, masked as anti-Zionism – what does the future hold? We know where this leads.

Added to this is the distortion of what Zionism is and how this has been defined for those who, as this respondent suggests, mask an antisemitic view. This has been exacerbated since 7 October 2023, where antisemitism seems to have been on the rise. One British Jew suggests:

> The feeling within the community has completely changed post 7/10 the overwhelming majority now don't feel safe living in the UK. Almost everyone I know has applied for

passports to a variety of different countries based on different pathways. For example, my husband has applied for a German passport as his grandfather came to the UK on the Kindertransport from Nuremberg.

The difference between what Zionism asserts and what anti-Zionism argues it asserts has become even more polarized in the milieu of the world since 2023. At the time of writing the conflict continues, Israeli forces continue to seek the destruction of Hamas and in so doing the lives of Gazans are threatened and taken. Israeli hostages continue to be held. There seems to be the feeling that conflates the actions of Israel as a justification for antisemitism, where Zionist can be synonymous with Jewish. Zionism has become a word that its opponents use to mean an idea that suggests not just the right to a Jewish homeland and state, but to an ideology that establishes this homeland violently at the expense of others. There are many Jews who identify as Zionist and would condmen the actions of Israel.

This means that criticisms of the actions of the state of Israel are not antisemitic:

> Equally, the criticism from within and outside Israel of racism and discrimination against minority groups within Israel is not antisemitic. Much of the criticism has been shrugged off by the Israeli government, but their own Or Commission (in 2000, after civil unrest at the beginning of the second intifada) plus the United States Department of State, have published reports that document racism and discrimination against specific racial and ethnic groups within Israel.

(Neuberger, 2019, 71)

However, this does not mean that all criticism of the State of Israel is not antisemitic. I am aware that the last two statements, before and after Neuberger's words seem antithetical to one another. There is a tendency to conflate the two. Similarly, the suggestion that Zionism is more than the right of a homeland and state goes beyond what most Jews would suggest. The problem becomes, as already identified, that those with antisemitic feelings try and phrase them in a way that it appears only to criticize Israel. It has led to legitimate criticism of Israel being both disguised and labelled as antisemitic measure. In 2017 Simon Schama, Simon Sebag Montefiore and Howard Jacobson wrote to the *Times* newspaper expressing their alarm 'that during the past few years, constructive criticism of Israeli governments has morphed into something closer to antisemitism under the cloak of so-called anti-Zionism'. They further suggest:

> We do not object to fair criticism of Israel governments, but this has grown to be indistinguishable from a demonisation of Zionism itself – the right of the Jewish people to a homeland, and the very existence of a Jewish state … Although anti-Zionists claim innocence of any antisemitic intent, anti-Zionism frequently borrows the libels of classical Jew-hating. Accusations of international Jewish conspiracy and control of the media have resurfaced to support false equations of Zionism with colonialism and imperialism, and the promotion of vicious, fictitious parallels with genocide and Nazism. How, in such

instances, is anti-Zionism distinguishable from antisemitism?" ... We do not forget nor deny that the Palestinian people have an equally legitimate, ancient history and culture in Palestine nor that they have suffered wrongs that must be healed. We hope that a Palestinian state will exist peacefully alongside Israel. We do not attempt to minimalise their suffering nor the part played by the creation of the state of Israel. Yet justice for one nation does not make justice for the other inherently wicked. Zionism is the right of the Jewish people to self-determination. We believe that anti-Zionism, with its antisemitic characteristics, has no place in a civil society.

(Sugarman, 2017)

Using antisemitic tropes such as Jews wanting power or being behind a new world order controlling governments and media often form part of so-called anti-Zionism. The argument seems to be that there is no issue with Jews, only the Zionism that seeks to spread the borders of Israel and limit the rights of people therein. This is creating a picture of Zionism that is not what most Jews would support; it is creating a straw man. Rather, it seems to obscure legitimate criticism of the actions of a government with rhetoric that is erroneous, antisemitic and dangerous.

Figure 5.2 A door plaque in Heaton Park Shul, Manchester dedicated to those who gave their lives defending Israel.

Thoughts for the classroom

The area of antisemitism is perhaps one of the most difficult areas to explore within the classroom. The first question perhaps should be: 'Does antisemitism need to be explored?' I wish the answer were no. However, the situation in which the world finds itself in means that, for the most part, it cannot be avoided.

UNESCO (2018) suggests an approach to educating against antisemitism that highlights the insidious nature of antisemitism itself, and the danger that it poses towards shared human rights acknowledging 'that the ideas behind anti-Semitism oppose, undermine and violate fundamental human rights principles. A human rights-based approach to education must, therefore, entail efforts to eradicate manifestations of anti-Semitism and protect the dignity of all people' (28). Further that critical thinking is an important part of the process; in the era of alternative facts, students should be equipped to challenge conspiracy narratives for themselves. In looking at modern and historical examples of antisemitism, it is hoped that students will be able to recognize how history repeats itself particularly in the prejudices that are expressed and acted upon. In so doing, teachers should:

- Explore the history of stereotypes.
- Explore the role of power dynamics in stereotypes.
- Acknowledge shared responsibility for rejecting stereotypes (UNESCO, 2018, 40).

Maybe in the early years of the primary school there is a possibility that it can be avoided, and the focus when teaching Judaism should be about Jewish beliefs and practices, meaning the lived reality of living as a Jew within the UK today. When the festival of Chanukah, for example, is taught, teachers do not just explore the story of Judah the Maccabee, but how it is celebrated by British Jews. This is a similar principle that lies behind the 'No Outsiders' initiative that seeks to represent different family types in books that are read in the classroom, and initiatives that seek to include people from diverse backgrounds in the material that is used in all classrooms (Moffat, 2017). The books that are suggested for use as a part of the approach illustrate that it's about inclusion and diversity, helping pupils see themselves in the curriculum, and providing positive examples of the world's peoples in all their diversity. Examples in this initiative include *Elmer* by David McKee, and *Odd Dog Out* by Rob Biddulph. In terms of representation of Judaism, this will require the teacher to use examples and books about Jews that are reflective of reality and do not perpetuate stereotypes. These might include such books as:

- *Belonging and Believing: My Jewish Family* Gill Vaisey (2021).
- *A Synagogue Just Like Home* by Alice Blumenthal McGinty and Laurel Molk (2022).
- *Eight Nights, Eight Lights* by Natalie Barnes and Andrea Stegmaier (2023).
- *Shabbat Is Coming!* by Tracy Newman and Viviana Garofoli (2014).
- *Sammy Spider's First Yom Kippur* (Sammy Spider's First Books) by Sylvia A. Rouss and Katherine Janus Kahn (2013).

This can also be enhanced at all stages of education through links with local communities and the inclusion of authentic voices. The inclusion of stories and examples of Jews is one way to encounter these voices but they can also be found in other ways.

- Visitors
- Visits to places of worship
- Video clips
- Video conferencing
- Books written from an insider's perspective.

All these experiences are valuable, though some may prioritize the face-to-face meeting over the other forms as they are more immediate and interactive. I have suggested elsewhere (Holt, 2022) that one of the bridges to learning in religion and worldviews classroom is with local and national communities. Jackson et al. also (2010) suggested this as one of their key recommendations: 'School leaders and RE teachers should develop community partnerships between the school and local faith communities, particularly those with an orientation towards social action, so that pupils can learn about the role of religions in society' (13). In developing this further, it is argued:

> One training teacher of RE lamented that he could not take pupils on exciting visits to Bethlehem or India. To some extent, as interesting as those visits would be, much more important are visits to/from local faith communities that explore with pupils the way that religion is lived within their communities. This will break down far more barriers than a global tourist activity.
>
> (Holt, 2022, 203)

Ofsted (2010) reflected on such an approach to religions more widely:

> A school decided to invite representatives from the local faith communities to its training on RE where they were introduced to the process of enquiry-based learning. As a result, they gained a greater appreciation of their role in supporting the overall programme for RE and were therefore able to make a richer contribution to it. Instead of simply imparting information, their meetings with pupils became conversations and discussions where they shared their experiences and views and contributed to the process of research and enquiry. Pupils' visits to local places of worship focused less on facts about the building and more on religious commitment and living.
>
> (48)

Thus, bridges are built within communities that will prepare pupils to be informed and respectful. Both schools and the Jewish community have responsibilities to facilitate this. One of the schools that I worked in held an annual Iftar meal; one year a speaker spoke about fish and chips being a Muslim food, about jeans being Muslim clothes. Making the point that accepting some of the existing British culture does not oppose Islam and can make a person more prepared to face the challenges. Although an example from Islam, similar events could be held in concert with the Jewish community. These are the voices that need to be heard in the classroom. It would help children and wider society if schools facilitated such opportunities and also if Jews themselves sought opportunities involved in this important task – both in schools and other places so that the negative view of Jews is challenged, not by teachers who 'have to' but by Jews who will reflect the true essence of their faith in their conversation and actions.

This is the first part of an approach to teaching Judaism that will hopefully challenge antisemitism. It does it in a way that does not address the stereotypes and the tropes, but by pre-empting them with experience and education. However, because of the way the world is, children as they get older will be exposed to such attitudes and teachers need to find a way to navigate and address the various issues that will arise. This may come in the explicit comments of people in various media and circumstances, but also in the study of the literature of the world. The use of plays such as The Merchant of Venice and characters such as Fagin in Oliver Twist will subtly introduce the various tropes that we find throughout the world. A teacher, if they must encounter these characters, and I'm not sure they do, must challenge the characterizations. This is not unusual; in recent years media companies such as the Disney Channel have issued 'health' warnings at the beginning of certain films and programmes. For example, when watching The Aristocats, a viewer will see this message:

> This programme includes negative depictions and/or mistreatment of people or cultures. These stereotypes were wrong then and are wrong now. Rather than remove this content, we want to acknowledge its harmful impact, learn from it and spark conversation to create a more inclusive future together. Disney is committed to creating stories with inspirational and aspirational themes that reflect the rich diversity of the human experience around the globe. To learn more about how stories have impacted society visit: www.Disney.com

Teachers must have the confidence to address antisemitism when it is found. Oftentimes using historical examples, while impactful and chilling, may suggest that antisemitism is something that belongs to the history books. This chapter has shown that it is part of the modern Jews experience, and the small and large aggressions should be highlighted and challenged.

There may be some trepidation on the part of teachers in knowing how to frame the discussion and perhaps they dare worried at being seen to 'take sides'. In many ways the idea that there are 'two sides' to the argument needs to be challenged. As explored in this chapter there is a difference between criticism of the actions of the government of Israel and antisemitism and so-called anti-Zionism. The problem also lies in the way that media speak about the various issues, and the conflation of various attitudes and approaches. Generalizations, stereotyping, and pillorying are ignorant at best and extremely harmful. It is not just a problem in society but also in schools:

> Those [parents] with children at mainstream schools are more likely to report their chil-
> dren experienced antisemitism at school (21%) than travelling to/from it (2%).
>
> (Lessof, 2024, 5)

Schools need to become 'safe' spaces where faiths are celebrated, and children feel as though their identities are recognized and valued. The presence in our schools of some Jews should be seen as an opportunity to share our common understanding and respect for each other on our overlapping journeys. Such contributions can enrich school life (see above), and help pupils feel as though their voices are important. Excluding pupils from inclusion or participation may make them feel isolated. McGarvey suggests that in such structures where people feel that their voices are not heard, the desire to participate diminishes:

> Enthusiasm to take part and be active in communities quickly dissipates when people realise the local democracy isn't really designed with them in mind; that it's designed primarily so that people from outside the community can retain control of it, over the heads of those who live there. … Listening to and valuing every child as an individual is crucial. As such, if the RE classroom contains people from beyond the big six, it is crucial that they have a voice to explore and express their beliefs.

Schools need to help children feel as though their backgrounds and life experiences as Jews are valued so that they can recognize their value and place in society.

Chapter 6

Expressions of Faith

Within Judaism expressions of belief are usually found in the way that a person lives. The chapters above highlight that a person's outlook on life, informed by the teachings of Judaism, finds expression in every aspect of a person's life. To separate expressions of belief from a person's life would be anathema to the overall message of Judaism. Every aspect of a Jew's life is imbued with the beliefs that they hold. As noted in the Introduction, while this may be true, it may be unconsciously so, in the sense that the way that a person lives is inherited and may not be conscious expressions of certain beliefs. It is, however, possible to suggest that the 'story' of the Jews with its attendant beliefs influences the way that Judaism is lived. Therefore, it is possible to speak of every act that a Jew performs as a potential expression of belief, though it may not be outwardly observable.

This contrasts, very much, with the discussion in the Series Editor's Foreword that outlines 'religion' as a modern and 'settled' term. The neat structures that Western colonialists had constructed based on a Christian lens, are not transferred to other religious traditions neatly, no matter how hard people tried. Within the classroom, this is one of the problems that a teacher will face when exploring Judaism. When the GCSE specifications are explored in England, we note that sections such as 'Living the Jewish Life' or 'Practices' deal with topics such as prayer (explored in this chapter) and ethics (see Chapter 7) alongside further expressions of belief such as festivals and life cycle rituals.

This is a result of the Department for Education issuing guidance for the reformation of the GCSEs that followed a common structure and tried to fit everything into a structure that had been inherited from a world religions paradigm. It is incumbent on teachers, who may need to teach within this structure, to highlight the reality of Jewish living compared to that which is found in the specification and their attendant textbooks. For those teachers who can construct an approach to Judaism not constrained by outside curricula, it will be useful to consider how to approach expressions of belief. This might be better done alongside the beliefs that are expressed. Separating the two is not always the most sensible approach and does not give the idea of a cohesive approach to a person's way of living. Elsewhere (Holt, 2022), I have suggested that one of the five 'bridges' to ensure effective learning within the classroom is through the underpinning of practices with beliefs. Those practices make no sense without an understanding of the attendant beliefs.

Throughout this chapter, the various expressions of worship will be explored within Judaism, alongside other expressions such as the celebration of festivals and life-cycle rituals will be touched upon, as they are an important expression of Judaism and community within the UK today. At this stage of the development of a worldviews approach within England it is important to reflect on how beliefs and practices are intertwined rather than separated.

Festivals

The Jewish Calendar, as noted earlier (see Introduction), is a lunar calendar that is linked to the solar calendar (lunisolar) and is different from the Gregorian calendar that is used in the UK. In the Hebrew calendar there are twelve months, each of twenty-nine- or thirty-days' length, dependent on the new moon. This totals a year of 354 days, which means that every two or three years an additional month is added to maintain the imperative that Pesach should fall at the time of the spring harvest (Abib):

> You shall observe the Feast of Unleavened Bread – eating unleavened bread for seven days as I have commanded you – at the set time in the month of Abib, for in it you went forth from Egypt; and none shall appear before Me empty-handed.
>
> (Exodus 23:15)

It thus maintains synchronicity with the lunar calendar (see Table 6.1). This is why festivals may be seen to shift dates slightly within the Gregorian calendar.

Another difference within the Hebrew calendar is that days begin and end at sunset (see Table 6.2); this links with the story of creation where each day is recorded in a specific way: 'And there was evening and there was morning, a first day' (Genesis 1:5). This is why Shabbat begins on Friday evening in the Gregorian calendar, as this is the beginning of the seventh day. Jewish festivals and holy days always commence a short time before sunset and terminate at nightfall the following day – approximately a 25-hour period.

There is not enough space in this chapter to explore all the festivals within the Jewish calendar (see Table 6.3). Some of the festivals that are perhaps seen to be most important or studied the most within classrooms will be explored below.

In discussing the importance of festivals, some British Jews indicated different ideas and experiences:

> I keep the Sabbath by not working. I go to the synagogue on the High Holidays. We hold a Seder at Passover. I sometimes build a Sukkah but do not always manage it. I celebrate the other festivals with greater or lesser amounts of observance.
>
> I enjoy the special food, special synagogue services for festivals and also really enjoy Pesach and Chanukah in others' homes.

Space does not allow for an exploration of all the different festivals, and so the examination here will focus on Shabbat, Rosh Hashanah and Yom Kippur, Pesach, Chanukah and Purim.

Table 6.1 The Months of the Year in the Hebrew Calendar.

Month number*	Hebrew month	Gregorian equivalent (approximate)**
1 (7)	Nisan	April/ May/ May
2 (8)	Iyar	April/ May/ June
3 (9)	Sivan	May/ June/ July
4 (10)	Tammuz	June/ July/ August
5 (11)	Av	July/ August/ September
6 (12)	Elul	August/September/ October
7 (1)	Tishrei	September/ October/ November
8 (2)	Cheshvan (or Marcheshvan)	October/ November/ December
9 (3)	Kislev	November/ January
10 (4)	Tevet	January/ February
11 (5)	Shevat	January/ February
12 (6)	Adar I (only in leap years)	January/ February/ March
12 (6)	Adar (Adar II in leap years)	February/ March/ April

*The numbering is based on differing times of the new year depending on which calendar is used. In the calendar of festivals based on the Torah, Nisan is the first month as the Torah outlines that 'In the first month, on the fourteenth day of the month, at twilight, there shall be a passover offering to the LORD' (Leviticus 23:5). It also outlines the timing of Rosh Hashanah: 'In the seventh month, on the first day of the month, you shall observe complete rest, a sacred occasion commemorated with loud blasts' (Leviticus 23:24). Whereas the agricultural or civil year begins after the autumn harvest, with Rosh Hashanah on the first day of Tishrei: 'You shall observe the Feast of Weeks, of the first fruits of the wheat harvest; and the Feast of Ingathering at the turn of the year' (Exodus 34:22).
**The earlier month indicates the date in which the first day could possibly fall, while the latest month is the date in which the final day will fall. This is based on the lunisolar calendar which adds an additional month.

Table 6.2 Days of the Week in the Hebrew Calendar.

Hebrew	Translation	Gregorian equivalent
Yom Rishon	First day	Sunset on Saturday to sunset on Sunday
Yom Sheni	Second day	Sunset on Sunday to sunset on Monday
Yom Shlishi	Third day	Sunset on Monday to sunset on Tuesday
Yom Revii	Fourth day	Sunset on Tuesday to sunset on Wednesday
Yom Hamishi	Fifth day	Sunset on Wednesday to sunset on Thursday
Yom Shishi	Sixth day	Sunset on Thursday to sunset on Friday
Yom Shabbat	Sabbath day	Sunset on Friday to sunset on Saturday

Shabbat/Shabbos

To a non-Jew, perhaps familiar only with Christian views of the Sabbath, it may appear odd to include Shabbat as a festival. It is variously described as a remembrance, a commemoration and observance and as a festive day to remember the creation of the universe and the day that the Almighty rested. Its pre-eminence in the life of Jews is shown in the various words that

Table 6.3 Festivals Within Judaism.

Festival	Time of year	Duration
Asara b'Tevet (Fast of 10 Tevet)	December/January	Sunrise to sunset
Tu Bishvat (New Year for Trees)	January/February	Sunrise to sunset
Ta'anit Esther (Fast of Esther)	March	Sunrise to sunset
Purim (Festival of Lots)	March	1 day
Ta'anit Bechorot (Fast of the Firstborn)	April	Sunrise to sunset
Pesach (Passover)	April	8 days
Shavuot (Festival of Weeks)	May/June	2 days
Shivah Asar b'Tammuz (Fast of 17 Tammuz)	July	Sunrise to sunset
Tisha b'Av (Fast of 9 Av)	July/August	25 hours
Rosh Hashanah (New Year)	September/October	2 days
Tzom Gedaliah (Fast of Gedaliah)	September/October	Sunrise to sunset
Yom Kippur (Day of Atonement)	September/October	25 hours
Sukkot (Festival of Tabernacles)	September/October	7 days
Shmini Atzeret (Eighth Day of Assembly)	October	2 days
Simchat Torah (Rejoicing with the Torah)	October	2 days
Chanukah (Festival of Dedication)	December	8 days
Shabbat/Shabbos	Every week	1 day

have been used to describe it, including 'shelter, palace, fortress, bride, and queen' (Diamant & Cooper, 2023, 16). The command to celebrate Shabbat is found throughout the Torah and two examples highlight two purposes of Shabbat. Firstly, as one of the commands of the Almighty given to Moses on Mount Sinai:

> Remember the sabbath day and keep it holy. Six days you shall labour and do all your work, but the seventh day is a sabbath of the LORD your God: you shall not do any work – you, your son or daughter, your male or female slave, or your cattle, or the stranger who is within your settlements. For in six days the LORD made heaven and earth and sea, and all that is in them, and He rested on the seventh day; therefore the LORD blessed the sabbath day and hallowed it.
>
> (Exodus 20:8-11)

The focus of Shabbat in this passage is focused on the Creation, 'honouring God as Creator' and 'that the world has a purposive Creator' (Lieberman, 2011, 5). The second command is in Deuteronomy:

> Remember that you were a slave in the land of Egypt and the LORD your God freed you from there with a mighty hand and an outstretched arm; therefore the LORD your God has commanded you to observe the sabbath day.
>
> (5:15)

In the context of the Exodus from Egypt, Shabbat is thus 'an affirmation that God not only created us but that He continues to care about His creation and about human history' (Lieberman, 2011, 5).

A third purpose of Shabbat for Jews is highlighted by Rabbi Menechem Schneerson, who suggested that it enables an experience of life that withdraws a person from the imperfect world:

> [W]e cease to struggle with the world, not because the task of perfecting it is on hold, but because on Shabbat the world is perfect; we relate to what is perfect and unchanging in it.
>
> (Lieberman, 2011, 4)

Echoing various Midrash that highlight Shabbat as a taste of the world to come, of Olam Haba, or also of the Messianic age, Rabbi Akiva taught:

> In the hour God said to Israel, 'I am giving you the Torah', God said, 'If you observing the mitzvah (commandment) of Shabbat, I will give you Olam Haba (the world to come)'. And Israel said before God, 'Master of the Universe! Show us an example of this Olam Haba'. God replied, 'This is Shabbat'.
>
> (in Ralston, 2015)

Echoed by Rabbi Irving Greenberg:

> According to the Genesis account, this world originally was and is still meant to be a paradise. But only when there is peace, with abundant resources and an untrammelled right to live, will the world be structured to sustain the infinite value of the human being. This is the heart of Judaism, the dream. Jewish existence without the dream is almost inconceivable. The drawing power of the vision has kept Jews faithful to their mission over several millennia. Expulsion, persecution, and destruction have assaulted but never obliterated the dream. Jews have repeatedly given everything, including their very lives, to keep it alive. And when catastrophe shattered the vision, Jews spent their lives renewing it. The question is: From where can these people draw the strength to renew their dream again and again? The answer of Jewish tradition is: Give people just a foretaste of the fulfilment, and they will never give it up. The Shabbat is that taste … The world of the Shabbat is totally different than the weekday universe: There is no work to do, no deprivation. On Shabbat, there is neither anxiety nor bad news. Since such a world does not yet exist in space, it is first created in time, on the seventh day of the week. Jews travel through time in order to enter a perfect world for a night and a day. The goal is to create a reality so complete and absorbing that these time travellers are caught up in its values and renewed. The Shabbat is the foretaste of the messianic redemption.
>
> (1988, 127)

Thus, the three purposes are reflected in the remembrance, observance and celebration in the activities of Shabbat. It is not only a day of rest from the labours of the world, but also a day to reconnect with the Almighty and to fully express one's devotion. There are rituals and activities that should be performed, activities that might be performed and activities which are forbidden. The observance of such will vary between Jews; some will be personal decisions about Shabbat observance, but some will reflect the tradition of Judaism, which a person will follow. Below, we will explore how Shabbat is celebrated, recognizing there will be diversity, followed by a discussion of the various activities that are encouraged and restricted.

Celebration

The celebration of Shabbat is to be a delight to Jews, a time of peace, as people are welcomed or throughout Shabbat, the phrase Shabbat Shalom (peaceful Shabbat) is offered in greeting. It begins on Friday evening with a festive meal, which in turn begins with the lighting of candles by the woman of the home. There is usually a minimum of two representing the command to 'remember' and 'observe', but there is no maximum. The lighting of the candles signifies the division between the end of the week and the beginning of Shabbat. As the candles are lit, a blessing is offered:

> Blessed are You, LORD our God, King of the universe, Who has sanctified us with His commandments and commanded us to light the Shabbat lamp.

This separation of the week from Shabbat is seen to be 'exquisite', in which 'one could sense in it the quiet of the approaching Sabbath, which above all meant rest and closeness to God' (Helmreich, 1976, 4–5). Praises are given to the woman by her husband in the form of the *Eshet Chayil* based on Proverbs 31. Blessings may also be offered for children who are present; these might include:

> For boys: May God make you like Ephraim and Menashe. For girls: May God make you like Sarah, Rebecca, Rachel, and Leah. May God bless you and keep you. May God shine light on you and be gracious to you. May God turn toward you and grant you peace.

Kiddush is offered over the wine:

> Blessed are You, God, Ruler of the universe, who creates the fruit of the vine.

Blessings are also offered over challah:

> Blessed are You, God, Ruler of the universe, who creates the bread from the earth.

There are usually sharing customs associated with the challah, it may be that the husband tears a piece and gives one to each person, or maybe each person rests their hands on the challah as the blessing is said, and then each person receives a piece. There may be two loaves of challah to represent the double portion of manna that was collected before the Shabbat would begin in the wilderness. Songs may also be sung, and the meal is shared. It may be that the talk around the table is not linked to the work of the week, but on thankfulness for the blessings received. For many families, the Shabbat meal in the home is the observance for the Friday evening, but many synagogues will offer Friday night services; some just before Shabbat begins, while others offer them later in the evening.

On Saturday morning, many Jews will attend Shabbat services at the synagogue. The Shabbat service can only begin when a minyan is present; in Orthodox traditions this is ten men, whereas in other traditions it can be ten adults. When the service begins, while there are variations between synagogues, services usually follow a similar structure:

- *Birchot Hashachar* (the morning blessings) are offered.
- *Korbanot* are recited – usually these are passages from the Torah related to sacrifices.
- *P'sukei D'Zimra*, songs of praise from the Psalms (a difference from weekday services is that Psalm 100 is omitted in many synagogues), are sung. The Nishmat prayer is offered at the end of the p'sukei d'zimra.
- *Shema Y'Israel* is recited.
- *Amidah* (the standing prayer), a series of blessings, is recited.
- *Tachanun*, where prayers are offered using passages of supplication from the Tanakh.
- The Torah is taken from the Ark and processed around the synagogue. This is followed by a reading of the Torah from the bimah. This is described as 'the emotional and intellectual heart of the service … [and] is an experience of communal study and a never-ending challenge to discover new meaning in it.' (Diamant & Cooper, 2023, 42–3)
- *Ashrei*, a prayer from the Psalms, is sung.
- The *Aleinu* prayer is recited, followed by the returning of the Torah to the Ark.
- A sermon is usually given by the rabbi.

This may be followed by light refreshments, especially if bar or bat mitzvahs have taken place as part of the service (see below). Speaking of the Shabbat service, one person has suggested:

> In exploring the focus of Judaism as the Almighty, the Torah and Israel and as a people it is very noticeable that a Shabbat service brings all three of these aspects together. Everything within the service focuses on Hashem; the reading of the Torah is the largest section of the service; the prayers often focus on Israel, but it is also a very social event, where people show how much they care for, and love, each other. We also celebrate people's births or engagements. And while I think about Shabbat and the purpose of it being focussed on the fourth commandment as a covenant between the Lord and Israel I think it helps me recognise that Shabbat is about focus on a Jew's relationship with Hashem and also with each other.

The rabbi gives the sermon, and often others are involved in the service. In many synagogues there will be a cantor (*hazzan*), who chants or sings the various aspects of the services. There are different approaches to the chanting of a cantor; they will usually be trained and often their singing will be akin to a performance, while increasingly in many synagogues they will serve the function 'more akin to being a song leader, creating a more participatory experience and allowing congregants to join in the singing' (My Jewish Learning, n.d.).

The synagogue is the centre of this Shabbat worship. Every aspect of the design of the synagogue will remind Jews of various aspects of belief and function, though it is possible for a Jew to attend and focus solely on the service and not on what is around them. One Jew commented:

> When non-Jews visit the shul they often speak of the importance of the ner Tamid, the eternal light. I have to say while I know it is a symbol of the Almighty it's not something I really notice. In fact, once it had been out for a week and no-one noticed.

These various features and their functions include:

- A *bimah*. A raised platform from which the Torah is read. In an Orthodox synagogue it will usually be in the centre facing the Ark (see Figure 6.1). In a Reform synagogue it will usually be at the front facing out (see Figure 6.2).
- The *aron kodesh* or ark of the Torah scrolls. Often a closed cabinet with a curtain covers it. This is opened when the Torah scrolls are to be read.
- The *ner tamid* or the eternal light symbolizing the presence of the Almighty. Usually placed above the aron kodesh.
- The tablets of the Ten Commandments usually above the aron kodesh.
- The *tallit* or prayer shawl (see Figure 6.3) that will be worn around the shoulders, by men in Orthodox services, possibly by all in a Reform synagogue.

Figure 6.1 The interior of Heaton Park Ashkenazi Shul, taken from the women's balcony.

Figure 6.2 The bimah in Jackson Row Reform synagogue, Manchester, facing the congregation.

Figure 6.3 Tallits.

- The seating: In a Reform synagogue men and women will sit together, in Orthodox, separately.
- A *menorah*: A seven-branched candlestick reminding Jews of the menorah that was in the Temple.

The remainder of Shabbat may be spent reading, eating an already prepared meal or visiting with family. Shabbat observance will differ between Jews and the difference in practice will be explored below.

Shabbat ends with the Havdalah (separation) ceremony, when three stars have appeared in the sky, or if the sky is overcast, when a blue thread cannot be distinguished from a white thread when they are held at arm's length. Some have interpreted this to mean thirteen-and-a-half minutes after sunset and see this as an expression of tosefet shabbat (the mitzvah of extending Shabbat). The Havdalah ceremony includes three objects:

- A multi-wick candle (or two candles if a multi-wick candle is unavailable) symbolizing the communal nature of Shabbat.
- Wine symbolizing the joy of Shabbat.
- Sweet spices symbolizing the sweetness of Shabbat.

As the candle is lit this marks the end of Shabbat, as this would have been forbidden during the time of Shabbat. Blessings are recited over each of the objects, though their exact wording will differ between communities:

Blessed are You,, Adonai our God, Ruler of the universe, Creator of the fruit of the vine.
Blessed are You, Adonai our God, Ruler of the universe, Creator of many kinds of spices.
Blessed are You, Adonai our God, Ruler of the universe, Creator of the fire's light.

At the conclusion of the blessings, a tradition among many Jews is to look at one's fingertips to see if it is possible to distinguish between the fingernails and flesh. This may recall Adam and Eve who, when leaving Eden, 'were covered by a protective shell, so looking at fingernails recalls the perfection of paradise' (Diamant & Cooper, 2023, 40). The ceremony then closes with a final blessing:

Blessed are You, Eternal our God, Ruler of the universe, Who distinguishes between the sacred and the profane, between light and darkness, between Israel and other people of the world, between the seventh day and the six days of the week. Blessed are You, Who distinguishes between the sacred and the profane.

Songs may be sung, or Shabu Shabu – a shout for the promise for a good week – is given. The candle is then extinguished in the wine.

Shabbat for Jews is a time of refocus and rest. One example of the benefits of Shabbat is shown in the Torah, where it is extended to the land:

When you enter the land that I assign to you, the land shall observe a sabbath of the LORD. Six years you may sow your field and six years you may prune your vineyard and gather in the yield. But in the seventh year the land shall have a sabbath of complete rest, a sabbath of the LORD: you shall not sow your field or prune your vineyard.

(Levitcus 25:2–4)

When land lies fallow, it is able to rest and to regain its nutrients that will make it more productive in the years that follow. This is just so for people; the rest provides strength and focus necessary for the following week.

Prohibited Activities

The positive mitzvah to rest on Shabbat is contrasted with the negative possibilities of what constitutes work. In ceasing from 'work', the outlining of what is considered melakha (work, plural: malakhot) is outlined in the Talmud as the thirty-nine Melakhot. It should be noted that with certain exceptions, these thirty-nine are also forbidden on festivals mentioned in the Torah (the exceptions mainly surround the preparation of food). The thirty-nine melakhot are often associated with creative activity or acts of creation. They are outlined in Mishna Shabbat 7:2 and are:

- ploughing earth
- sowing
- reaping
- binding sheaves
- threshing
- winnowing
- selecting
- grinding
- sifting
- kneading
- baking
- shearing wool
- washing wool
- beating wool
- dyeing wool
- spinning
- weaving
- making two loops
- weaving two threads
- separating two threads
- tying
- untying
- sewing stitches
- tearing

- trapping
- slaughtering
- flaying
- tanning
- scraping hide
- marking hide
- cutting hide to shape
- writing two or more letters
- erasing two or more letters
- building
- demolishing
- extinguishing a fire
- kindling a fire
- putting the finishing touch on an object and
- transporting an object (between private and public domains, or over four cubits within public domain)

In the modern world there are elements of the melakhot that are debated and have had to be applied. One such example is the use of electricity on Shabbat.

Further, in Jewish law, there are prohibitions about carrying objects between private and semi-public areas; a private area or domain would be a house, whereas a semi-public is most other places. The *Book of Jeremiah* teaches:

> Thus said the LORD: Guard yourselves for your own sake against carrying burdens on the sabbath day, and bringing them through the gates of Jerusalem. Nor shall you carry out burdens from your houses on the sabbath day, or do any work, but you shall hallow the sabbath day, as I commanded your fathers ... If you obey Me – declares the LORD – and do not bring in burdens through the gates of this city on the sabbath day, but hallow the sabbath day and do no work on it.

(Jeremiah 17: 21–2,24)

There is also a restriction of carrying items for further than two metres in public. All these restrictions would apply to items such as keys, tissues, medication, babies, nappies, glasses, books, and even pushing prams and wheelchairs. This has led to the development of a more modern understanding of eruv which is a geographic location that is contained within a 'fence' or physical boundary. An eruv is correctly termed an 'eruv chatzerot'. This is a merger of many different areas or domains into one. Essentially making the larger geographic area into one, it has been described as 'a large back garden'. Eruvs can be found around the world, most are concentrated within Israel, and they are also eruvs in Manchester, London, New York, Rio, Perth, and many more cities.

In Manchester, for example, these boundaries consist of existing walls, rivers, fences, and in some places, a specially installed wire that runs high above the ground. Each Friday before Shabbat begins, the eruv is checked if it is intact and is therefore able to be used during Shabbat. An eruv doesn't give *carte blanche* to carry anything, but rather that which is prohibited between domains. Things like a mobile phone would still be forbidden.

For many Reform Jews, an eruv would be seen to be unnecessary, as the rules about carrying on Shabbat between domains would be seen to be not relevant today. Indeed, eruvs are not without their critics, who cite concerns about their effects on non-Jews and question whether the practice is a workaround rather than being in the spirit of the law.

Thoughts for the classroom

The inclusion of Shabbat as a festival may seem unusual for students who are unfamiliar with the Jewish faith; how can a day full of restrictions be a cause of celebration? Considering this, it is important that the teacher ensures that Shabbat as a festival and a day of joy is emphasised throughout its teaching. It is not a day of restrictions but of opportunities. While the description of Shabbat observance seems fairly settled above, the variety of ways that it is observed by Jews should be noted. David Graham (2024b) highlights that while 'the social and religious significance of Shabbat cannot be overstated' (3), it is possible to see a variety of practices and views of its importance among British Jews. Some of Graham's findings include:

- 61% have a Shabbat meal most weeks.
- 20% do not turn lights on or off, and avoid operating electrical products.
- 51% light candles in their home most Friday evenings.
- 23% do not drive on Shabbat.
- 27% regularly attend synagogue on Shabbat.
- 50% rest from their jobs.
- 58% spend time with friends or family.
- 29% read or learn about Judaism.
- 31% take a break from technology.

This highlights, for Graham (2024b), the continued importance of Shabbat today:

Yet the idea of Shabbat remains timeless and very much present in modern life: a recurring break or rest from the everyday, marked by ritual or by simply doing things differently. For the religiously inclined, it presents an opportunity to focus on spiritual wellbeing and growth. For Jews who are less observant, it may be more akin to the reboot button on a computer, an opportunity for a pause before getting things going again. Either way, as Ahad Ha'am maintained, this weekly pause for Shabbat is an important part of the cement that glues the Jewish people to their identity.

(9)

Regardless of whether Graham's conclusion is supported by the data, the diverse nature of its observance is evident, and it will be interesting for students to hear from a range of Jewish voices about their Shabbat experience.

Rosh Hashanah/ Yom Kippur

The celebration of Rosh Hashanah and of Yom Kippur is possibly the most important 'festival' within Judaism; one self-identified 'secular' Jew in the UK has suggested that 'of all the things I do not do as a Jew, the one thing that I will always do is to remember and celebrate Rosh Hashanah, whatever that might look like'. Indeed, David Graham (2024a) found that 'of all the major Jewish holidays … Rosh Hashanah is the most widely observed. Almost three-quarters (74 per cent) of Jews in Britain observed Rosh Hashanah rituals at home (e.g. lit candles or ate apples and honey)' (3). As such there is an argument that it perhaps should be more focused on within the classroom than it is. In some ways, it seems to have less importance in the classroom than Pesach (see below), maybe because it does not have a 'story' associated with it. It could be argued that Rosh Hashanah, Yom Kippur and the 'Days of Awe' or 'High Holy Days' are the most important days within the Jewish calendar. Graham (2024) has highlighted the synthesizing nature of these days:

> The High Holy Days are a time for self-reflection, a time when families to come together and celebrate, and a time when the synagogues are at their fullest and Jewish community life at its strongest.
>
> (2024a, 9)

Focusing as they do on the individual, the family and the community, all aspects of the High Holy Days should be explored within their teaching within the classroom, and their celebration or observance within the community.

Rosh Hashanah and Yom Kippur mark the beginning and end of the High Holy Days; the *Unetanneh Tokef*, a part of Jewish readings at these times, highlights this:

> On Rosh Hashanah it is inscribed,
> On Yom Kippur it is sealed.
> How many shall pass away and how many shall be born,
> Who shall live and who shall die,
> Who shall complete the normal span and who not,
> Who shall perish by fire and who by water, Who by violence of man or beast,
> Who by hunger and who by thirst,
> Who by earthquake, plague or execution;
> Who shall have rest and who shall wander, Who secure and who tormented, Who at ease and who afflicted;
> Who shall become poor or rich, find failure or find fame.
>
> (Westminster Synagogue, 2011, 56–7)

Rosh Hashanah is seen to be the Jewish New Year, and is full of different activities that are both celebratory and reflective. Examples of practices include:

- *Tashlich*: usually takes place in the afternoon of Rosh Hashanah. In this activity, Jews recite verses from the Tanakh and throw bread crumbs into water. As the beginning of the Days of Awe, this is representative of casting one's sins away, there may even be the belief that fish take the crumbs away, as the person hopes the Almighty will take their sins. This was not a popular part of celebrations until early medieval times, but is now fairly widespread.

- Rosh Hashanah services in the synagogue are usually elaborate affairs, often being compared to royal celebrations. The shofar is blown one hundred times during the service to remind Jews to reflect on their decisions over the past year, and focus on the Almighty in *teshuvah* (repentance/return). The promise is that evil can be overcome and forgiven for as the Talmud teaches: 'There are three things that can annul evil decrees, and they are: Prayer, charity, and repentance.' (*Bereshit Rabbah* 44:12)
- Various prayers are offered in the synagogue service including the Amidah (see above) and the Unetanneh Tokef (see above). Prayers may also begin with a nuash (or musical theme). Speaking of the Unetanneh Tokef and Rosh Hashanah more widely, Reuven Hammer (2005) suggests:

Many consider this poem to be the pinnacle of the Rosh Hashanah liturgy. The poet has painted a picture of the most solemn day of the year, which to him is Rosh Hashanah, not Yom Kippur. All other concepts associated with the day have been stripped away. 'Awesome and terrible' are the only fitting words to describe it … But this is not a day of suffering without hope. No matter what one has done, says the poet, the severe decree — the penalty of death — can be averted.

(88–9)

Rosh Hashanah begins the period of ten days where prayer, charity and repentance should be performed in earnest to avert the judgement. Another prayer offered is *Avinu Malkeinu* ('Our Father, Our King'), prayer to the Almighty, asking for forgiveness, to be remembered favourably in the *Book of Life*. Its closing phrase is 'Our Father, Our King, graciously answer us, although we are without merit. Deal with us charitably, and lovingly save us'.

- A large family meal is shared, and some foods that will be eaten include apples and honey (honey to represent the wish for a sweet new year); a round challah is a reminder of the never-ending round of live, wine over which *kiddush* is offered, pomegranates to represent something new, something that hasn't been eaten in a while, and tradition suggests that it has 613 seeds to represent the mitzvot;.

The Holy Days or Days of Awe in between are focused on repentance, prayer and charity. The final day of Yom Kippur fulfills a command in the Torah:

For on this day atonement shall be made for you to cleanse you of all your sins; you shall be clean before the LORD.

(Leviticus 16:30)

Here the judgement of the Almighty will be confirmed. It is a day of fasting for men over the age of thirteen, and for women over twelve. Some others will be exempt from the fast because of health. This fast is seen to be a penitential act for sins, and also as a way to focus on the spiritual aspects of life. Some of the ancient practices associated with Yom Kippur and the ridding oneself and the community of iniquity are found in the Torah. Here two goats are brought before the congregation, and then sacrificed 'the people's goat of sin offering' so that 'expiation for himself and his household, and for the whole congregation of Israel' (Leviticus 16: 15, 17). The other goat is brought forward and Aaron confessed 'over it all the iniquities and transgressions of the Israelites, whatever their sins, putting them on the head of the goat; and it shall be sent off to the wilderness through a designated man. Thus the goat shall carry on it all their iniquities to an inaccessible region; and the goat shall be set free in the wilderness' (Leviticus 16:21–22). This is seen as purely symbolic and a scapegoat is represented today by the confessing of sins and the healing of rifts between people. This is recalled in the morning service, but is further expressed earlier in the evening service on *Yom Kippur* and *Kol Nidre*. Kol Nidre begins the Yom Kippur service, and is considered to be a statement rather than a prayer. Its formulation will differ but usually three people will begin with the following being recited three times:

> By the authority of the court on high and by the authority of this court below, with divine consent and with the consent of this congregation, we grant permission to pray with those who have transgressed.
>
> (The Rabbinical Assembly, 2010, 204)

The service continues with the following also recited three times:

> All vows, renunciations, bans, oaths, formulas of obligation, pledges, and promises that we vow or promise to ourselves and to God from this Yom Kippur to the next – may it approach us for good – we hereby retract. May they all be undone, repealed, cancelled, voided, annulled, and regarded as neither valid nor binding. Our vows shall not be considered vows; our renunciations shall not be considered renunciations; and our promises shall not be considered promises.
>
> The entire congregation of the people Israel shall be forgiven, as well as the stranger who dwells among them, for all have erred.
>
> (The Rabbinical Assembly, 2010, 205)

The assurance is later given that 'ADONAI replied, "I have forgiven, as you have asked"' (The Rabbinical Assembly, 2010, 205).

Other parts of the observances of Yom Kippur include:

- The wearing of white to symbolize purity.
- Fasting for twenty-five hours including the abstination from sexual activity.
- *Shacharit*: The morning synagogue service where Leviticus 16 and the sacrificial rites are read. The haftarah reading is Isaiah 57:14–58:14, which speaks of the importance of ritual being a means to motivate people to action to build a just world (see Chapter 7).

- *Musaf* (additional sacrifice): This service immediately follows shacharit and recites a list of atrocities suffered by the Jews since the time of the Romans until the Shoah.
- *Yizkor*: The Yizkor service is a memorial to those who have died. It may include a list of people in the community who have died in the last year. The influence of the deceased on a person's life is reflected upon. The souls of those who have died will be prayed for.
- *Mincha*: The afternoon synagogue service, where the story of Jonah is read and Torah command to love neighbour.
- Ne'ilah: This service signals the end of Yom Kippur with the blowing of the *shofar* which recalls when it was blown at Sinai as the Torah was given. It might also represent the victory for Jews over the sins of individuals and the community represented in the festival.
- *Havdalah*: The service that ends of Shabbat is carried out.

This is a day of great solemnity when the judgement for the coming year is fixed.

Pesach/Passover

Within UK schools, it is possible to suggest that Pesach (or Passover) is the most often taught Jewish festival. There are many possible reasons for this, but most likely it is that it celebrates a seminal event within Judaism, and is focused on Moses and the Exodus. It is a remembrance of the Almighty intervening in the persecution of the children of Israel and their ultimate deliverance and return to the land of Israel. In contrast to Rosh Hashanah and Yom Kippur, which some may see as more important observances (whatever importance means), the story of Pesach brings the celebration alive and enables it to be accessible at the various Key Stages, and we are able to see a progression in how it is taught.

Pesach is also one of the festivals that are celebrated among British Jews. In 2024, the Institute for Jewish Policy Research found that four out of every five Jews in the UK attended a seder meal (Graham, 2024). This figure drew from all sections of the Jewish community. Although it is an important celebration of 'the belief that God intervenes in people's lives, and belief in the divinity of the Torah', it may also serve a purpose in establishing and reminding Jews of a shared identity: 'For example, 54% of those [Jews] who don't believe in God or any higher or spiritual power say they attend seder annually. But there is no contradiction here; this simply attests to the reality that for many Jews, seder attendance is as much an ethno-cultural celebration as it is a religious one' (Graham, 2024, 5).

Graham (2024) also notes that 'those who have children (of any age) are more likely to attend every year than those with no children' (4), perhaps suggesting that it is an important festival in passing on the Jewish faith, perhaps more so because of the involvement of the children in various activities of the celebration (see below). It is a celebration that places children at its heart, and thus encourages celebration among Jews and focuses in the school classroom.

The celebration of Pesach is commanded in the Torah:

And Moses said to the people, 'Remember this day, on which you went free from Egypt, the house of bondage, how the LORD freed you from it with a mighty hand: no leavened bread shall be eaten. You go free on this day, in the month of Abib. So, when the LORD has brought you into the land of the Canaanites, the Hittites, the Amorites, the Hivites, and the Jebusites, which He swore to your fathers to give you, a land flowing with milk and honey, you shall observe in this month the following practice: Seven days you shall eat unleavened bread, and on the seventh day there shall be a festival of the LORD. Throughout the seven days unleavened bread shall be eaten; no leavened bread shall be found with you, and no leaven shall be found in all your territory. And you shall explain to your child on that day, "It is because of what the LORD did for me when I went free from Egypt"'.

(Exodus 13:2–8)

Remembrance of the freeing of the Jews by the Almighty lies at the heart of Pesach and the command to 'explain to your child' is taken very seriously in its celebration. Within the *Haggadah* (literally 'telling', a text setting forth the order of the seder meal), the first question (and there are three subsequent ones explored below) is asked by the youngest child: 'Why is this night different from all other nights?' (Scherman & Zlotowitz, 2008, 25). The story of Pesach is then told.

The Story of Pesach

The background to the story of Pesach begins with Jacob/Israel and his sons including Joseph, who became a ruler in Egypt. With a famine in Canaan, Joseph's brothers, his father and their families totalling seventy people (Exodus 1:5) moved to Egypt to be under the protection of Joseph. After the generation of Joseph and his brothers passed away, the Torah records that 'the Israelites were fertile and prolific; they multiplied and increased very greatly, so that the land was filled with them' (Exodus 1:7). There are various esti-mates as to how much time passed between the death of Joseph and the decision of the Pharaoh that 'the Israelite people are much too numerous for us' (Exodus 1:9). Estimates generally range between sixty-four years and 500 years; the time of sixty-four years is based on the tradition that Moses was the great-great nephew of Joseph based on the genealogy found in Exodus 6, though it is suggested that this may be incomplete. *The Kehot Chumash* suggests that Moses was born on 7 Adar 2368 since creation, and that Joseph was born 2199, suggesting a time of 169 years between their births, with Joseph dying at the age of 110 (Genesis 50:26). This would suggest a time of fifty-nine years, but estimates place the time differential as much later. Indeed, Exodus 12:40 suggests that the Israelites lived in Egypt for a period of 430 years, subtracting eighty for the age of Moses, when he spoke to Pharaoh (Exodus 7:7), and Joseph was appointed to a position of authority at the age of thirty, with his father joining him nine or more years later, as there had been seven years of plenty and two of famine in between. This means the Israelites lived in Egypt for approximately seventy years before Joseph died, meaning that 360 years passed between Joseph's death and the Exodus, meaning that when a new king arose in Egypt, who knew nothing of Joseph, it had been approximately 280 years. These numbers seem low when one considers that Josephus records the burdens placed upon the Jews (see below) as lasting for over 400 years (Josephus, 1999, 96), and the Torah records that approximately 600,000 Israelites formed part of the Exodus (Exodus 12:37–8), suggesting an extended time period for that many descendants to come out of the original seventy. I think that the chronology is neither fixed nor sure, and there are many different interpretations; all we can say for certain is that a period long enough for the acts of Joseph to have been forgotten had passed.

The Pharaoh was concerned about the number of Israelites; to stop them from increasing further and thus becoming a threat in 'fighting against us' (Exodus 1:10), the Egyptians 'set taskmasters over them to oppress them with forced labour; and they built garrison for Pharaoh: Pithom and Raamses' (Exodus 1:11). The enforced labour did not have its desired effect on the Israelites, rather 'the more they were oppressed, the more they increased and spread out' (Exodus 1:12). The tasks and burdens inflicted on the Israelites increased, and then the actions of the Pharaoh became even darker than oppression:

> The king of Egypt spoke to the Hebrew midwives, one of whom was named Shiphrah and the other Puah, saying, 'When you deliver the Hebrew women, look at the birthstool: if it is a boy, kill him; if it is a girl, let her live'.
>
> (Exodus 1:15–16)

Fearing the Almighty more than the Pharaoh, the Hebrew midwives averred and did not fulfil the Pharaoh's command. When asked why they had not, they replied that the Hebrew women were far more accomplished and 'vigorous' than Egyptian women, and the midwives arrived too late to witness the birth. For Jews, the hand of the Almighty was with his people:

> And God dealt well with the midwives; and the people multiplied and increased greatly. And because the midwives feared God, He established households for them.
>
> (Exodus 1:20–21)

In response, however, the Pharaoh became even more determined, ordering 'all his people, saying, "Every boy that is born you shall throw into the Nile, but let every girl live"' (Exodus 1:22).

The narrative of the Torah provides a short overview of the birth of Moses. Alongside this, there are many traditions that have arisen that fill in some gaps and provide Jews with a greater understanding of who Moses is, and the miraculous nature of his life. It begins with the description that 'A certain man of the house of Levi went and married a

Levite woman' (Exodus 2:1) meaning that Moses' parents were both of the priestly tribe. Further in Exodus we learn that Moses' father, this man of the house of Levi' is Amran, and that he is married to Jochebed. It is suggested that Jochebed was the daughter of Levi, and was 130 when she married Amran, at which point she miraculously regained her youth. When Moses was born, it is recorded that the room filled with light, indicating to Jochebed that Moses was special. For this reason, she took extra effort to conceal him from the Egyptians, which she did for a period of three months. At the point that she could no longer hide Moses, she placed him in a wicker basket in the reeds of the River Nile. Moses' sister, Miriam, stayed near him to keep an eye on what happened to her brother. The Torah records that at this point, a daughter of the Pharaoh came to bathe in the Nile and discovered the basket with Moses in it. 'She took pity on it and said, "This must be a Hebrew child"' (Exodus 2:6).

All of this serves as a prelude to the story of the Exodus, which is celebrated at Pesach. Although time has been taken to establish the narrative of the birth of Moses, it highlights the situation in which the Israelites found themselves. It was the hardest of situations, their persecution and situation were horrendous. It was a circumstance in which nothing short of the intervention of the Almighty could bring about change.

Although there are many other aspects of Moses' story, we fast forward to a time in the future when he received his commission to free the children of Israel. Forty years later, Moses had a vision of the Almighty known as 'the burning bush' in which a bush was on fire but did not burn. The Almighty spoke to him, telling him that he had seen the suffering of his people in Egypt and that Moses was to return to Egypt and lead the people of Israel into their Promised Land of Canaan. It was in this experience that the Almighty identified himself as Ehyeh-Asher-Ehyeh, 'I am' (see Chapter 1).

Moses returned to Egypt as he had been commanded and asked the Pharaoh to set the slaves free. The Pharaoh refused. To persuade him, God sent a plague which turned the River Nile to blood. Pharaoh agreed to release the slaves, but after Moses took this 'plague' away the Pharaoh changed his mind. This happened eight more times with eight worsening plagues in Egypt.

1 A plague of frogs invaded Egypt.
2 Gnats attacked both people and animals.
3 Swarms of insects covered Egypt.
4 All the Egyptian livestock died.
5 People were afflicted with boils.
6 Hail and fire fell on Egypt from heaven.
7 A Plague of locusts covered all Egyptian land.
8 The land of Egypt was covered by total darkness for three days.

It was the tenth and final plague that enabled the Israelites to escape Egypt. The Israelites were to kill a lamb and paint the blood on their door posts. This would mean that the final plague would pass over the Israelite homes. This final plague was the most brutal; the

Angel of Death killed the firstborn son in all the Egyptian homes. This terrible event and the preceding nine convinced Pharaoh to let the slaves go.

After the Israelites had left Egypt, Pharaoh changed his mind about letting them go. His army caught up with the Israelites on the shores of the Red Sea. With the power of the Almighty, Moses parted the waters which allowed the Israelites to pass safely through. The waters then came together and the whole Egyptian army was drowned. The Israelites were now safe to make their way to the Promised Land and reclaim their covenant. They may have felt that their troubles were at an end. The threat from the Egyptians had lessened but there were many more trials to be faced. Jews believe that the people of Israel needed to be prepared to enter the Promised Land. The journey of the Exodus lasted for forty years and helped them learn more about themselves and their relationship with the Almighty.

There were challenges along the journey, and there was murmuring at different points. Throughout their journey, however, the love of the Almighty was with them. There were many signs of his providence. For safety when they had crossed the Red Sea, the Almighty sent a pillar of smoke to guide them by day, and a pillar of fire to guide them by night, which many Jews interpret today as a symbol of the presence of the Divine (Shechinah, see Chapter 1). When Israelites were thirsty, Moses struck a rock with his stick and water came gushing out. When they were hungry the Almighty sent manna (sweet food) over-night. This would last for one day, except on the Sabbath when they were to gather twice as much as the day before so they wouldn't have to work. The Israelites even complained that there was no variety in this food. The camp of Israel was also infested by snakes. Moses told people to look upon him and the staff Almighty had given him, and they would be saved. But because this seemed so easy, many people didn't look and were poisoned.

An important part of the Exodus was the Sinai experience where Moses received the Torah and the mitzvot (see Chapter 3).

Celebration

The celebration of Pesach begins for many Jews with a 'spring-clean' of the house to ensure that there is no chametz (leaven) in the home.

> On the very first day you shall remove leaven from your houses, for whoever eats leav-
> ened bread from the first day to the seventh day, that person shall be cut off from Israel.
>
> (exodus 12:15)

This is in commemoration of when the people of Israel left Egypt in a hurry and so did not have time to make leavened bread before leaving. Although, the requirement is to remove any chametz that is more than the size of an olive, many Jews try and remove all trace of chametz, even cleaning every surface and nook to ensure that no leaven is left behind. As indicated below, in observing the laws of kashrut many Jews have separate pans, fridges and cutlery for meat and dairy; for many observant Jews, this will also extend to a separate set of pots, pans and utensils, specifically for use at Pesach so there is no trace of chametz. For many other Jews, this is seen to be unnecessary, even here the objects may be thoroughly washed or sterilized.

The five grains that are chametz, if it sits in water for more than eighteen minutes, are wheat, barley, rye, oats and spelt. As Jews get rid of any trace of chametz from their home, they can use it up, throw it out, burn it or give/sell it to non-Jewish friends or neighbours.

Some of the foods containing chametz are obvious such as bread, pasta, biscuits, crackers, beer and so on; but others such as ketchup may or may not contain chametz and so the ingredients label should be read carefully to ensure that every type of chametz is removed. This proscription against leaven being eaten or being found in the home, or in one's domain (many interpret this to include a person's car in addition to the home) is for the time duration of Pesach:

> You shall not eat anything leavened with it; for seven days thereafter you shall eat unleavened bread, bread of distress – for you departed from the land of Egypt hurriedly – so that you may remember the day of your departure from the land of Egypt as long as you live. For seven days no leaven shall be found with you in all your territory, and none of the flesh of what you slaughter on the evening of the first day shall be left until morning.
>
> (Deuteronomy 16:3–4)

Of note, as it is sometimes misunderstood by outside observers, it is not yeast that is forbidden, but rather the fermented grains, and so wine made of fermented grapes is permitted, and is an essential part of Pesach celebrations.

Some Jews have additional restrictions on the food they can eat during Pesach, for example, many Ashkenazi Jews do not eat kitniyot (small things) referring to rice and other grains. Sephardi Jews have never restricted their use during Pesach, and Reform Jews (nineteenth century) and Masorti Jews (2015) have allowed their use as they do not see any authority to include them in the definition of chametz.

On the night before the Pesach Seder meal there is a final search of the home for any remaining chametz. The search begins with a blessing outlined in the *Haggadah*:

> Blessed are You, Hashem our God, King of the universe, Who has sanctified us with his commandments and has commanded us concerning the removal of chametz.
>
> (Scherman & Zlotowitz, 2008, 14)

For many Jews, this is turned into a game for the children who are searching for a piece of chametz that has been hidden by their parents. Some Jews conduct this search by candlelight, but this tradition varies. The search ends with any chametz wrapped in a bag ready to be burned the next morning and the words:

> Any chametz which is in my possession which I did not see, and remove, nor know about shall be nullified and become ownerless, like the dust of the earth.
>
> (Scherman & Zlotowitz, 2008, 14)

On the first night of Pesach families gather for a seder (order) meal. This meal has specific foods (see below) and is conducted using the order set out in the *Haggadah*. Candles are lit with a similar prayer to the one on Shabbat:

> Blessed are You, Hashem, our god, King of the universe, Who has sanctified us through His commandments, and commanded us to kindle the flame of Pesach.
>
> (Scherman & Zlotowitz, 2008, 14)

The seder consists of fifteen different sections; many think to mirror the fifteen steps in the Temple in Jerusalem. These fifteen stages are:

1 *Kaddesh:* The Kiddush (blessing on the wine) is recited, and the first glass of wine is drunk.
2 *Urechatz:* Hands are washed.
3 *Karpas:* Eating karpas (usually parsley, celery or boiled potato) which has been dipped in salt water.
4 Yachatz: The middle matzah is broken and the larger piece is put aside as the afikomen (what comes after).
5 *Maggid:* The story of the Exodus is told focusing around the four questions asked by the youngest child. A second glass of wine is drunk.
6 *Rachtzah:* The washing of the hands prior to the meal.
7 *Motzi:* A blessing recited over bread products.
8 *Matzah:* A blessing over the matzah to be eaten.
9 *Maror:* A blessing is recited for the eating of the maror (bitter herbs).
10 *Korah:* The eating of a sandwich of matzah and bitter herbs.
11 *Shulchan orek:* The meal is served.
12 *Tzafun:* The eating of the afikomen which has been hidden during the meal.
13 *Barech:* A blessing after the meal ends is recited and a third glass of wine is drunk.
14 *Hallel:* Psalms of prayers are recited, and a fourth glass of wine is drunk.
15 *Nirtzah:* The conclusion, where a prayer is offered that the Almighty will accept the observance and some Jews will pray for the messiah to come quickly.

A fifth cup of wine is often poured for the prophet Elijah, symbolizing the hope for redemption, the return of Jews to Israel and for some the opening of the Messianic Age. For some Jews this fifth glass of wine is drunk for to celebrate the return of Jews to Israel as their homeland today. A seder plate (see Figure 6.4) is usually used in the meal which contains space for different foods (see Figure 6.5).

Each food has symbolism to remind Jews of various aspects of the Exodus story:

- *Matzah:* Unleavened bread (soft or hard) is eaten in remembrance of the leaving of Egypt in a hurry so bread could not rise.
- *Maror and Chazaret* are bitter herbs and remind Jews of the bitterness of slavery. The Egyptians 'made life bitter for them with harsh labour at mortar and bricks and with all sorts of tasks in the field' (Exodus 1:14).

Figure 6.4 A children's seder plate.

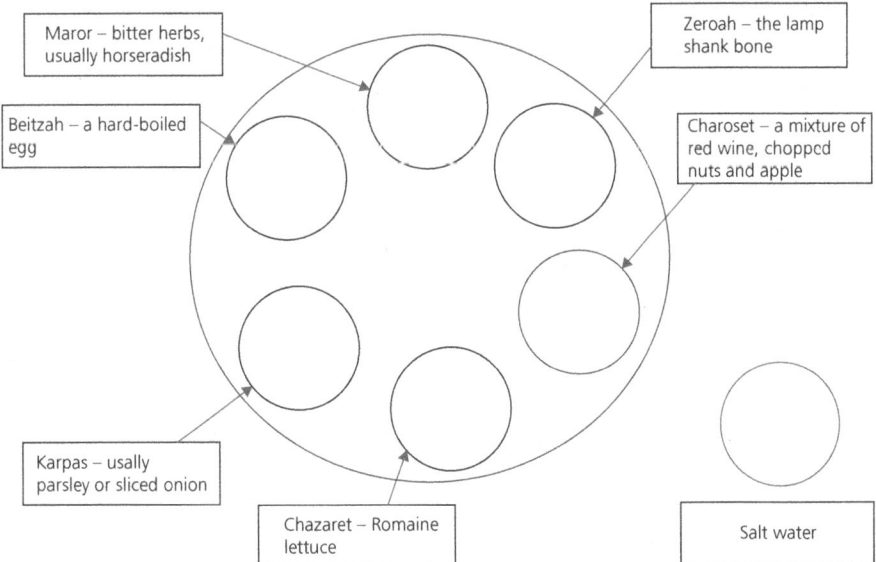

Maror – bitter herbs, usually horseradish

Beitzah – a hard-boiled egg

Karpas – usally parsley or sliced onion

Chazaret – Romaine lettuce

Zeroah – the lamp shank bone

Charoset – a mixture of red wine, choppcd nuts and apple

Salt water

Figure 6.5 Outline of the meal on the Seder plate at Pesach.

- *Charoset*: On the first eating of the maror, it is often dipped in charoset, which could represent the mortar, which were used in their labour as slaves. Some Jews use a total of forty ingredients in the making of charoset, symbolizing the forty years spent in the wilderness.
- *Zeroah*: A lamb bone to symbolize the sacrifice of a lamb made by the Israelites, and the painting of its blood on the doorposts, enabling the angel of death to pass over their homes.
- *Beitzah*: The hard-boiled egg is a symbol of the festival offering in the Temple and reminds Jews of the mourning at the destruction of the Temple and the hope that it can be rebuilt.
- *Salt water*: There are different interpretations of the significance of the dipping of the maror in the salt water. Some suggest it is the tears of the slaves in Egypt. Others suggest that the first dip reminds Jews of the dipping of Joseph's tunic into blood which began the story of the move to Egypt. The second dip of maror may remind the dipping of hyssop into the lamb's blood to paint on doorposts.

There are many other aspects of the celebration of Pesach as a seven-day festival; though for many Jews the first and last days are those that are specifically focused on. *Shvi'i shel Pesach* celebrates the day that the Israelites reached the Red Sea and witnessed the miracle of the parting or splitting of the sea.

Pesach is important as a Jewish festival, perhaps as the defining festival of Judaism. It remembers what is considered by many to be the foundational event that establishes the Law and illustrates the justice of the Almighty. Its continued commemoration throughout history is a reminder to Jews that justice is the purpose of the world, while many may see the inequality throughout the world as 'just the way it is'. Jews recognize 'the socio-economic-political reality in which people live will eventually be perfected', indeed the reality of the world 'is a deviation from the ideal and that redemption will overcome this divergence' (Greenberg, 1988, 34). This lies at the heart of Jewish identity and is lived out in the way that they seek to fulfil their purpose in life, to do good and repair the world (see Chapters 2 and 7). The re-enactment of the story of the Exodus reminds them of the Almighty's intimate involvement in their lives, and his continued presence in history and the world. It is a festival that points both backwards into history, and also into the future. It is a festival of hope for the redemption of the world.

Chanukah

Chanukah (also Hanukah) is celebrated around the Jewish world and is perhaps one of the most noted from outside of the Jewish community. For Jews, religiously it 'is a relatively minor holiday' where 'work is not forbidden, as it is on the Sabbath and for the high holidays of Rosh Hashanah and Yom Kippur' (Economist, 2024), but has increased in popularity, leading to Yitz Landes to comment in an American context that it has become: 'a symbol of how Jews can be Americans [that is] also legible to non-Jews: it works with other winter holidays'.

The Story of Chanukah

It is the festival that draws on the story of Judah the Maccabee found in the apocryphal texts of the Maccabees (see Chapter 4). The story celebrated at Chanukah remembers events during the second century BCE when the Maccabean revolt (also known as the Hasmonean Rebellion or Civil War) freed Judea and Jerusalem from the rule of the Seleucid Empire, and more particularly it enabled the Second Temple to be rededicated. Under the Seleucid Empire, the Jews in Judea had been generally able to follow their own traditions, but Antiochus IV Epiphanes invaded Jerusalem and 'came upon the Jews with a great army, and took their city by force, and slew a great multitude of those that favoured Ptolemy and sent out his soldiers to plunder them without mercy. He also spoiled the temple and put a stop to the constant practice of offering a daily sacrifice of expiation for three years and six months' (Josephus, 1999, 670). There is the suggestion that Antiochus was intervening in a dispute between different factions of Jews, some of whom wanted a Hellenizing of the traditions and beliefs, known as Tobiads who has been expelled from Jerusalem. Whatever the cause, Antiochus went further when he outlawed Judaism and subjugated the Jews and traditions. In 167 BCE he 'compelled the Jews to dissolve the laws of their country, and to keep their infants uncircumcised, and to sacrifice swine's flesh on the altar' (Josephus, 1999, 670), and ordered an altar dedicated to Zeus be built in the Temple.

This was not taken well by the Jews, and Mattathias, 'one of the priests who lived in a village called Modin', along with his five sons Johanan, Simeon, Eleazar, Jonathan and Judah (later known as Judah HaMakabi 'Judah the Hammer') led a rebellion against Antiochus and his occupying force. In 166BCE Matthatias died, and Judah began to lead the rebellion. In 164 BCE the rebellion was successful despite the Jewish armies being vastly outnumbered, the Temple was retaken and rededicated. The rededication was a process and there was a question about whether it 'would be presumptuous for humans to restore the Temple' when it was the prerogative of the Almighty (Greenberg, 1988, 266). The Maccabees waited but in the meantime removed the idol of Zeus at New Year, and the desecrated altar was also removed, it was not smashed but taken apart as it had been the original altar, and then removed other elements associated with the desecration. In rededicating the Temple, Maimonides explains:

> When the Jews overcame their enemies and destroyed them, they entered the Sanctuary; this was on the twenty-fifth of Kislev. They could not find any pure oil in the Sanctuary, with the exception of a single cruse. It contained enough oil to burn for merely one day. They lit the arrangement of candles from it for eight days until they could crush olives and produce pure oil.
>
> (*Mishneh Torah, Scroll of Esther and Hanukkah* 3:2)

This was reminiscent of the dedication of the tabernacle (Leviticus 8–9) by Moses, and of Solomon's Temple (1 Kings 8:66 and 2 Chronicles 7:1–3), both of which took eight days. The menorah and its light had always been a symbol of the presence of the Almighty. Some may question why there was not more oil available, but it could be suggested that the hunt was for oil that had not been tainted by the occupying force. Josephus in his book *Jewish Antiquities* narrates how at the end the festival of lights was celebrated by the Maccabees:

> Now Judas celebrated the festival of the restoration of the sacrifices of the temple for eight days, and omitted no sort of pleasures thereon; but he feasted them upon very rich and splendid sacrifices; and he honoured God, and delighted them by hymns and psalms. Nay, they were so very glad at the revival of their customs, when, after a long time of intermission, they unexpectedly had regained the freedom of their worship, that they made it a law for their posterity, that they should keep a festival, on account of the restoration of their temple worship, for eight days. And from that time to this we celebrate this festival, and call it Lights. I suppose the reason was because this liberty beyond our hopes appeared to us; and that thence was the name given to that festival. Judas also rebuilt the walls round about the city, and reared towers of great height against the incursions of enemies, and set guards therein. He also fortified the city Bethsura, that it might serve as a citadel against any distresses that might come from our enemies.

> (1999, 409)

This story and its celebration sit behind the celebration of Chanukah as the festival of lights today. Chanukah is a word that means 'to dedicate' and remembers the rededication of the Temple.

Although its celebration is taken for granted by most Jews today, it is the only festival that is not related directly to events narrated, or commands, in the Tanakh. It is, however, celebrated in many different contexts and is a reminder of the presence of the Almighty, and his involvement in the lives of Jews today. One of the most poignant celebrations is told by Rabbi Hugo Gryn:

> As I light the menorah in my comfortable London home, surrounded by our children, the oldest of whom is getting married tomorrow, I go back to Chanukah forty-two years ago, the bitter, cold winter of 1944, to a miserable Nazi concentration camp called Lieberose in Silesia. From our less-than-meagre rations we saved our margarine, from bits of wood carved out bowls for oil lamps, and out of blanket and uniform threads fashioned wicks of a sort. Then on the first night of Chanukah, in our crowded barrack-room (Block 4 it was), the melted fat in its place, we sang the blessings about God's miraculous saving power. And then disaster! Margarine does not burn! It just fizzled out.

> And my anger over precious and seemingly wasted calories, and the less than good-natured teasing of non-Jewish fellow prisoners. Though I was then a middle-aged 14-year-old, I burst into tears. My father, who also saved his rations, and whose idea the

celebration was in the first place, and without whose support I would certainly not be alive to tell this tale, tried to comfort me.

'You and I', he said, 'have seen that it is possible to live as long as three weeks without food. We once lived almost three days without water. But you cannot live properly for three minutes without hope!'

Sadly, my father did not survive … But my life was blessed by his life and you will understand why, to this day, beyond the theology and the history of Chanukah lights, there shines for me an image of love, and always the inextinguishable rays of hope.

(Gryn, 2010, 20–1)

It is that hope that underpins the observance and celebration of Chanukah for Jews today.

Celebration

Chanukah, along with Purim, are festival days where Jews are not commanded to rest. Perhaps the most well-known tradition associated with Chanukah is the use of the Chanukiah (Hanukkiah, sometimes known as the Chanukah menorah), the nine-branched menorah on which a candle is lit each night of Chanukah (see Figure 6.6). The use of eight branches, with the central candle (*shamash*/ servant) to light, relates directly to the miracle

Figure 6.6 A Chanukiah by wonderwoman627, www.storyboardthat.com *Creative Commons.*

of the oil in the Temple and the eight days. Some also suggest that the use of eight is to not replicate the use of the menorah in the Temple.

The festival of Chanukah takes place over eight nights. On the first night, it is traditional that the candle on the right is lit, and then on each subsequent night the lighting continues from right to left. The newest candle is lit first, meaning that the lighting goes from left to right on that night. This tradition developed gradually and perhaps because it is an easily replicable practice within the home. The Chanukiah is often placed in the window to celebrate and spread the news of the miracles of the oil, while others place it near the door opposite the menorah for the reminder of mitzvot as they enter. The candles are traditionally lit at sundown, except on Shabbat, when it is lit before the beginning of Shabbat, usually an hour before. On each night there are traditionally two blessings that are recited:

• Blessed are You, Lord our God, King of the universe, Who has sanctified us with His commandments and commanded us to kindle the Hanukkah light[s].
• Blessed are You, LORD our God, King of the universe, Who performed miracles for our ancestors in those days at this time.

On the first night, the *shehecheyanu*, a blessing used on most special occasions, is recited:

• Praised are You, Lord our God, King of the universe, For granting us life, for sustaining us, and for helping us to reach this day.

Other celebrations each evening may be the retelling of the story, not just of the miracle of the oil, but perhaps of the greater miracle of the liberation of the Jews from oppression. This is a story and message that has resonance for many Jews today and throughout history, as they have lived as minorities and sometimes under oppression. Irving Greenberg suggests its significance to remind Jews of the need for universal rights both for themselves and others:

> In this time, too, many universal cultures – Marxism and Communism, triumphalist Christianity, certain forms of liberalism and radicalism, fascism, even monolithic Americanism – have demanded that Jews dissolve and become part of humankind. All these philosophies have claimed that Jews can depend on their principles and structures to provide for Jewish rights. The Maccabee revolution made clear that a universalism that denies the rights of the particular to exist is inherently totalitarian and will end up oppressing people in the name of one humanity. Universalism must surrender its overweening demands and accept the universalism of pluralism.
>
> (1988, 278)

There are also many other messages that can be drawn by Jews from the story of Chanukah. Some could include the importance of standing for right; although Mattathias, his sons and their followers, faced overwhelming odds they knew that what was happening was wrong, and they had a responsibility to stand up for it. Linked with this idea is the belief that one person, like a single flame, can transform the darkness around it. Further, the command to publicize the miracle means that it is not sufficient for a Jew to celebrate in private, rather they should show their belief to the world, proudly standing as one who worships and celebrates the Almighty.

Included in the narrative retelling of the story in Jewish homes there may be various elements that are highlighted. For example, the story of Judith might serve as a particular inspiration both to remind Jews of the impact an individual can have, and of the important role of women. The story is told in the Apocryphal Book of Judith. In this story, Judith, a rich and beautiful widow's town of Betulia was threatened by the Assyrian General, Holofernes, she was dismayed by the reaction of some of the Jews who did not seem to trust the Almighty. She entreated them: 'Let us humbly wait for his consolation, and the Lord our God will require our blood of the afflictions of our enemies, and he will humble all the nations that shall rise up against us and bring them to disgrace' (Judith 8:20). She undertook to go to the camp of Holofernes, who became besotted with her, so much so that he invited her into his tent:

And the heart of Holofernes was smitten, for he was burning with the desire of her. And Holofernes said to her: Drink now, and sit down and be merry for thou hast found favour before me. And Judith said: I will drink my lord, because my life is magnified this day above all my days. And she took and ate and drank before him what her maid had prepared for her. And Holofernes was made merry on her occasion, and drank exceeding much wine, so much as he had never drunk in his life.

(Judith 12:16–20)

Judith cut Holofernes' head off and escaped to her allies, declaring the death of Holofernes and reminding them of the goodness of the Almighty. Upon discovering their General dead the Assyrians fled, the Book of Judith records:

One Hebrew woman hath made confusion in the house of king Nabuchodonosor: for behold Holofernes lieth upon the ground, and his head is not upon him. Now when the chiefs of the army of the Assyrians had heard this, they all rent their garments, and an intolerable fear and dread fell upon them, and their minds were troubled exceedingly. And there was a very great cry in the midst of their camp. And when all the army heard that Holofernes was beheaded, courage and counsel fled from them, and being seized with trembling and fear they thought only to save themselves by flight: So that no one spoke to his neighbour, but hanging down the head, leaving all things behind, they made haste to escape from the Hebrews, who, as they heard, were coming armed upon them, and fled by the ways of the fields, and the paths of the hills.

(14:17–18 and 15:1–2)

As Judith helped to bring out the freedom of the Jews, so as women light the candles, it may be seen that they are performing acts on behalf of others.

Figure 6.7 A wooden dreidel.

Another tradition of Chanukah is the playing of a game of dreidel. A dreidel (see Figure 6.7) is a spinning top and is known by various names including *goyrl* (destiny), *varfl* (throw), and *sevivon* (to turn or rotate). Tradition suggests that the game was played by Jews hiding in the caves during the Maccabean rebellion and is linked with the study of Torah. Others suggest that it is a development of a game traditionally played in Europe.

The dreidel has four Hebrew letters, one on each side:

- nun נ
- gimel ג
- hei ה
- shin ש (sometimes replaced with pe פ)

These letters are believed to be an acronym of 'nes gadol hayah sham', meaning 'a great miracle happened there'. The letter 'pe' is used in Israel 'poh' instead of 'shin', meaning that 'a great miracle happened here'.

When the game begins, each person has an equal number of objects (pennies, chocolate, matchsticks, etc.) normally between ten and fifteen. Each person places one of their objects into the centre (the pot). Each person takes a turn in spinning the dreidel. Depending on which letter is facing upwards determines what happens:

- nun – the player does not need to do anything
- gimel – the player gets everything in the pot

- hei – the player gets half the pot (if an odd number it is rounded up)
- shin – the player adds another object into the pot.

When a person runs out of pieces they are usually out of the game, though it is possible to ask for a loan from another player. For the most part the game of dreidel is just a fun game to play on Chanukah to remember the events from the Maccabean rebellion and the miracle of the oil. Some Jews have suggested deeper meanings, but these are not universally accepted. Suggestions include the four countries/empires that historically oppressed the Jews: Babylonia, Persia, the Seleucid Empire, and Rome; the four dimensions of the human psyche: ego, body, reason, and evil; or as a reminder of times of threat and persecution.

A more recent development to the celebrations of Chanukah surrounds the giving of gifts. A gift is traditionally given to children on each of the eight nights of Chanukah. Many see this as a recent tradition, though others see small gifts of money as having a long history. Greenberg (1988) suggests that 'American Jews have turned Hanukkah into the great gift holiday … Christmas is so pervasive in America and the children's sense of being shut out was so fierce that Hanukkah was rededicated as the season for giving' (278). This type of approach was shown in the television series *The Goldbergs* season 3, episode 10 where the mum created 'Super Hanukkah':

> 'My mom was always trying to figure out ways to make Hanukkah exciting and compete with our neighbours the Kremps, who always had these amazing blow-out Christmas parties', says the show's creator, Adam F. Goldberg. 'We weren't particularly religious, but you grow up feeling envious and wishing you could just have that experience, so that's really what this episode is about'.
>
> Rather than eight nights of gifts – which, Goldberg adds, usually only yielded one real gift and seven nights of filler in his family – Beverly's idea of Super Hanukkah means having 'all the presents opened on one morning under a Hanukkah bush, which is essentially Christmas, and that drives Pops insane because The Goldbergs don't celebrate Christmas. They celebrate Hanukkah'.
>
> (Sneitker, 2015)

This raises an interesting point about the acculturation of Judaism within a modern context. Indeed, Dianne Ashton (2013) highlighted that 'the women's organization of the Conservative movement recently argued that "any child who has built a sukkah [booth constructed for prayers and meals during the autumn holiday of Sukkot] will not feel deprived of trimming a [Christmas] tree." In their view, those children would not need Hanukkah to be any more elaborate than rabbinic standards made it' (7). Perhaps a different approach is taken within the television series *Friends* in the episode 'The One with the Holiday Armadillo', where Ross is trying to teach his son about Chanukah, but he has only ever known Christmas. The message of the programme seems to be that Christmas and Chanukah are not in competition. Sophia Zohar (2021) suggests its positive impact in observing the clash of cultures:

> 'The One with the Holiday Armadillo' tells the classic Jewish tale of the inner conflict we never need to have. Can Judaism and Jewish traditions exist in a world where the secular culture is so heavily Christian? The episode is brilliantly crafted, as this conflict plays beautifully into the strained dynamic between Ross and his son from his first failed marriage. But just as the episode ends by showing us that Ross and Ben really do love each other, the episode carries another message: Jewish identity has its own pull, and Judaism is, as Ben says in the end, 'awesome!' It can exist powerfully beside other traditions simply through proud, unapologetic practice. No smoke, no mirrors, no armadillos needed. (in the words of Monica Gellar, 'now that's a sentence I never thought I would say')

For Jews living in the UK, this perhaps has resonance as they strive to navigate the cultural norms alongside observance of Jewish customs. Indeed, in 2023 the Institute for Jewish Policy Research found that nearly 25 per cent of British Jews have a Christmas tree in their homes as well as a Chanukiah, though very few of those describe themselves as Orthodox or Traditional, and some will be accounted for with mixed-faith families. The suggestion is not, however, that Jews are abandon their faith for a new one, rather it:

> says something about their desire or willingness to absorb wider cultural norms into their lives and the extent to which they see their Jewishness as a completely exclusive part of who they are. Maintaining a Jewish identity in a non-Jewish society has long been a challenge; the ways in which we adopt non-Jewish customs and practices says a great deal about who we are and how we manage those dynamics.
>
> (Lessoff, 2023, 6)

This provides an interesting discussion of religion, culture, assimilation and observance. While possibly a focus for further exploration, none of this discussion should detract from the joy and celebratory sense that Chanukah brings for Jews who observe the festival.

Purim

One Jewish man once expressed the thought surrounding festivals that 'They tried to kill us, they failed. We had a party'. While flippant, and perhaps jarring to our sensibilities, as we have looked at the celebrations of Pesach and Chanukah, and now in looking at Purim this is essentially the approach that seems to have been taken. Purim is a celebration of the story of Esther and the Almighty's intervention in the saving and protection of the Jews. These celebrations and stories help provide Jews with a sense of identity, and a concrete expression of the love of the Almighty and his influence in the history and ongoing lives of Jews.

The Story of Purim

The story of Purim is recorded in the book of Esther within the Tanakh. It begins with King Ahasuerus, who banishes or executes (depending on the authority cited) his wife, Queen Vashti, for refusing to appear at the command of the King to 'display her beauty to the peoples and the officials' (Esther 1:11). Tradition suggests that she was justified in this as the command may have been to appear naked. For this apparent slight, and at the urging of his advisor Ashasuerus she was put away. The story continues with the King searching for a new wife, and Esther (Hadassah) at the urging of her 'foster father' and father's niece, Mordecai, presented herself to the king and became part of his harem. Over the course of time 'Esther won the admiration of all who saw her … The king loved Esther more than all the other women, and she won his grace and favour more than all the virgins. So he set a royal diadem on her head and made her queen instead of Vashti' (Esther 2:15, 17). In all of this, Esther did not reveal her background and identity as a Jew to the king.

All of this serves as a prelude and contextualization of the actions of the king's adviser, Haman. Having been appointed Haman expected the people to bow to him, but he noticed that Mordecai would not, and when questioned Mordecai explained that he could not because he was a Jew. Haman was furious but was loathe to act against Mordecai because it might inflame his people. Chillingly, 'Haman plotted to do away with all the Jews, Mordecai's people, throughout the kingdom of Ahasuerus' (Esther 3:6). Haman schemed and presented a plan to the King:

Haman then said to King Ahasuerus:

There is a certain people, scattered and dispersed among the other peoples in all the provinces of your realm, whose laws are different from those of any other people and who do not obey the king's laws; and it is not in Your Majesty's interest to tolerate them. If it please Your Majesty, let an edict be drawn for their destruction, and I will pay ten thousand talents of silver to the stewards for deposit in the royal treasury.

(Esther 3:8–9)

Ahasuerus gave Haman his authority to act and a decree was issued to 'destroy, massacre, and exterminate all the Jews, young and old, children and women, on a single day, on the thirteenth day of the twelfth month – that is, the month of Adar – and to plunder their possessions' (Esther 3:13). Preparations were made for the extermination order to be carried out. Meanwhile there was much mourning and fasting among the Jews; Mordecai came before the palace gates in sackcloth to mourn the decision. Esther sent servants to placate him and to find out what was wrong. Mordecai told her of the edict and told her that she should speak to the king and plead on behalf of her people. Esther was reticent to do such a thing, the example of Queen Vashti was probably in her mind, and she told him:

If any person, man or woman, enters the king's presence in the inner court without having been summoned, there is but one law for him – that he be put to death. Only if the king extends the golden sceptre to him may he live. Now I have not been summoned to visit the king for the last thirty days.

(Esther 4:11)

Mordecai responds, depending on how one reads with, with compassion or with a rebuke. Most Jews would suggest compassion, reminding her that she, too, would suffer the same fate as her people. Further, if she did not act, then his faith in the Almighty meant that 'if you keep silent in this crisis, relief and deliverance will come to the Jews from another quarter, while you and your father's house will perish' (Esther 4:14). He then suggested, in perhaps the most oft quoted passage from Esther: 'And who knows, perhaps you have attained to royal position for just such a crisis' (Esther 4:14).

Seemingly galvanized, Esther replied that if she were to do this Mordecai should gather the Jews together and fast on her behalf for three days and nights. After this period fasting she would go into the court of her husband 'though it is contrary to the law; and if I am to perish, I shall perish!' (Esther 4:16). Mordecai and the Jews of the city did as Esther asked, and she went into the king and found favour with him as he extended the golden sceptre towards her. He greeted her with:

'What troubles you, Queen Esther?' the king asked her. 'And what is your request? Even to half the kingdom, it shall be granted you'.

(Esther 5:3)

Before answering with her complete request, she asked the king to invite Haman to court for a feast that she had prepared. When Haman and the king had arrived at the feast, the king repeated his question, promising again up to half of his kingdom. She suggested that the king and Haman return tomorrow. Haman was strengthened and thrilled by the attention and celebrated his good fortune with his family and friends, declaring that he had 'great wealth' and 'the king had promoted him ... above the officials and courtiers' and celebrated that he would be with the king and queen on the next day (Esther 5:11–12). There was only one thing that annoyed Haman, and that was Mordecai who still refused to bow to him.

Then his wife Zeresh and all his friends said to him, 'Let a stake be put up, fifty cubits high, and in the morning ask the king to have Mordecai impaled on it. Then you can go gaily with the king to the feast'. The proposal pleased Haman, and he had the stake put up.

(Esther 5:14)

Overnight, the king discovered in his records that Mordecai had denounced two of the opponents of his, and he wondered what honours had been given to Mordecai, to which his servants reported, 'None.' At that point Haman entered, and the king asked for his advice as to what he could do to honour the person who had found his favour. Thinking it to be himself, Haman responded that the person should be dressed in royal clothes, to ride on the king's horse, a crown be placed upon his head, and the horse to be led by one of the king's attendants. The king ordered Haman to do as he had suggested for 'Mordecai the Jew' (Esther 6:10). Despondent Haman returned home and was soon to return to Esther's feast.

The king repeated his question a third time, at which point she made her request:

> 'If Your Majesty will do me the favour, and if it pleases Your Majesty, let my life be granted me as my wish, and my people as my request. For we have been sold, my people and I, to be destroyed, massacred, and exterminated. Had we only been sold as bondmen and bondwomen, I would have kept silent; for the adversary is not worthy of the king's trouble'. Thereupon King Ahasuerus demanded of Queen Esther, 'Who is he and where is he who dared to do this?' 'The adversary and enemy', replied Esther, 'is this evil Haman!' And Haman cringed in terror before the king and the queen.
>
> (Esther 7:3–6)

The king left in a rage while Haman begged for his life from the queen. When the king returned, he saw Haman lay prostrate on the couch on which Esther too lay; and thought that Haman meant to 'ravish' Esther (Esther 7:8). Haman blanched, realizing his precarious standing. One of the servants told the king of the stake that Haman had prepared for Mordecai, at which point the king ordered for Haman to be impaled upon it.

Mordecai and Esther were honoured by the king with riches and position, and Esther made one more request:

> 'If it please Your Majesty', she said, 'and if I have won your favour and the proposal seems right to Your Majesty, and if I am pleasing to you – let dispatches be written countermanding those which were written by Haman son of Hammedatha the Agagite, embodying his plot to annihilate the Jews throughout the king's provinces'.
>
> (Esther 8:5)

Thus, it was done, and the Jews were saved through the providence of the Almighty. The news was greeted with joy, and celebrations commenced, which it was enjoined upon Jews to do each year in remembrance of these events.

> Mordecai recorded these events. And he sent dispatches to all the Jews throughout the provinces of King Ahasuerus, near and far, charging them to observe the fourteenth and fifteenth days of Adar, every year – the same days on which the Jews enjoyed relief from their foes and the same month which had been transformed for them from one of grief and mourning to one of festive joy. They were to observe them as days of feasting and merrymaking, and as an occasion for sending gifts to one another and presents to the poor.
>
> (Esther 9: 20–22)

It is known as Purim, meaning 'lots' as Haman had cast lots to decide the day of the extermination of the Jews.

Celebration

As suggested the festival of Purim is a joyous festival, one of 'merrymaking', where celebration takes place, gifts are given and acts of charity (tzedakah) are performed. An important aspect of the events of Purim is that they took place in the Diaspora, it did not take away the vulnerability of being 'a stranger in a strange land' (see Exodus 2:22), it did show the importance of the Almighty in the daily life of a Jew. Indeed, the suggestion is that the lessons of Purim are to savour 'the sweetness of life ... today, for that is all one really has for sure'. Secondly, that while the dream of redemption and restoration was not fully realized, Jews should 'celebrate the victory while poking fun at it, to enjoy it fully while appreciating to today' (Greenberg, 1988, 236). In the vernacular, Jews should take the win and live in the moment, the future is unsure but the providence of the Almighty is with them wherever they may be, whether in Israel or in the Diaspora.

Much time has been taken to tell the story of Purim above because the telling of the story lies at the heart of the celebration of the festival by Jews. As the story is retold in the synagogue the whole gamut of human emotions is encountered. In tandem with celebrations lie Pesach, a re-enactment is important to remember the despair, the terror, and the resulting relief and joy. As the story is told, it is a sombre, raucous and joyous affair. It is a mitzvah to listen to the story, and as the Megillah (scroll or book of Esther) is read various actions take place. Whenever Haman's name is read (a total of fifty-four times) noise is made by the stamping of the feet (sometimes with his name on the soles of shoes) or the rattling of a ra-ashan (ratchet). In this way the name of Haman is 'blotted out' fulfilling the command in the Torah to 'blot out the memory of Amalek from under heaven', of whom Haman was a descendent (Deuteronomy 25:19). A small number of Jews avoid the use of a ratchet, but it is now almost universal around the world. Often, the name of Mordecai is greeted with cheers, especially when he is appointed the king's chief counsellor.

Other elements of celebrations of Purim around the world include the dressing up in fancy dress costumes including masks. This is perhaps symbolic of the disguising of Esther, meaning her living secretly as a Jew in the King's court. Or maybe it refers to the dressing of Mordecai in sackcloth, and then later in the King's robes. Another suggestion is that because charitable acts are a central part of the celebration people dress up so the recipients of good works won't be embarrassed because they do not know from whom they are receiving gifts. Perhaps the most important suggestion of the meaning of costume is regard to the Almighty and in contrast to the festivals of Chanukah and Pesach, 'the miracle of the holiday of Purim was disguised in natural events ... Only after the fact, when one looks at the entire story, does one realize the great miracle that transpired' (Zaklikowski, 2025). Indeed, the name of the Almighty is not mentioned in the Book of Esther, but he is undoubtedly there guiding events towards their resolution, and there is no doubt in Mordecai's mind that a solution would be provided. The fasting and study of Torah by the Jews to prepare for Esther's audience with the king is similarly remembered in the study of the Torah as part of the celebrations.

Other traditions include the burning of effigies of Haman, a Purim play that is a comedic dramatization of the story, and the eating of *hamantaschen* (Haman's pockets) by many Jews, especially those of an Ashkenazi heritage. Other pastries such as fazuelos or baklavas are eaten in different communities. Foods differ around the world, but one of particular note is the eating of kreplach – a dumpling with meat 'hiding' in the middle; another allusion to the hidden nature of the Almighty in the story. It is a day of joy, as one Jew has observed:

> One has to love the Purim holiday. At what other time can one eat, drink (even get drunk!), send and receive gifts, make jokes and kid around, even have the rabbi encourage everyone to make noise in the synagogue (at the proper time, of course), and get mitzvah points for doing this!
>
> (Greenberg, 1988, 243)

In tandem with the joyous celebrations there is also a serious side to the celebration of Purim:

> Jews are pledged to work for the end of oppression of the weak everywhere; a temporary, partial victory should not blind one to the persistence of evil in the world.
>
> (Greenberg, 1988, 245)

This may take on an extra importance for Jews today who live in the Diaspora, or even in Israel, as they may experience antisemitism (see Chapter 5).

Thoughts for the classroom

There are many opportunities to utilize and explore Jewish festivals within classrooms at any Key Stage. What is, perhaps, most important is the way that each festival marks important aspects of Jewish history and belief, and in the way that the celebrations and observances help people understand the concepts that are central to Judaism. In each of the festivals it is impossible to overlook the importance of the Almighty in the history of the Jews and in the lives of Jews. The light that is central to Chanukah, and to the retelling of the story of the Exodus, is a constant reminder to Jews of the immanent nature of the Almighty. He has chosen them; he has delivered them and will continue to be intimately involved in their individual lives and the life of the community. In exploring bridges to learning that can be utilized in the planning and teaching of religion in schools, the third bridge is to link between beliefs and practices (Holt, 2022). It is impossible to understand the experience of Jews today, and their celebration of festivals without linking them with the underpinning beliefs.

Within the teaching of religion in schools one of the pedagogies suggested is the 'experiential approach' (see Holt, 2022 and Grimmitt, 2000), one aspect of which might be 'to have pupils "experience" some of the practices of religious believers' (Holt, 2022, 67). There are many positive aspects to this approach in the sense that eating some of the foods of Pesach and reflecting on that experience might help pupils begin to understand the multi-sensory and 'spiritual' elements of celebration. This is often described as religion-neutral, in the sense that teachers are having pupils experience aspects of religion in a non-confessional and safe space. It is also remembered by pupils, which enables them to appreciate aspects of faith. However, such activities need a lot of consideration before being undertaken. The concerns that people may express are twofold. Firstly, the mundanification of what are 'spiritual' or 'sacred' practices. How does the teacher safeguard against making the sacred mundane, as it does not have the same intents and purposes as within Judaism. As such a teacher needs to be very conscious of the reasons why they are doing something, and the aim of the activity. Do the benefits outweigh the potential concerns? Does this activity desanctify some of the religious actions of Judaism and make them mundane?

The second concern is that students are being asked to 'perform' a Jewish ritual act. The purpose of such an activity is to have pupils feel what it is like. As indicated by the previous concern, without the same purpose and belief supporting it, it is impossible to get the same feeling. Within the classroom there seems to be an inconsistent approach to the re-enactment of, or participation in, ritual acts. For example, the playing of the dreidel game may be considered fine, where the repeating of ritual actions of prayer would not. Where is the line drawn, and how do teachers know what is appropriate or not?

In the recreation of a Passover meal, the retelling of the story of Purim with the pupils using groggers every time Haman's name is mentioned, the playing of dreidel the teacher should always consider why they are having pupils recreate the activity and the safeguards they need to put in place not to mundanify it. Indeed, various celebrations could be seen by some to be superficial cultural appropriations, that exoticise Judaism, and focus on its colour and excitement, detached from the beliefs that such celebrations celebrate. The richness and diversity of Judaism, especially in Britain, lies at the heart of teaching Judaism in the classroom. It might also be that some activities might be suitable but others not so. Care should be taken not to design activities unthinkingly.

In a related consideration suggested in the Introduction, does the recreation of events maybe suggest a possible Christianization of such? To what extent does the utilization and recreation of Jewish activities indicate a cultural appropriation? This concern high-lights the need to, if experiential activities are undertaken, situate them very firmly within Judaism and the purpose that they have for Jews. Consider the recreation of Passover meals within some traditions of Christianity. The Council of Christian and Jews (2023) outline the undesirability of this:

> 'Christian Seders' run the risk of both appropriating modern Jewish customs and ritu-als, and of promoting the notion that Christianity replaces Judaism. (referred to as Supersessionism and Replacement Theology)
>
> In 'Christian Seders', those attending may well imagine that the matzah and wine symbol-ise Christ. But using them in this way is to replace a living Jewish ritual with a Christian

theology. Christians would undoubtedly be uncomfortable with non-Christian groups adapting Holy Communion to portray an alternative understanding of Christ.

Replacement theology in 'Christian Seders' can reinforce Christian anti-Judaism, which has a long, shameful, and dangerous history. Rather than Christianity replacing Judaism, both religions should be respected as separate living faiths.

(4)

Extreme care should be taken that teachers do not frame the activities in any way but the way that they are understood by Jews. In a similar way, pupils should not do such. The Jewish purpose of the seder remains the focus of the discussion and why it is important for Jews today.

Each of the festivals relates to a specific belief or story that can be taught to students of any age. Within the Early Years Foundation Stage, and Key Stages 1 and 2 a lot of focus in schools tends to be around festivals. What is key, however, is that pupils are not just asked to recount events or list how they are celebrated. Rather, what they provide for and teach Jews should be central to each of these discussions. Each of the festivals above shows the nature of the Almighty, and the closeness of the relationship between the Almighty and his people. As the students get older some of the more challenging questions about why the Almighty would allow certain circumstances to develop could be explored, and this would enable further questions about the Almighty and his nature to be explored.

One of the key aspects of exploring festivals in the classroom is the opportunity that teaching about them provides in breaking down barriers and helping students see similarities and differences with their own experiences. This is why their importance by Jews, as well as how they are celebrated become key. Drawing on the discussion above about how to explore anti-semitism in the classroom (see Chapter 5), we can see the importance of authentic Jewish voices in our classrooms in whatever form they take. Celebration is a universal concept that people of all ages will recognize; and in exploring what a Jewish celebration looks like then children are able to see that there are universal experiences that mean that people are more similar than different. To help hear Jewish voices then books similar to those listed above might be used. In addition there are books such as:

- *Chanukah Lights Everywhere* by Michael Rosen and Melissa Iwai (2006).
- *Hanukkah – Celebrations & Festivals* by Leslea Newman and Rotem Teplow (2024).
- *New Year at the Pier: A Rosh Hashanah Story* by April Wayland and Stéphane Jorisch (2009).

There are also television programmes that sometimes address the issues. Perhaps becoming dated is an episode of *The Rugrats* that celebrated Chanukah; others have been suggested as appropriate in the discussion of the individual festivals above. Similarly, there is a whole genre of Jewish music videos that outline the celebration of various festivals. They are joyous and able to teach at the same time. Musical groups that share such videos include Six13 and the Maccabeats. They tend to release new 'parodies' each year; the Maccabeats catalogue includes:

- Defying Gravity (We'll Rise Above). 2024 Hanukkah Anthem
- An Encanto Purim
- It's Shabbat! (Baby Shark Parody)
- Les Misérables Passover

    Six13s include:

- A Wicked Chanukah
- A Billy Joel Passover
- A Star Wards Chanukah
- Eralution of Taylor Swift (Chanukah Version)
- Bohemian Chanuka (a Queen adaptation)
- A Lion King Passover

All of these tell the story, show how it is celebrated and begin to discuss their importance in a way that is authentically Jewish and engaging for the students.

Similarly, there are activities that students could consider as they engage with the story and draw similarities with their own experiences. One activity that could be used to explore one of the stories behind some of the festivals is a fortune line. In a fortune line (see Figure 6.8) twelve events from the story are plotted, and students would be asked to explain how one of the figures would have felt at those points. After plotting a line graph, a second figure could be chosen to compare their feelings at different points, and students could explore reasons for such. After doing so, because the words on the y axis are blunt instruments, the students could suggest different words that would explain the figures'

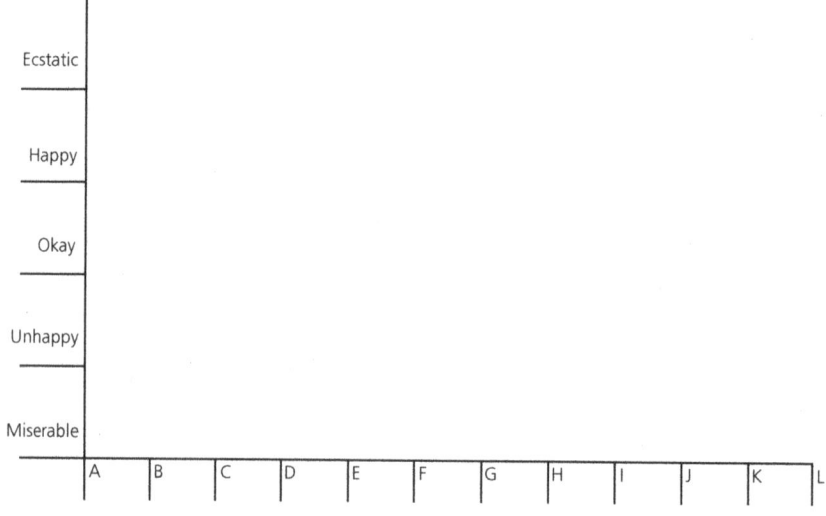

Figure 6.8 A Fortune Line.

feelings in a better way. Dependent on age and understanding, the students could be given the events by the teacher or select the events for themselves.

A further activity could be to look at some of the ways that a festival is celebrated and begin to think of some of the ways that these link to pupils' own experiences. One example is to use a template similar to Figure 6.2 (see above) and have children consider foods that they could use to symbolize an important event in their lives, that help them remember the good and the bad. Some may see this type of task as trivializing certain aspects of Jewish experience, but the key thing is that illusory barriers of 'them' and 'us' as children realize that remembrance is an important part of any community.

This may lead to discussions at different Key Stages of the importance of remembrance in terms of individual and community identity. This might link to aspects of sociology of religion and the function and purpose of religion, as well as the links between religion and society. Events such as festivals are, for the most part, communal activities that ensure the passing on of the faith and the establishment of an identity. Within Judaism, where an increasing number of Jews are identifying as secular, these celebrations still form part of a person's heritage and identity. The thoughts of three British Jews illustrate this point:

> Festivals are more important from the point of view of getting together with family.
> Some of us go to the synagogue and we all get together and sometimes also with friends to spend time together.
> I sometimes visit friends and celebrate but not often.

In keeping the practices of Judaism alive, even if just in festivals, it ensures that it continues to exist and be passed on. Consider the purpose of religion as explored by Durkheim:

> The general conclusion of the book which the reader has before him is that religion is something eminently social. Religious representations are collective representations which express collective realities; the rites are a manner of acting which take rise in the midst of the assembled groups and which are destined to excite, maintain or recreate certain mental states in these groups. So if the categories are of religious origin, they ought to participate in this nature common to all religious facts; they too should be social affairs and the product of collective thought.
>
> (2001, 10)

This collective thought and society are expressed through all religious practice, but in particular in its celebration of festivals.

Laws of Kashrut

As has been explored within Chapters 3 and 4, the mitzvot are a central part of Jewish life. As such the living of them is an expression of Jewish spirituality. There are strict laws about food and diet in Judaism that are outlined in the Torah. The food which a Jew is allowed to eat is called kosher. The proper way of preparing such food is also called kosher. The food which is forbidden to all Jews to eat is non-kosher or treifah.

Kashrut is the name given to the different laws which decide whether meat is kosher or not. It is the responsibility of a Jewish mother to make sure that the food laws are kept within her own home. These laws can be found in the book of Leviticus (Chapter 11) in the Torah, and Jews believe that keeping these laws called the kashrut helps to keep their identity. One Jew in the UK has expressed this thought:

> I think it is really about separation, identity and mindfulness. It sets us apart from others and makes us more aware about what we eat and its effect on us.

Kosher foods include:

- All domestic birds and their eggs.
- Animals with split hooves which chew the cud, and their milk.
- All fish with scales and fins.
- All plants, including fruit and vegetables.
- Eggs and milk can be eaten if they are taken from animals which are kosher.

Shellfish and pork are not allowed at all, but even some of those foods allowed must be eaten separately. Meat and milk cannot be cooked together, eaten together or used together. This is based on a passage from the Torah:

> You shall not boil a kid in its mother's milk.

> (Exodus 23:19)

Most Jewish kitchens have two sinks and two sets of saucepans to be used separately for milk products and meat products so that they can never come into contact even accidentally (see Figure 6.9). The usual practice is to wait six hours between the eating of meat and dairy, though some Jews wait between one and three hours, for some there is a difference depending on which was eaten first (the waiting time between eating dairy and then meat is often much shorted, and there is a Talmudic suggestion that no time period is needed in this case).

Meat has to be treated in a very specific way. The ritual killing of meat for food is called *shechita*. This means animals must be killed by a certified butcher who follows strict guidelines. Every animal must be killed by passing a very sharp knife across its throat to cut the jugular vein. It is claimed that this is the most painless method of killing an animal.

The Torah orders all animals killed for food to be free from blood. To begin with the animal is hung up until all the blood has drained out. Then the meat is soaked in salty water before it is cooked. The use of shechita has its critics, Louis Jacobs (1999) has responded to these criticisms:

> But while obedience to the will of God is perhaps the most powerful motive in keeping these laws, a number of Jewish thinkers and teachers have pointed out that shechita, contrary to what its enemies affirm, is the most humane method of killing animals for

food. It should not need repeating that the most distinguished medical authorities have affirmed that this method results in instantaneous loss of consciousness on the part of the animal, so that the method is as painless as any method can be ... All killing of animals for food involves some pain to the animal, so the next logical step would be for the law to enforce vegetarianism.

(Jacobs, 1999, 81)

Recognizing the diversity of approach, even within Jewish communities, one UK Jew has suggested that her own morality has led her to vegetarianism:

I do not think Orthodox forms of kashrut are important to everyone. Personally, I consider not eating meat as part of my Judaism, but I appreciate this is not a common belief.

One further category of food is *pareve* or parve (neutral) is a food that does not contain meat or dairy, and as such can be eaten with both. This includes grains, pulses, vegetables, fruits, eggs from kosher birds, and kosher fish. The 'kosherness' of food and products is usually certified by a rabbi, and for much produced food today, there is a kosher certification agency that grants an *heschner* (seal of approval). The process of certification usually includes a visit to the factory/premises to inspect ingredients, processes and equipment. Period checks are then made, allowing the company to issue products with a certification symbol. There are also guides and websites available for people to check the kosher status of a product.

In response to a question about the difficulty of keeping kosher, one Jew responded:

It is very straightforward, it is what I have always done since being a child, it is just a natural part of life.

Figure 6.9 A kitchen in a synagogue showing the separation of meat and dairy.

There are differing levels of observance of the laws of kashrut. One British Jew recognized that:

> Every Jew has a different level of commitment, implementation of the rules of kashrut so obviously for the religious Jews they will feel they're very important.

Graham & Boyd (2024) suggest that 49 per cent of British Jews see the laws of kosher as having importance; the statistics behind the observance of kashrut include:

> Excluding vegetarians, two in five (40%) Jewish families only buy kosher meat for the home, and 39% separate meat and milk at home.
>
> These practices are more or less universal among haredi and Orthodox Jewish families, and very common among Traditional ones at a level of around 75%. They are far less common among Reform/Progressive families (about 15%), and almost non-existent among non-practising secular/cultural ones (3%).

(9)

Thoughts for the classroom

Within schools one of the topics that most interest children is the food laws of Judaism, and they are important to explore because they highlight the living of Judaism as a way of life. Judaism isn't just something that happens in the synagogue but something that happens in every moment of every day. This highlights that the Almighty is worshipped in every act of living. Children should not be left with the impression, however, that all Jews keep the laws of kashrut; as can be seen there are different levels of observance. Categorizing activities or the designing of menus will help students solidify their understanding of the laws, but teachers should be careful not to attempt to 'justify' the laws, for Jews who follow the requirements they do so because they are commanded by the Almighty, not because of any perceived health benefits, even if there may be some.

Life-cycle rituals

Within Judaism, as with many religions, there are rituals and ceremonies that mark certain points in a person's life. These are generally seen to surround birth, coming of age, marriage and death. These are important in perpetuating Judaism, as symbols of Jewish identity, and adhering to traditions established in the Torah and throughout history. Other rituals may accompany other life events such as the bathing in the mikvah (see Chapter 7). This chapter will now briefly explore two of these and the ways in which they may be observed and celebrated.

Birth rituals

An important aspect of the welcoming of a child is the 'naming'. This is usually done at a *brit milah* for a boy or a *brit bat* (also known as *simchat bat*, which means 'the Joy of the Daughter', or *zeved bat*, which means 'the Gift of a Daughter') for a girl. The name, depending on tradition, may be chosen from the people in the Tanakh, but more likely a deceased relative (an Ashkenazi custom) or a living relative (a Sephardic custom). The name is usually announced, and the meaning behind its choice is given, with associated prayers such as that 'baby Ruth will embody the kindness and generosity' of Ruth in the Tanakh (Diamant & Cooper, 2023, 161). It may also be part of the custom to bring the baby in front of the congregation on Shabbat where they are welcomed by all.

Brit milah

Brit is one of the Hebrew words associated with the covenant (see Chapter 3). Brit milah, the circumcision of boys, traces its history within Judaism back to the time of Abraham, and its requirement as a symbol of the covenant with the Almighty:

> You shall circumcise the flesh of your foreskin, and that shall be the sign of the covenant between Me and you. And throughout the generations, every male among you shall be circumcised at the age of eight days.
>
> (Genesis 17:11–12)

It is for this reason that a Jewish family will usually have their son circumcised at the age of eight days. It is tradition that a father is responsible for the brit milah, but usually a mohel (a ritual circumciser) will act in his stead assisted by a sandek (patron) usually a grandfather will hold the baby's legs. The ceremony can be performed anywhere; some choose a hospital for it to be performed in, while most take place in the home surrounded by friends and family.

The mohel may lead the service, but it could as easily be a rabbi or even a member of the family. Usually, the father recites the blessing for the milah, though the mohel could do so:

> Blessed are You, Adonai our God, Ruler of the universe, who has sanctified us through Your mitzvot and ordained circumcision.

Which elicits the response:

> Amen! Just as he has entered into the covenant, so may he enter into the study of Torah, the marriage canopy, and the performance of good deeds.

At this point, the boy is circumcised. Kiddush is offered over a glass of wine, with a prayer and the announcement of the boy's name. Following the explanations of the name by the parents, a celebratory meal takes place.

There are some Jews who do not circumcise their sons, seeing it as an anti-quated and violent procedure. Indeed, there are countries such as Iceland which have proposed bans on non-medical circumcisions which raises issues of freedom of religion and belief. As with all the commandments, many Jews see there as being no explanation behind the ritual, but see it as a commandment of the Almighty.

Brit bat

The welcome service for a baby girl is not a new innovation, indeed there is a long tradition in Sephardi Jewish communities. However, the brit bat as a common service has its roots in the 1970s and the desire for a service to welcome the baby girl. Although some families choose to carry out this ceremony when the baby is eight days old, in a similar way to boys, some families choose to wait until the mother is sufficiently recovered to enjoy the service. The service can take place in the syna-gogue or within the home. A home service will usually include:

- The *Birkat haGomel* may be recited. This prayer of thanksgiving by the mother is usually offered on the first Shabbat after the birth, but if it hasn't been offered then it, along with other blessings will be offered.

    Blessed are You, Adonai our God, Sovereign of the universe, who has bestowed every goodness upon us.

Followed by the response:

    Amen. May the One who has bestowed goodness upon us continue to bestow every goodness upon us forever.

- Prayers and readings are offered.
- The baby girl may be wrapped in a tallit; her name is announced and a prayer for her life will be offered. In some services candles may be lit, the baby's hands or feet might be washed, or she may be immersed in a small mikveh (see Chapter 7).
- The meaning of the name is explained.
- Gifts are given and further prayers may be recited.
- A celebratory meal takes place.

This service highlights the equality of boys and girls, and enables the community of Jews to celebrate the birth of a baby girl.

Coming of age

The Talmud teaches:

    At five years of age the study of Scripture; At ten the study of Mishnah; At thirteen subject to the commandments; At fifteen the study of Talmud; At eighteen the bridal canopy; At twenty for pursuit [of livelihood]; At thirty the peak of strength; At forty wisdom; At fifty able to give counsel; At sixty old age; At seventy fullness of years; At eighty the age of 'strength'; At ninety a bent body; At one hundred, as good as dead and gone completely out of the world.

(Pirkei Avot 5:21)

At the age of thirteen (twelve for a girl), a boy becomes responsible for his own actions: 'subject to the commandments'. While not a rite required in the Tanach, a service began to be held for boys who had completed their first fast at Yom Kippur, at the age of thirteen. During the Second Temple Period, it was not unusual for boys to be counted as part of the minyan. This age began to take on added importance and the bar mitzvah developed as a celebration of the boy's first *aliyah* (call to read from the Torah). There were associated celebrations for a girl's twelfth birthday, but these were not religious rites; rather they will have been family celebrations where blessings may have been recited. In the twentieth century more formalized rites of a bat mitzvah were developed especially in Reform communities, and in some Orthodox traditions.

Initially the bat mitzvahs differed from bar mitzvahs, as they were held on Friday evenings where girls would read from the haftara (a selection of readings from the Nevi'im) rather than the Torah. In many Reform synagogues today the two ceremonies are nearly identical, and the terms bar and bat mitzvah may be replaced by the less gender-specific b-mitzvah. In many Orthodox traditions the prohibition of women reading from the Torah persists, and so they may read from the book of Esther or the Psalms, or they will give a d'rash (see below). These may also take place in the home rather the synagogue, but these practices vary, though most Orthodox Jews will celebrate it in some way.

There are various phases to the preparation for, and celebration of, a bar or bat mitzvah:

- There is a period of preparation where the young people will learn to read the Torah and haftara sections of the service in Hebrew. They will also prepare a d'rash, or lesson based on the readings that they are preparing. For some, this will also include learning how to wear tefillin.
- Before the service a parent may place a tallit on the shoulders of their child.
- *Aliyah*: In this part of the ceremony the young person is called up to the bimah to read or chant from the Torah. They may also read the haftara portion. This is the part of the ceremony that indicates the young person has come of age. Family members may be involved in reciting blessings from the Torah before each portion of the reading, or they may be involved in the opening of the ark, or the returning of the Torah scrolls.
- *D'rash*: The young person will offer a teaching, or a lesson based on the Torah readings. They will explain what they have read and usually apply it to life today.
- The rabbi and/or parents may offer their own thoughts and recite blessings.
- There will be a celebratory meal or party where the young person will receive gifts.

Thoughts for the classroom

Within this chapter, time has necessarily been taken to explore various expressions of Jewish devotion. The expressions chosen have been illustrative and are in no way to be seen as a comprehensive outline of the ways that Jewish beliefs are expressed and lived. One such example that has not been explored is prayer, including the various ways that prayer is offered in an individual's life. This has been alluded to at various points within the book, for example, when speaking of the celebration of Shabbat, but space has not allowed a detailed exploration of this, and other aspects of Jewish practice.

Exploring aspects of Jewish festivals will hopefully enable the reader to utilize the underlying beliefs to begin a much more in-depth study of Jewish practices, both those explored here and those not. There are many opportunities for using expressions of Jewish belief in the classroom, which provide concrete examples of how beliefs are put into practice. Using the concept of brit and chesed helps a person understand both the nature of the covenant, and its expression in festivals, the rites of passage and various laws of Judaism.

When looking at religious beliefs, it is important to build bridges to help students understand what is being taught. Two of these bridges are with their own experiences and with local and national communities (Holt, 2022). The exploration of two of the life-cycle rituals will leave further scope for exploration of marriage and death rituals. The ones chosen will enable both bridges to be utilised. The completion of a 'Journey of Life' by students to highlight important aspects in their own lives that have happened, and that they hope will happen, will provide a springboard for the exploration of important points in a Jew's life. This type of activity breaks down illusory barriers of 'them' and 'us' as students recognize the similarities in the life experiences of all people. One tendency that might need to be thought through as a teacher is the representation of Jewish practices and communities. Sometimes it is tempting to use examples from Israel or the United States, for example, *You Are So Not Invited to My Bat Mitzvah*. These will be engaging, but if this is all students see then they build a skewed view of Judaism. It is much more beneficial for students to see expressions from the local area, either with local voices from the local community or prepared videos by organisations, such as TrueTube and the BBC's 'Being … ' series of programmes, that highlight the lived reality of Jews in the UK.

Part 2

Contemporary Issues

Chapter 7

The Ethical Dimension

As we get further through the book, the threads of Judaism become increasingly intertwined. In exploring the 'ethical dimension' of Judaism, mention should be made of Ninian Smart's (1998) suggestion that the ethical dimension refers to the law that a religion has as an expression of the doctrines and narratives. Many of these have already been explored in various of the preceding chapters. As we move forward in this chapter, elements of mitzvot, as found in the Torah, and how they relate to contemporary issues will be explored. What cannot be overstated is the focus on Judaism as a lived religion, and this goes beyond what is usually meant by such; it is not only important to recognize how Jews live today, but also to recognize that only by living can what it means to be a Jew is seen. Judaism is a religion of action, and while there are beliefs that underpin action, these may not be the motivator and it may just be that things are done because they are commanded, or because they have always been done. This chapter begins with a discussion of 'Justice' as one of the expressions of the ethics of Judaism, however, it could be seen to be not just 'one' of the expressions, but 'the' ethical expression. Every aspect of Jewish ethical behaviour is rooted in justice and *tikkun olam*. The remainder of the chapter will look at issues such as care for the environment, the sanctity of life, same-sex relationships and the role of women; but it is possible to see them as expressions of justice.

Justice

Justice lies at the heart of Judaism. The Almighty is just (see Chapter 1), and as such humanity is to act in the same way. In *Pirkei Avot*, it is recorded:

> Moses received the Torah at Sinai and transmitted it to Joshua, Joshua to the elders, and the elders to the prophets, and the prophets to the Men of the Great Assembly. They said three things: Be patient in [the administration of] justice, raise many disciples and make a fence round the Torah.
>
> (1:1)

Justice permeates every aspect of life and is multifaceted. It affects the way that a person behaves in relation to their job: 'It is not your responsibility to finish the work, but neither are you free to desist from it' (Pirkei Avot 2:16). Similarly in the business practices that are undertaken, a person should seek to act justly and not to cheat others:

> You shall not falsify measures of length, weight, or capacity. You shall have an honest balance, honest weights, an honest *ephah*, and an honest *hin*.
>
> (Leviticus 19:35–6)

Honesty in all a person's words and dealings contributes to the exhibition of justice in the ways that a Jew interacts with others. The Torah commands a person not to deceive:

> Do not wrong [deceive] one another, but fear your God; for I the LORD am your God.
>
> (Leviticus 25:17)

Echoing the ninth commandment:

> You shall not bear false witness against your neighbour.
>
> (Exodus 20:13)

There is also the responsibility to deal justly with foreigners:

> The stranger who resides with you shall be to you as one of your citizens; you shall love him as yourself, for you were strangers in the land of Egypt: I the LORD am your God.
>
> (Leviticus 19:34)

This is developed further in the principle of *Geneivat da'at* ('theft of the mind' or 'stealing knowledge') which rejects an approach of dissimilitude and false representation. This goes to the motives of people that lie behind their actions. It is not enough to be seen to act justly, but it must be truly honest. In the *Talmud*, it is written:

> As Shmuel said: It is prohibited to deceive people, and even to deceive a gentile ... It is taught in a baraita that Rabbi Meir would say: A person may not importune [yesarhev] another to eat with him, making it seem as though he genuinely wants his company, but in reality he entreats him only because he knows that the other will not eat with him, i.e., will not accept the invitation. And similarly, one may not send another person many gifts merely because he knows that the other will not accept them.
>
> (Chullin 94a:5,10)

The Talmud gives many examples of how these principles may be exhibited in the practices of individuals. One such example surrounds the sale of wine:

> And needless to say, one may not intermingle new produce with old produce, in the event that the old produce is superior, as with grains, since intermingling lowers its value. Actually, they said: With regard to wine, they permitted one to mix strong wine with weak wine, because one thereby enhances it. One may not intentionally mix wine sediment with the wine, but one may give the buyer wine with its sediment; the seller is not required to filter the wine.
>
> (Bava Metzia 60a)

The command to deal justly with others thus can be seen to influence every area of life. Even in the antisemitic trope of Shylock in Shakespeare's *Merchant of Venice*, we see in Shylock's willingness to abide by the terms of the contract that he had drawn up, even though it was to his disadvantage, an example of the importance of dealing justly and honestly with others.

This justice is not limited to one's personal and business dealings; rather it is a way of life. Robinson suggests:

> It is clearly the duty of every Jew to seek justice. In a world unredeemed, a world that is damaged, it is the job of every Jew to participate in *tikkun olam/repair of the world*. In areas of social justice, social action, Judaism has set itself clear mandates. 'You shall do what is right and good', we are told in Deuteronomy 6:18.
>
> (2000, 243)

The world is not as the Almighty created it; as Adam and Eve were cast out of the Garden of Eden, imperfection came into the world. Thus, as we look around the world there is evident injustice and inequality. In the principle of *tikkun olam*, a Jew is to repair the world and to act to do that which is good. Originally in the Mishnah, tikkun olam is used in a way that speaks about repairing or bringing about justice within the legal system to ensure that society is just and running smoothly. This has developed over time into any action that seeks to bring repair or justice to the world. Maimonides suggests that the world can be changed through three types of action: reading the Torah, acts of loving-kindness and religious obligations:

> He is saying that with wisdom, and that is the Torah; and with enhancement of [good] traits, and that is acts of loving kindness; and with the fulfilment of command-ments, and that is the sacrifices [referred to in the mishnah as service] – there will be a continuous refinement of the world and ordering of its existence in the most complete way.
>
> (*Rambam on Pirkei Avot* 1:2)

As a person lives the mitzvot they can change the world; and indeed, are preparing it for the Messianic Age (see Chapter 2). This is not the only purpose of good acts; they should be performed to change the world today. These good acts could be described under the terms *tzedakah* (justice and righteousness) and *g'milut hasadim* (acts of loving-kindness). Tzedekah has come to refer to acts of charity in seeking to bring justice to the world; the Talmud teaches that acts of tzedakah are equal to all the mitzvot:

> Charity [tzedakah] and works of kindness are as important as all commandments of the Torah. Charity applies to the living, works of kindness apply to the living and the dead. Charity applies to the poor, works of kindness apply to poor and rich. Charity is through a person's money, works of kindness through his money and his person.
>
> (*Jerusalem Talmud Peah* 1:1 20)

Tzedekah is charity of any kind; this may be in the gifts of time, of wealth, of respect, of kindness or of goods. The *Mishneh Torah* suggests that there are different levels of tzedakah, and a Jew may reflect on these as they consider their intention in performing such acts, going from the best of intentions and working down:

1 Helping a person become self-reliant: 'The highest level beyond which there is none is a person who supports a Jew who has fallen into poverty [by] giving him a present or a loan, entering into partnership with him or finding him work so that his hand will be fortified so that he will not have to ask others [for alms]' (*Mishneh Torah, Gifts to the Poor, 10:7*).
2 Tzedekah with no ulterior motive, as the person given does not know the recipient's identity (and vice versa): 'A lower [level] than this is one who gives charity to the poor without knowing to whom he gave and without the poor person knowing from whom he received. For this is an observance of the mitzvah for its sake alone' (*Mishneh Torah, Gifts to the Poor, 10:8*).
3 'When the giver knows to whom he is giving, but the poor person does not know from whom he received' (*Mishneh Torah, Gifts to the Poor, 10:9*).
4 'When the poor person knows from whom he took, but the donor does not know to whom he gave' (*Mishneh Torah, Gifts to the Poor, 10:10*)
5 'Giving [the poor person] in his hand before he asks'. The person receiving is not humbled by having to ask (*Mishneh Torah, Gifts to the Poor, 10:11*).
6 'Giving him after he asks' (*Mishneh Torah, Gifts to the Poor, 10:12*).
7 'Giving … less than what is appropriate, but with a pleasant countenance' (*Mishneh Torah, Gifts to the Poor, 10:13*).
8 'Giving … with sadness' (*Mishneh Torah, Gifts to the Poor, 10:9*) or perhaps better described as begrudgingly.

Often, acts of tzedakah are most obviously given in charitable financial donations, in this way justice in the world can be found as those with less are able to be raised in their needs and standing. The giving of 10 per cent of one's income (tithing or *ma'sar kesafim*) is not an uncommon practice, but the *Shulchan Arukh: Yoreh De'ah* suggests:

> The amount of charity one should give is as follows: if one can but afford, let him give as much as is needed. Under ordinary circumstances, a fifth of one's property is most laudable. To give one-tenth is the average disposition. But to give less than one-tenth is niggardly.

> (249)

Though the giving of more than one-fifth is discouraged as it may place the giver in need. One example within the Torah about the responsibility to care for the poor is found within the law of *peah* (corners) regarding the harvest:

> When you reap the harvest of your land, you shall not reap all the way to the edges of your field, or gather the gleanings of your harvest. You shall not pick your vineyard

bare, or gather the fallen fruit of your vineyard; you shall leave them for the poor and the stranger: I the LORD am your God.

(Leviticus 19:9–10)

This is a way to deal justly with the poor and utilize wealth in a way that is for the benefit of others. Today, for Jews who are not farmers, this may apply in the donation of leftover food or wealth to charities. Jews can share 'the bounty and fruits of our lives, not hoarding what we have to ourselves. We can give of our crops, our creative work, our money, time, or talents' (Danan, 2022). The world is supposed to be just, and it is a Jew's responsibility to work for this. As such, whether in issues of law or inequality Jews will work to do good and repair the world. Inequalities can be with regards to the financial and other needs of people and the fair distribution of wealth; it can also mean combatting prejudice and discrimination in all its forms. Consider the following prayers that are used in different congregations:

You have taught us to uphold the falling, to heal the sick, to free the captive, to comfort all who suffer pain.

(Stern, 1983, 383)

Help [those who govern] understand the rules of justice You have decreed, so that peace and security, happiness and freedom, will never depart from our land.

ADONAI, God whose spirit is in all creatures, we pray that Your spirit be awakened within all the inhabitants of our land. Uproot from our hearts hatred and malice, jealousy and strife. Plant love and companionship, peace and friendship, among the many peoples and faiths who dwell in our nation. Grant us the knowledge to judge justly, the wisdom to act with compassion, and the understanding and courage to root out poverty from our land.

May it be Your will that our land be a blessing to all who dwell on earth, and may You cause all peoples to dwell in friendship and freedom. Speedily fulfil the vision of Your prophets: 'Nation shall not lift up sword against nation, neither shall they learn war anymore'. 'For all of them, from the least of them to the greatest, shall know Me'. And let us say: Amen.

(The Rabbinical Assembly, n.d.)

Only in repairing the world can a person be seen to be fulfilling the command of the Almighty to rule over the world and to be wise stewards. There are many Jewish charities and organizations that work to make the world a better place, and it is through support of these that many Jews may perform tzedakah, though it is important to note that tzedakah is not limited to these organizations or given only to benefit Jews. In the UK, such charities include:

- Jewish Council for Racial Equality (JCORE).
- World Jewish Relief, which works to help provide relief and help people to become self-reliant.
- Jewish Care focused on health and social care support.

- Jewish Women's Aid supporting women and children who have experienced domestic and sexual abuse.
- Jami (Jewish Association for Mental Illness), a subsidiary of Jewish Care focusing on providing mental health support.
- Tzedek, a charity working to reduce poverty.

Environmental ethics

Possibly the greatest problem in the world today is that of the many threats to the environment. Inextricably linked with the concept of justice is the way that Jews are to care for the world. They are to act with justice towards the natural world, for as the Psalms teach: 'The earth is the LORD's and all that it holds, the world and its inhabitants' (24:1). The earth belongs to the Almighty. The way it belongs to the Almighty is shown in the following prayer:

> Master of the universe, in whose hand is the breath of all life and the soul of every person, grant us the gift of Shabbat, a day of rest from all our labours. With all of our senses may we perceive the glory of Your works. Fill us with Your goodness, that we may attest to Your great deeds. Strengthen us to become Your faithful partners, preserving the world for the sake of future generations. Adonai our God and God of our ancestors, may it be Your will to renew Your blessing of the world in our day, as You have done from the beginning of time.
>
> (Nevins, n.d.)

The natural world was not just created by the Almighty, but as suggested above, each day it continues to be spoken into existence. The Almighty is intimately involved in the world. As such when the Almighty gave the command to 'till it and tend it' (Genesis 2:15), the concept of *L'vadah ul'shamrah*. This concept is not to leave the world alone, but to nurture and care for it so that it flourishes each day. The story is told in the Talmud of Choni Hameageil which explains one associated reason that Jews should care for the world:

> One day Choni was journeying on the road and he saw a man planting a carob tree. He asked, 'How long does it take [for this tree] to bear fruit?' The man replied: 'Seventy years'. Choni then further asked him: 'Are you certain that you will live another seventy years?' The man replied: 'I found [already grown] carob trees in the world; as my forefathers planted those for me so I too plant these for my children'.
>
> (*Depths of Yonah* 2:2.15)

This links with the old adage that the world is not inherited from our ancestors, but it is borrowed from our descendants. It should be enough to care for the world because it is a command of the Almighty, but there is the added responsibility of taking care of it for future generations, as Pirkei Avot suggests: 'It is not your duty to finish the work, but neither are you at liberty to neglect it' (2:16).

When Jews consider the various threats to the world, it might be considered that these have developed because humans have forgotten their relationship to the world, and therefore the threats are both physical and spiritual. In many ways, asking what humanity's role is in relation to the world is forgetting that there is not really a separation between the world and humanity. If Jews see themselves as separate from the natural world then it may become a commodity that can be ignored and exploited, perhaps not even consciously. However, if Jews see themselves as integrally linked then the responsibility becomes innate. In many ways this links with the discussion of Martin Buber's I-It versus I-Thou explored in Chapter 2; people find themselves not in a relationship with an 'it' but with a living organism:

> Throughout all of this the tree remains my object and has its place and its time span, its kind and condition. But it can also happen, if will and grace are joined, that as I contemplate the tree I am drawn into a relation, and the tree ceases to be an It.

(Buber, 1970, 58)

This relationship with 'Creation – happens to us, burns into us, changes us, we tremble and swoon, we submit. Creation – we participate in it, we encounter the creator, offer ourselves to him, helpers and companions' (Buber, 1970, 130). Thus, when Jews consider their responsibility for climate change, pollution, deforestation, and many other issues that threaten the world, the choices to be made are clear.

Sanctity of life

As indicated in Chapters 1 and 2, humanity is created in the image of the Almighty. As such they have a special relationship, role and value within creation. The Talmud teaches the importance of preserving human life:

> Therefore, Adam the first man was created alone, to teach you that with regard to anyone who destroys one soul … the verse ascribes him blame as if he destroyed an entire world, as Adam was one person, from whom the population of an entire world came forth. And conversely, anyone who sustains one soul … the verse ascribes him credit as if he sustained an entire world.

(Sanhedrin 37a:13)[1]

So important is the need to preserve life is the associated belief of *pikuach nefesh*, that a mitzvot can be broken to save a life. Providing commentary on a passage from the Torah, the Talmud suggests:

> 'You shall therefore keep My statutes, and My ordinances, which if a man do, he shall live by them' (Leviticus 18:5). This teaches that one should live by God's mitzvot, and not

---

[1] The original source suggests 'one soul from among the Jewish people'; most authorities who quote this today in relation to sanctity of life omit this and expand it to all of humanity.

that he should die by them. This verse serves as a source for the halakha that one may violate a prohibition in order to save a life.

(Avodah Zarah 27b:10)

Thus, if a doctor needed to save the life of a person on Shabbat, they would be allowed to. The sanctity of life is therefore associated with the preservation of life and not just with the command not to take it. There are exceptions to the pikuach nefesh which are normally in relation to saving one's own life. A person cannot kill another person to save their own life, and adultery and idolatry are also excluded from that which a person can do to save their own life (see Sanhedrin 74a–b).

These beliefs in the sanctity of life and the need to preserve life have implications for Jewish attitudes to issues such as abortion. With regards to abortion, Jewish responses most often relate to the idea of when the foetus is a life. For some Jews, the foetus is a part of the woman, and as such her life takes precedence, and the majority of, if not all, Jews, would accept abortion to save the mother's life. Though there may be the suggestion that this should not be the case 'If the head of the foetus emerges' for 'it should not be touched' (*Mishneh Torah, Murderer and the Preservation of Life* 1:9). Some may also use this to argue that the foetus is not a life until this point, while others use the Talmud to suggest that 'until forty days from conception the foetus is merely water. It is not yet considered a living being' (*Yevamot* 69b:10).

Having queried the status of a foetus as a life, there is Talmudic interpretation that suggests that the killing of a foetus is the killing of a life:

'One who sheds the blood of a person, by a person [ba'adam] his blood shall be shed' (Genesis 9:6). The word ba'adam literally means: In a person, and is interpreted homiletically: What is a person that is in a person? You must say: This is a foetus that is in its mother's womb. Accordingly, a descendant of Noah is liable for killing a foetus.

(*Sanhedrin* 57b:5)

It would appear then that as with many aspects of the Torah and the Talmud, there is debate about the 'life' of a foetus. As indicated above, for most Jews, this would mean that the life of the foetus should not be taken except to save the life of the mother. However, there are also Jews who would suggest that there may be other circumstances in which it would be accepted. Within Orthodox Judaism, Rabbi Eliezer Melamed has extended the understanding of what might constitute saving a life, 'he points out that "since emotional illness is generally considered a threat to life, she may abort her foetus to protect her life"' (Berkowitz, 2021, 1139). This approach is normative within forms of Masorti and Reform Judaism, though they may also add the acceptability of abortion in cases of rape and incest.

For Jews, as with everybody, abortion is a serious decision that should be considered by those who are seeking such. Abortion is a complex and emotive issue and the need to show compassion towards the woman is paramount within Judaism. For many Jews a consideration of abortion would also include discussion with the mother's family including the father (if appropriate) and the rabbi. The sanctity of life is seen to be applied by those who would permit and those who would restrict abortion within Judaism. The sanctity of life is applied to both the mother and to the foetus.

The role of women

It is perhaps an 'interesting' place to situate a discussion about the role of women in a section on the ethics of Judaism. Judith Plaskow (1991) describes elements of her awareness of the place of women in Jewish belief and practice:

> As I became more involved with traditional practice, other starker disabilities of women presented themselves. The legal inability of women to initiate divorce, for instance, entails that a woman with an obstinate or missing husband must remain unmarried for the rest of her life. The fact that, in traditional Judaism, women are not counted in a minyan (quorum required for public prayer) or called to the Torah amounts to our exclusion from the public religious realm ... Such experiences and they are part of the lives of thousands and thousands of Jewish women-did and do make me feel that there are aspects of Jewish and feminist identity that are irreconcilable.
>
> (xi)

In different forms of Judaism, many of these same restrictions continue. In Orthodox shuls or synagogues, there will be a separation of men and women. Tradition has prescribed this. Indeed, in reflecting on the possibility of change within some areas of Judaism, Plaskow has suggested that such 'a deeply patriarchal tradition ... will require a revolution as great as the transition from biblical to rabbinic Judaism' (1991, xiii).

When reading Jewish history, and even scripture, a person encounters an overwhelmingly male-focused narrative. Though there are exceptions women are spoken about and perhaps valued in relation to men. Greenspahn (2009), has suggested:

> In this androcentric (male-centred) orientation, women are looked at from a male point of view, so that it is always their impact on someone else that matters. They are the 'other', to use modern, scholarly parlance.
>
> (247)

Many Jews have begun to reclaim or to rediscover the voice of women within Judaism. In the Midrashic tradition (see Chapter 4), there are examples of the stories of women being given greater detail and focus. There are also modern stories and initiatives that seek to highlight the voices of Jewish women, past and present. One such example is *The Red Tent* by Anita Diamant (1997), which reimagines the story of Dinah, daughter of Leah and Jacob, whose story is often lost in comparison to her twelve brothers. Focused on a red tent, a place where women would go during the time of menstruation, it highlights issues of purity. It should be said that there is no evidence that the women of Jacob's family used such a tent, but the relation to ancient, and perhaps modern, attitudes towards menstruation is important. When a person reads this, they may be reminded of the practices associated with the mikveh, a bath of ritual purification that is still in use today. Based on a tradition in the Torah that a person should bathe in water to remove impurity, indeed a woman's time of menstruation is described as being 'in her impurity seven days' (Leviticus 15:19). The Torah also suggests that 'a spring or cistern in which water is collected shall be pure' (Leviticus 11:36). It is with this as a background that the use of a mikveh developed, where a mikveh is used following menstruation or childbirth. There are other traditions that require the use of a mikveh for all Jews, not just for women, such as when a person converts to Judaism, before Yom Kippur, and for some Jews before Shabbat.

The use of the mikveh for the purposes of removal of impurity considers among most Orthodox Jews, but there are varying attitudes within Reform and Masorti Jews. Some Jews do not use the mikveh, while for others if it is used it is not for the sake of removal of impurity, but the marking of a transition in life, or preparation for an important event. For some the mikveh has been re-appropriated 'into a space for women to celebrate Rosh Chodesh, to mark a milestone, or to bring closure to a crisis' (Nadell in Greenspahn, 2009, 168). In some Jewish views, the concept of mikveh especially had to be rejected, before the practice could be transformed. Reflecting on her previous support of the mikveh, Rachel Adler (1997) highlighted that in doing so she had created:

> A theology for the despised ... where worldly power went unchecked, the slave remained a slave, the poor stayed poor, the woman was subject to her husband, but the meaning of indignity was inverted and transfigured: Humiliation was triumph, rejection was salvation, and death, eternal life. My theology upheld the rules and practices that sustained women's impurity by holding out to the impure a never-before-experienced sense of purity.

(204)

She rejected the premise completely. However, for many Jewish women today, the mikveh has been reclaimed, one such example is the Mayyim Hayyim mikveh:

> Mayyim Hayyim is a resource for learning, spiritual discovery, and creativity where women, men, and people of all genders and ages can celebrate milestones like weddings and b'nai mitzvah; where conversion to Judaism is accorded the honor and dignity it deserves; where survivors of trauma, illness or loss find solace; and where those who immerse monthly can explore the ritual on their own terms. Mayyim Hayyim is a fountain of creativity that, since its opening in 2004, inspired new liturgies and curricula, publications, music, artwork, and plays.

(Mayyim Hayyim, n.d.)

The mikveh serves as a practical example of how attitudes to, and the voices of women, have changed in the modern world. For some the beliefs of impurity remain, but for others they have transformed into an empowering message for women. This is replicated in other areas of Jewish belief and practice.

In the role of women in religious life it has always been the role of a woman to keep a kosher home, and to be responsible for the religious observances within the home. One such example can be seen in the observance of Shabbat (see Chapter 6). While women are seen to be equal with men, for some this does not mean that they are the same. Each might be seen to have different responsibilities and roles. This debate has been especially shown in the place of women in the formal religious life in synagogues, including:

- Publicly reading the Torah (ba'al kriah)
- Being part of a minyan
- Being called for an aliyah to read the Torah
- Being a cantor (shalich tzibbur)
- Being a rabbi and halakhic arbiter
- Being able to wear a tallit and tefillin

Within Masorti and Reform Judaism, these rights are taken for granted for men and women, while within Orthodox communities they would be very rare for women. Again, this illustrates the debate about whether halakhah is subject to change, or if it remains forever unchangeable.

It is possible to explore much more of the debate and practices associated with the role of women. In exploring Judaism today, it is important that diverse voices are heard; not least of these would be women. For Jews, this would continue in the tradition of women like Deborah, a leader and a prophetess who assured victory for the Israelites and ushered in peace in the land; or Abigail who took upon herself the sin of her husband turning away the wrath of David. In a rereading of Jewish scripture and history these voices are increasingly coming to the fore. In establishing the *Shalvi/Hyman Encyclopedia of Jewish Women* the stated aims of its editors it 'to make available to all who are interested in Jewish history and culture the varied accomplishments of Jewish women and their many contributions to the Jewish historical experience over the course of the past three millennia' (Sartori & Rosenbaum, 2021). It is important that when exploring the Jewish experience today that these stories and experiences should be utilised.

Same-sex relationships

The traditional view found within most, if not all traditions, of Orthodox Judaism seems to be based on Leviticus 18:22:

Do not lie with a male as one lies with a woman; it is an abhorrence.

There are many writings within Orthodox Judaism that confirm this approach to same-sex relationships with regards to marriage and sexual activity. Many reasons are suggested, some drawing on it being an imitation of the practices of those not of Israel (see Leviticus 18:3), or perhaps committing the sin of Onan where semen is wasted, i.e. not used for the purpose of procreation (see Genesis 38). Some of the language used, even by those Orthodox Jewish writers who are trying to take a softer approach may still identify it as a choice and therefore, it is seen as a 'problem'.

There are Orthodox Jews who have begun to discuss and perhaps ameliorate this stance towards same-sex relationships. In light of developments in understanding the nature of sexual identity, and that it is innate rather than a choice, leads to a problem in interpreting the Torah. As sexuality is something that a person is born with this means that its prohibition means 'that, for some people, the Torah has forbidden all plausible sexual activity. In other words ... the purport of the commandments of the Torah is: God has created us with sexual desires; these must be completely suppressed and never expressed. The commandment ... is in essence a commandment to live a life of total celibacy and sexual abstention' (Rapoport, 2004, 21). The idea that people are born with certain dispositions is not new; it can be found in the writings of Maimonides, but its application to same-sex relationships is perhaps new. It does mean that some Jews would now reject so-called 'conversion therapy'. The rejection of same-sex relationships remains in place for most Orthodox Jews but this is slightly ameliorated by what Rabbi Jonathan Sacks has called the need for Jews 'to understand his or her [those who are in same-sex relationships or have same-sex attraction] plight, caught between two identities and two cultures', and further that this needs to be accompanied with 'Compassion, sympathy, empathy, [and] understanding' (Rapoport, 2004, ix). This is a step beyond the language of condemnation that may have been used in the past.

Within Reform and Masorti forms of Judaism there has been the recognition that considering modern developments in understanding the innateness of sexual identity, there is a need to reconsider the outright rejection that is found in the Torah, and in many historical attitudes.

Within the Masorti Jewish community within the UK most Jews accept same-sex relationships, and highlight:

> People of all gender identities and sexual orientations are welcome in Masorti communities. Most Masorti synagogues also offer same-sex ceremonies and marriage registration. We have a Masorti LGBT+ Network that regularly runs activities.
>
> (Masorti Judaism, n.d)

Indeed, since 2014, same-sex marriages have been accepted and approved to be conducted within synagogues. At the time, Rabbi Jonathan Wittenberg suggested: 'This is an important step forward. As a movement, we will continue to strive to be inclusive and to honour the dignity of all people, within the framework of Jewish law' (Rocker, 2014). It is important to note that as Rocker suggests, the acceptance of same-sex relationships is done so within the framework of Jewish law. In accepting same-sex relationships Masorti Judaism is not rejecting the law. Some argue that the interpretation of Leviticus is with regards to the sexual immorality of the Canaanites, and it is this that was being rejected.

Other Jews have suggested that even allowing for the prohibition within Leviticus, it is in keeping with Jewish tradition to reinterpret the law, and on the basis of modern approaches to innate sexuality, and the recognition that sexual activity is not just for procreation, Kirschner (1988) argues that:

> Halakhah has the capacity to recognize and to reckon with advances in empirical knowledge ... In our own times, new understanding of human sexual diversity also requires the reconsideration of an ancient judgment ... For those who are already persuaded by the empirical evidence of sexual diversity, the Jewish imperative is clear: to rescind the ancient denunciation of [same-sex relationships] and to recognize that all persons, in their unique sexual being, are the work of God's hands and the bearers of God's image.
>
> (457–8)

This is the approach taken within Reform and Masorti communities throughout the UK. There are many charities and organizations that seek to support those who are Jewish and LGBTQ+. First and foremost are individual synagogues, and there are also groups such as:

- *Keshet UK* which works in areas of education and training across the different Jewish communities in the UK, so that the 'vision of a world where no one is forced to choose between their LGBT+ and Jewish identity' is realized (KeshetUK, 2023).
- *Rainbow Jews*: A charity providing education and school resources to celebrate LGBT Jewish history and heritage in the UK.

There are also individual voices of Jews that can be used to illustrate the experience of gays and lesbians living in the UK and practising Judaism. There are also important figures such as the late Rabbi Lionel Blue who was the first Jewish Rabbi to come out as gay in the UK.

Thoughts for the classroom

In this chapter, we have only explored the issue of justice, and then how that might apply to a small number of issues. There are many issues in the modern world that have not been explored; this does not mean that they are not important but that the ones that are included are indicative of the way that Jews strive to make ethical decisions.

Their approaches to ethics are representative of the underpinning beliefs that are described in the rest of the book. What is notable, however, is the issue of interpretation. In most of the issues explored there is scope for personal decision making, and this must be based on a person's interpretation of how best to serve the Almighty and others. Perhaps in the issue of environmental ethics, there is little to disagree with, though individual practice may differ. However, in discussing issues such as same-sex relationships and abortion there are different responses within Judaism, and maybe authority can be found in the different approaches. Indeed, in the issue of same-sex relationship it is possible to see a microcosm of issues of authority and interpretation throughout Judaism. For many Orthodox Jews, the question is settled because it is revealed in the Torah, though it is tempered by the need to show love and compassion. Whereas within other forms of Judaism where the Torah may not be seen to be set in stone, but able to be interpreted as in in ages past, there might be an acceptance of such relationships. It is important in exploring many ethical issues to recognize the differing worldviews among Jews around the globe. Some Jews who like the status quo use interpretive lenses from that cultural perspective, whereas younger, and perhaps more Westernized, Jews view Judaism and their relationship with the Almighty, others and the world through their own lenses. Maybe within Judaism, there is room for both approaches, but the importance of recognizing the deeply held views of others is paramount in gaining understanding.

Chapter 8

Authority and Diversity in the Jewish World

In the Introduction to this book we listed several Jewish traditions that are to be found within the UK. In some ways these only scratch the surface as there are secular Jews who have many different approaches towards the beliefs and practices of Judaism. Up to this point Orthodox, Reform and Masorti as the main traditions have been mentioned and drawn upon. It is important to note this threefold presentation is not the whole story. In this chapter we will explore a variety of different traditions that can be found in the UK and around the world. As this task is undertaken it is important to note the concept of authority in each and whether that authority can be extended beyond that particular tradition. It is interesting that there are many teachings and beliefs that go across the various traditions. It will not be possible to identify every tradition or individual worldview that expresses Judaism in this chapter, but hopefully in identifying some of the larger groups a better understanding of the diversity within Judaism can be developed.

Considering the Series Editor's Foreword alongside the Introduction to this book to outline the various traditions is to miss the rich diversity of individual worldviews that will be a panoply of different approaches to, and across, Judaism. There will be individuals who utilize selected aspects of more recognized organized worldviews. The presentation further on is not to negate this worldviews approach, but the delineations do exist, and it will be useful to establish them to enable a context to the worldviews of individuals. The chosen traditions are not to suggest that this is the limit of expressions found within the UK. There are many more to be found.

Authority is an interesting concept within Judaism; in the different stages of Judaism there have been various people who have communally exercised authority. It is useful to define what is meant by authority. Authority might be the source of truth or guidance to which people go, and in this case the only source of authority is the Almighty. In many traditions of Judaism, the decisions and guidance of the Almighty can be found in the laws and writings found in the various sources of authority (see Chapter 4). The diversity comes in which people are authorized or given the authority to interpret and teach those laws.

Within rabbinic Judaism, in which Judaism has lived for nearly two thousand years, the authority may be seen to lie with the rabbis, or with the community more widely.

Those rabbis will include those people who have passed on, and those who live today. In response to a question about where authority lies in Judaism, one British Jew responded:

> It is collective. People often look to the Orthodox Chief Rabbi or, increasingly, some of the senior Progressive Rabbis but this is not the whole picture. Individual synagogues or even individuals may address the need for change themselves. We are always speaking out, it's part of being Jewish, we don't need authority!

In many ways authority in Judaism is personal; for some Jews this will mean that they should study and make decisions for themselves. For others, it is a choice about who to listen to for guidance. This may manifest itself in the different traditions that delineate themselves from others. Clive Lawton (2016) highlights this in his discussion of diverse forms of authority:

> Orthodox rabbis dispute the right of Progressive rabbis to make authoritative rulings. Indeed, the Orthodox feel that as Progressive rabbis have received their qualifications from those who in their opinion do not hold the right views, they are therefore not proper rabbis. This means that key decisions taken by Progressive rabbis are disputed by Orthodox rabbis, and this invalidates, for example, conversions to Judaism, marriages, divorces and other issues of personal status performed by Progressive rabbis. Disputes around matters of personal status are probably the most intractable challenges facing the Jewish community today, and are centred on the dispute as to who is legitimately a rabbi.
>
> (60)

The various traditions briefly explored in this chapter will be Orthodox, Masorti, Reform and Kabbalah; though these can be understood as umbrella terms, and with regard to Kabbalah, a spirituality rather than a 'denomination'.

Orthodox

Orthodox Judaism is a group of different traditions that are viewed by many as sharing an approach to halakhah that generally sees the Written and Oral Torah as directly revealed by the Almighty, and that as such it should be interpreted as such. This would suggest a strict interpretation of the various laws that would include the observance of Shabbat and the various 'restrictions' outlined in Chapter 6, or the living of kashrut laws, or the covering of a married woman's head with a wig or a scarf. It is not, despite this, monolithic; there are various groups and approaches that will interpret the application of the law and the various beliefs of Judaism in different ways.

Orthodox is an appellation that began to be used in the nineteenth century, when it was used in distinction to Reform. Orthodox was seen to mean 'traditional'. Orthodox Judaism has its roots in response to Haskalah (the Jewish Enlightenment) and the suggestion that societal changes also necessitated change in Jewish practice. There was a turn, in

Europe, and then later in the United States towards a more strictly Orthodox approach to Judaism. Orthodox Judaism has an important place in British Judaism. Prior to the nineteenth century, when Jewish migration from Eastern Europe began to increase, the Jewish population in Britain tended to be Sephardi. The nineteenth century saw migration from Eastern Europe, and this saw a rise in mainly Ashkenazi Jews. The majority of Orthodox Jews in the UK today are from an Ashkenazi background.

Modern Orthodox Judaism is a strand within the UK who try and balance adherence to the halakhah with engagement in wider society. One of the largest umbrella groups is the United Synagogue which represents many Orthodox Jews in the country, operating over sixty synagogues across the UK. The Chief Rabbi is the leader of this group and is seen to be the highest authority. Though it is important to note that individual rabbis and synagogues can interpret law in their local circumstance. The Chief Rabbi serves as a communal figure who provides guidance and represents the Jewish community. As with all rabbis within Modern Orthodoxy, the Chief Rabbi is seen as a guide rather than an absolute authority. In addition to the relative autonomy of local rabbis, there is also the possibility of personal reflection of halakhah by the individual.

This authority is also reflected in *beth din* (house of judgement), a series of courts which deal with a wide range of legal and religious issues, including divorce and marriage, the laws of kashrut, disputes over financial matters and conversions. Though not legally binding, their decisions are important within the Orthodox Jewish community, and the London *beth din* is seen to be particularly important.

A group within the Orthodox tradition are the Charedi, or as they are sometimes known, the Ultra-Orthodox, though this term does have negative connotations. Charedi comes from a Hebrew word *chared*, meaning to tremble, perhaps drawing on a passage from Isaiah:

> All this was made by My hand, And thus it all came into being – declares GOD. Yet to such a one I look: To the poor and brokenhearted, Who is concerned about [alt: trembleth at] My word.
>
> (66:2)

In line with many aspects of Orthodox Judaism, Charedi Jews believe in the immutability of the Torah, and for this reason the study of the Torah as a spiritual act lies at the heart of Charedi spirituality.

The rabbi has a significant role in Charedi Judaism as a spiritual and legal authority. They serve as a guide for the community in matters of Jewish law, ethics and personal conduct. Within Charedi Judaism there are the gedolim (great rabbis), whose rulings and opinions on religious matters are considered binding. Charedi Jews focus on rabbinic authority rather than individual interpretations of Jewish law. This reflects the belief that tradition and the community consensus are the focus of what it means to live as a Jew today.

In contrast to other forms of Orthodox Judaism, Charedi Jews will often maintain a degree of separation from wider society. They may view secularism as a challenge to

Judaism, and thus may limit access to certain aspects of society which may distract from a religious life. This separation from society is emphasized in the traditional forms of dress such as black hats, long coats and modest clothing for women – as a way of maintaining their separation and visibly expressing their religious identity.

One form of Charedi Jews is known as Chasidic; founded by Rabbi Israel ben Eliezer (1698–1760), known as the Baal Shem Tov (Master of the Good Name). He integrated Kabbalah, a mystical understanding of Judaism as a way for all people to develop this connection with the Divine (see below). This is seen to provide an alternative to an intellectual elite that some saw as developing in the interpretation of halakhah. Further authority within Chasidism, in addition to that explored above, is within the concept of *tzaddik*, a leader or spiritual guide who might function between the community and the Almighty; they will be known as a *Rebbe* and he will serve as a leader in the community, and will be succeeded by a son or close follower. In contrast to a rabbi, their role is often more 'spiritual' rather than administrative, in that they are to guide people to a connection with the Almighty. Within the Chabad-Lubavitch tradition of Chasidism, Rabbi Menachem Mendel Schneerson (1902–94) is seen to be an important example of a rebbe.

Masorti

Masorti (tradition) or Conservative Judaism is seen by many to bridge the gap between Orthodox and Reform Judaism, in that it combines a continuing commitment to halakhah while being open to modern interpretation (see Chapter 7). Masorti Jews view halakhah as central to Jewish identity, and it is also living in the sense that it can evolve in response to changing circumstances and contemporary knowledge. The laws of Shabbat, kashrut and ritual will be observed; there may be adaptation to the modern world. This may manifest itself, for example, when many Masorti synagogues observe separate seating for men and women, and also allow women to serve as rabbis, read Torah and take on leadership roles. The inclusivity of Masorti Judaism is an important principle, as is the responsibility to heal the world (tikkun olam). Masorti will be heavily involved in the local community, especially in activities linked to tikkun olam. They will support local food banks, be involved in interfaith activities, and try to raise the standard of living for all of those within society.

As with other forms of Judaism, rabbis play an important role in the community life of Masorti Judaism, and also in supporting personal decision making. They seek to maintain a balance between tradition and modern circumstances. Masorti Judaism UK is an umbrella organization supporting the different Masorti communities within the UK. They will provide guidance on halakhah but do not issue rulings that are binding on the community, as synagogues serve as autonomous communities, where the community is able to shape approaches to ritual and interpretations of halakhah. Each synagogue will have links to a *beth din* that will rule on matters of divorce, marriage and conversion.

Reform

Reform Judaism is seen to have developed in the nineteenth century in response to Haskalah (the Jewish Enlightenment) and sought to interpret Jewish life in light of modern society, including developing social, scientific and cultural landscapes. As seen throughout this book, Reform is characterized by a desire to keep the Jewish laws, within the context that halakhah is always able to be interpreted, that it is a dynamic thing that is able to respond to changing circumstances. The central beliefs of Judaism (see Chapters 1–4) remain central within Judaism, and as they seek to find their place in the wider world the responsibility of tikkun olam (see Chapter 7) becomes a major focus of living a Jewish life.

Within the UK the Movement for Reform Judaism is an umbrella organization that represents many of the Reform Jewish communities in the UK. The Movement for Reform Judaism provides support for synagogues, rabbis, educational programs and social justice initiatives throughout the Reform community. Other groups such as the Reform Synagogues of Great Britain support Reform communities by developing communities, and by offering training for leaders and rabbis. There are different sources of authority within the Reform community:

- Rabbis lead services and offer guidance on different matters to individual Jews, and to the wider community. In this role they are important voices in interpreting halakhah.
- Personal decision making plays an important role in reform Judaism. Individuals will consult Torah and rabbis in making decisions, but they are able to be guided by their conscience in making decisions in a Jewish context.
- The Movement for Reform Judaism provides non-binding guidance, often in the form of position statements on particular issues in the community.
- Each synagogue has a board comprising a lay leadership who work alongside the rabbi, often ensuring that the community's needs are met and are reflective of the Jewish principles important to the community.

The Board of Deputies of British Jews

One organization that many see as 'the voice of the British Jewish Community' is the Board of Deputies of British Jews (Board of Deputies of British Jews, 2024), founded in 1760. It does not claim to be an authoritative group, rather it is an elected group of 300 deputies representing synagogues and Jewish communities from across the country, and from across the different traditions in the UK. It is an advocacy groups and speaks out on matters of interest to British Jews. The Board of Deputies outlines four divisions engaged in this work:

- *Security, Resilience and Cohesion.* In this area the Board engages in interfaith activities and 'works to combat antisemitism and extremism, as well as to promote and defend Jewish rights and freedoms in the UK' (2024).

- *International Division.* As suggested in the name this area works to speak up and speak out about issues affecting Jews around the world, including antisemitism but covering many issues.
- *Communities and Education.* This area is involved in many different areas including the oversight of Jewish schools, educating the community about issues in the modern world, ensuring that the representation of Jews and Judaism in schools and in the community is accurate, and protects the heritage of Judaism.
- *Finance, Fundraising and Organization.* Engaged in the smooth running of its operations.

Examples of its outreach activities include meeting with politicians and community leaders to celebrate Jewish festivals, and to discuss antisemitism, and issues of concern such as the assisted dying bill. In many ways they are a unifying voice, and this is shown in their weekly *Community Briefing* that highlights the work that it undertakes, and comments on the issues that are being spoken about in wider society.

Kabbalah

It is incorrect to place Kabbalah as a separate tradition within Judaism, rather it can be found across traditions and is better described as a mystical or esoteric dimension to Judaism. It can be found in different traditions and can be seen to be integral to some forms of Chasidism. It is through Chasidism that mystical ideas such as being able to connect with the Almighty and the concept of *devekut* (cleaving to the Almighty) were made accessible to the wider community. It has been identified that there are two streams of Kabbalah: one of which 'reserved study only by the best students' and the approach of Chasidism 'to bring the wisdom and practice of Kabbalah to the average person' (Kurzweil, 2007, 3).

There are various concepts throughout this book that are central aspects of a Kabbalistic understanding of Judaism, those beliefs such as Ein Sof, the Sefirot, creation (see Chapter 1) and tikkun olam (see Chapter 7). Study, meditation, prayer and the observance of mitzvot are important ways for Jews to connect with the Divine; indeed, the three daily tasks of a Kabbalist are prayer, study and acts of kindness. The purpose of following Kabbalistic principles is to connect to the Divine; this is done through the five levels of the soul:

1 *Nefesh* (the vital, physical life force).
2 *Ruach* (the emotional and moral spirit).
3 *Neshamah* (the intellectual and spiritual self).
4 *Chayah* (the life force connected to divine essence).
5 *Yechidah* (the unity of the soul with God).

Kabbalah is perceived as a way that Jews can move beyond a focus on the details of the law and to see the Almighty behind those laws. Kurzweil (2007) suggests that 'if you focus on the details of just one tree, you miss the magnificence of the forest' (19). This is not to suggest that laws should be ignored, but that Jews are able to encounter the spiritual meaning of them with Kabbalah. The Zohar, a central text within Kabbalah, is seen to be a spiritual commentary on the Torah attributed to Rabbi Shimon bar Yochai in the second century; while many see it as the work of Rabbi Moses de Leon in thirteenth-century Spain; de Leon presented it as a discovery of the second-century text. It is central for Kabbalists in enabling a connection to the Almighty and gaining insights into the nature of reality.

Authority with Kabbalah can be summarized as coming from several sources; firstly the Torah and, more widely, the Tanakh; the Zohar containing mystical interpretations of the Torah; other Kabbalistic texts; and historical rabbis such as Isaac Luria (1534–72) who is seen to have systematized Kabbalah into a framework that could be studied, and Chaim Vital. However, in addition to these sources a person's own experience and spirituality are an important aspect of authority with Kabbalah. One of the main focuses of Kabbalah is spiritual purification and a connection to the Divine; this is made possible by living a life of holiness and devotion which enables a person to access and interpret truths. These are developed within a Jewish framework, with insights enhancing rather than detracting from halakhah. Thus, authority within Kabbalah rests on traditional texts as well as personal spiritual experience. Indeed, Kurzweil (2007) suggests that 'the laws, customs, practices, holidays, and rituals of Judaism are best understood in light of Kabbalistic teachings' (1).

Thoughts for the classroom

Within the established traditions the question of authority lies upon the teachings of the Tanakh, the Talmud and the rabbis. It is interesting, in exploring these expressions that are popular in Britain today, to see that each one has adapted the question of authority for the modern world. For Orthodox this is about the restatement of traditional norms and a timeless application of halakhah. For Reform and Masorti this has been about trying to understand the nature of halakhah in the modern world and even reinterpret it to differ-ent extents. While, in all forms of Judaism there continues to be an autonomy that, to an extent, is both amplified and restricted within these traditions.

These three traditions also show the need for teachers to go beyond a binary representation. At various points in this book, we have explored the importance of recog-nizing Orthodox and Reform understandings, but it is evident that even this level of diversity is insufficient. Drawing on elements explored in the Introduction to this book, a binary approach to Judaism is a false dichotomy. Most people would acknowledge that in many debates to describe an either/or approach is simplistic at best. Perhaps they persist because extreme positions are easy to caricature and easy to pull apart in terms of their limitations. They encourage polarity and they make arguments easy to have and oppos-ing views to be torn down. While polarity helps position oneself into one of two camps, it misses the richness and diversity that we can find by honestly engaging with both sides of the debate. Sometimes in the polarities we can engage in some rich thinking, but it is not the only place where it can be found. In Judaism the establishment of dichotomies and polarities creates what might be termed a duolithic view. It is a lazy approach to teaching and misses the rich diversity that we can find in the 'messiness' and lived reality of religions.

Chapter 9

Judaism and Contemporary Britain

Throughout the previous chapters there have been many examples of how Judaism is lived in Britain today. This is an important aspect in striving to teach Judaism in the class-room. Judaism is a religion that is rich in history, and many aspects of its beliefs and expressions have been influenced or established by events throughout history. In the previous chapter, we tried to explore the various nuances of authority within the Jewish community, and as this chapter moves forward, we will try and understand what this means for the lived experience of Jews in Britain today. As has already been discussed, the experience of the individual Jew is dependent on many factors that contribute to their worldview. In this chapter, we will explore various aspects of what could be considered the Jewish experience in Britain today. The values and teachings of Judaism will form a significant part of this, but it will also be influenced by gender, culture and many other aspects of a person's life experience. Thus, to try and articulate what it is to live as a Jew today in Britain is perhaps folly, if the individual nature of religious experience is not noted.

Numbers

Many aspects of Jewish history, unfortunately, were covered in the discussion of antisem-itism (see Chapter 5), but this does not tell the whole story. The first record of Jews being in Britain was following the Norman Invasion, most likely in about 1070. There were Jewish communities in mainland Europe and in King William's lands in France. It is suggested that it was natural for some to follow their feudal Lord across the channel (Roth, 1964, 4). Though there were examples of tolerance and friendly relationships, there were still restrictions on the activities of Jews. They were excluded from many trades, though they were able to be involved in medicine and in money lending. The latter because many Christians saw usury, or the charging of interest, as a sin, and so Jews were some of the only people able to be involved in this industry. It was a little over 200 years later that the Edict of Expulsion was issued, and Jews were forced from England, not resettling until, officially 1656, when Oliver Cromwell indicated that the Edict would no longer be enforced. Though there is evidence of a Sephardi community living 'unofficially' in England since the 1630s. What is also of note is that despite Cromwell's pronouncement, Parliament did not rescind the Edict, but it was ignored.

In terms of numbers of Jews in the UK, one of the most important sources is the Census data, though it is important to note that the religion question was only added in 2001. Other data sources have been used to compile the data, but caution should be taken.

- 1933: c. 300,000 (United States Holocaust Memorial Museum, 2024)
- 1940s: c. 400,000 (Migration Watch UK, 2014)
- 1945: 450,000 (United States Holocaust Memorial Museum, 2025)
- 2001: 266,745
- 2011: 269,568
- 2021: 277,613

With a decline in the post-war years to the end of the twentieth century, there seems to be a slight increase in those people identifying as Jewish; one suggestion why this may be so is the increase in birth rates among the 'Ultra-Orthodox' or Charedi communities (University of Manchester, 2007). The Census is a blunt instrument as it does not define who is Jewish, rather it allows for self-identification. There are other metrics available. In 2016 Mashiah and Boyd (2017) recorded that there were 454 active synagogues in the UK, the highest number since before the Second World War (8). As suggested in the previous chapter this represents a diversity of groups, with 52.8 per cent being Central Orthodox, 19.4 per cent being Reform, 13.5 per cent Strictly Orthodox, 8.2 per cent Liberal, 3.3 per cent Masorti and 2.9 per cent Sephardi (Mashiah & Boyd, 2017, 9). Comparing Census details with reported synagogue membership, the JPR suggest that there are approximately 141,503 Jewish households in the UK, with 79,597 or 56.3 per cent holding membership of a synagogue. These figures are inexact, but they highlight that possibly over half of British Jews are involved with their local synagogue. The Institute for Jewish Policy Research often publishes reports and data sets that try to interrogate the data for religiosity, practice and identification among British Jews. Their 2024 report (Graham & Boyd, 2024) gives a similar number as the Census, and highlights the comparative small-ness compared to Israel and the United States, but also recognizes:

> The British Jewish community is both large and small – large enough to have built a vibrant and dynamic Jewish life in the country with numerous synagogues, Jewish schools, youth movements, cultural centres, festivals and events, but small enough to see many regional communities struggling to maintain their infrastructure, and for indi-vidual Jews to sometimes feel vulnerable and isolated.
>
> (2)

Within the sociology of religion are the linked concepts of retrenchment and assimilation. On the one hand, there is a 'strain toward greater assimilation and respectability' and on the other, a strain 'towards greater separateness, peculiarity, and militance'. Armand Mauss (1994, 5) further suggests that

> along the continuum between total assimilation and total repression or destruction is a narrow segment on either side of the centre; and it is within this narrower range of

socially tolerable variation that movements must maintain themselves, pendulumlike, to survive.

In many ways this is the experience of Judaism within Britain. This can also be related to the experience of many immigrant communities over the past couple of centuries. In terms of Jews in Britain, particularly in the interwar years, there was a general desire to fit into, and flourish in, society. This was not common to all Jews, but a number may need to not display other aspects of Jewish identity, perhaps only feeling the need to wear a kippah or tallit when attending the synagogue. This was more than likely not a renunciation of Judaism as a faith but a recognition that any 'difference' had the potential to be used to cause division and discrimination. There may have seemed to be a tenuousness to the position of Jews in British society, which may continue into society today. The visibility of Jews and their representation in society may reflect a more secure feeling as being a part of British society. It could also be that subsequent generations of Jews were being born into a country where religious tolerance seemed to be more settled, and so they did not feel the need to hide any aspects of their identity. Rather than this generation being more religious, it is fairer to say that the groundwork had been laid so that there was an environment that was more conducive to expressing faith as a minority. However, as indicated in Chapter 5 there does seem to be evidence of antisemitism in aspects of society, which does not make Jews feel completely confident in their British-Jewish identity:

> British Jews continue to grapple with the tension between being out and proud in multi-cultural Britain, and toning down or hiding their Jewishness for fear of standing out or falling victim to hostility. In that regard, they remain insiders/outsiders – feeling part of modern Britain and acculturated into wider British life, yet also exposed, or not fully seen or understood.
>
> (Graham & Boyd, 2024, 2)

As indicated in the Introduction and earlier in this chapter, there is a diversity in the religiosity of British Jews. This is highlighted in television programmes such as *Friday Night Dinner* which observes a Shabbat meal that is held in the home of seemingly secular Jews. There is little evidence of it being Shabbat apart from it taking place on Friday night.

Education in Jewish communities

One of the ways in which Jewish identity is expressed, preserved and developed within the UK is through a focus on education, both formal and informal. One British Jew has identified that there are 'lots' of opportunities for education in the British Jewish community:

> There are many well-established youth groups, like Maccabi, JLGB, synagogue learning opportunities beyond cheder, lots for young Jews interested in environment, LGBTQ+ etc

Further:

> There are many opportunities across the spectrum ... Both cultural and synagogue based

In terms of formal education in 2014/15 there were 30,900 Jewish children attending 139 Jewish schools across the UK (Staetsky & Boyd, 2016, 3). The number of children is expected to rise to 40,000 in the mid-2020s with there being an actual number of 14,325 Jewish schools in 2021 (Boyd, 2023, 3–4). Examples of the diverse range of schools include:

- The King David High School in Manchester. A voluntary aided academy. The ethos of the school is described in the following way:

> At our Modern Orthodox, Zionist high school, we are committed to fostering a vibrant and holistic educational environment that integrates high academic standards, good practice, religious intent, emotional wellbeing, and experiential Jewish learning, both formal and informal. Our ethos is built upon the pillars of Torah, academic excellence, emotional and social development, and a deep connection and love to Zionism, the land of Israel, the State of Israel, Yiddishkeit (love for Judaism) and the Jewish People.
>
> (The King David High School, n.d.)

- Eden Primary School in Muswell Hill. The first primary free school to be established. It describes its ethos:

> Eden Primary is a Jewish school where everybody is welcome. The school's Jewish ethos embraces children from across the spectrum of Jewish belief and the wider community on an equal basis. Jewish, universal and British values are embedded in all that we do.
>
> (Eden Primary, n.d.)

- Immanuel College in Hertfordshire. A private Jewish primary and secondary school.

> We aim to enable your child to cultivate their individuality and relish their Jewish identity as a familiar and integral part of their everyday. Of course, we seek to help your child live the core Jewish values of justice, fairness, honesty and consideration of others as well as respond to their place in a multi-cultural and pluralistic society. Finally, we aim to enable them to develop as leaders and entrepreneurs with a desire for positive social action.
>
> (Endlar, 2025)

It is interesting to note the reasons why Jewish parents send their children to Jewish schools, and this links to the retrenchment and assimilation that were discussed earlier in the chapter. On the one hand, there is a desire for the children to be immersed in the Jewish community life and establish a Jewish identity. On the other hand, children need to be prepared for life in the wider community, and this means that some parents may opt for their children to experience 'a broader ethno-cultural context and to mix with a more diverse student body' (Boyd, 2023, 9).

This rise in specifically Jewish schools may have been buoyed by the Free Schools and Academies initiatives that allowed for greater freedom in establishing schools. It has not been without its controversy within the Jewish community. Most Jewish schools are registered and seek to provide a balanced diet so that there is a balance between Jewish life and the recognition of the diversity of modern Britain. However, there are examples where schools have failed to teach wider religious content (Humanists UK, 2023) and schools that are unregistered (this is not a uniquely Jewish issue). In some areas unregistered schools are teaching teenage boys Torah and Talmud but little else. Many within the wider Jewish community see these examples as problematic, and most schools do fulfil the requirements of a broad and balanced curriculum. Again, this highlights the challenge of being part of a wider British society in which antisemitism is experienced. The desire to be in a safe space is paramount within the Jewish community.

Although the word 'synagogue' has been used throughout this book, one British Jew outlined that he 'prefers the term "shul", which is Yiddish for school. This helps me understand more what the building is for, it is a house of learning'. In this way it is possible to see more informal educational programmes in shuls around the UK that seek to teach people of all ages about Judaism. These will take place in classes, and in worship services (see Chapter 6). For example, the Liberal Jewish Synagogue in London offers adult education classes in Hebrew and in Judaism. Seed Shuls in London, Manchester and Borehamwood offer a range of classes for all members of the family. The Norwich synagogue offer classes for children and families exploring things such as festivals, mitzvot, the Torah and Hebrew.

The more socially and culturally based education activities are exemplified by groups such as Maccabi GB whose self-proclaimed mission is 'to create inclusive sporting, community and educational experiences that strengthen Jewish identity, enhance wellbeing and inspire engagement in the Jewish community, Israel and beyond' (2024). Their programmes include:

- UK Events including an Interfaith fun run.
- International Events such as the Maccabiah Games, an international sporting competition for Jewish teenagers.
- Tackling Antisemitism in Sport. Working with the Government and sporting bodies to reduce antisemitism.
- Grassroots Sport Clubs. Supporting and running many different sports clubs around the country.
- Grassroots Community Tournaments in many sports.
- Leadership: 'Providing young people with leadership, sporting, and community experiences to enhance their confidence, wellbeing, and Jewish life'.

- School Sport working specifically with Jewish schools.
- Stand Up! Education. An interfaith project bringing Muslim and Jewish educators into the classroom to combat discrimination.
- Student Sport bringing together university Jewish society for sporting competitions.
- Streetwise. A programme of assemblies and similar events to help Jewish youth keep themselves safe.
- Yellow Candle. An informal educational programme to remember the Shoah.

As can be seen from the range of events, Maccabi GB are very much focused on developing a sense of community between Jewish young people, based on a sense of Jewish identity. To see a thriving community of young Jews is an important aspect to identify within British Judaism, in that this perhaps more than any other point highlights the living nature of Judaism, and its potential for future flourishing.

Thoughts for the classroom

The teacher should be prepared for an accurate and authentic discussion of misconceptions as they arise. One of the issues that may arise for students if this is not done is that they may feel that some issues are taboo, and that when issues are quickly passed over then there may be something to hide. This is a similar approach when teaching about issues of Islamophobia and links with violent extremism. We may not want to teach about them because they are not 'mainstream' teachings or practices, but if they are not addressed as they arise then students will get their information elsewhere. This is not to suggest that they are taught at the expense of the central beliefs and practices of Judaism, nor should they be the focus of curriculum questions, but they should be addressed as appropriate. I have argued elsewhere that when such topics are covered it 'should be done thoughtfully and not to sensationalise the subject matter. These are lived religions that demand thoughtful consideration' (Holt, 2019, 16).

One further aspect that will help the teacher be prepared to address some of the misconceptions about Judaism is the complex interplay between religion and culture. In many, if not all, religious traditions there is the idea of purely religious ideas and teachings that lie at the heart, or even on the periphery of the religion. There is also the recognition that elements of religion are influenced by the culture of the society within which the religion is found. In Buddhism, for example, there are specific beliefs and practices associated with Japanese Buddhism and Tibetan Buddhism; they are seen to be different cultural expressions of a central truth (Holt, 2023a). Within the modern world, aspects of Republicanism have been seen to provide the context to, and influence, the presentation of some forms of Christianity. This has been the same throughout history, and sometimes the separation of culture and religion is very difficult, as they have formed a symbiotic relationship. This process is described by Peter Berger (1969) who suggests that social institutions such as the law, education, family, language, rules and values are not only the product of human inventiveness but also are the very things that shape human experience. The dialectical process of constructing and being constructed by society proceeds in a particular way: externalization, objectification and internalization:

> Externalization is the ongoing outpouring of human being into the world, both in the physical and the mental activity of men. Objectivation is the attainment by the products of this activity (again both physical and mental) of a reality that confronts its original producers as a facticity external to and other than themselves. Internalization is the reappropriation by men of this same reality, transforming it once again from structures of the objective world into structures of the subjective consciousness.

> (4)

The recognition that the expression of Judaism that is found today may be different to that which may have been understood in previous ages. This discussion will help situate beliefs and recognize the various influences that have an impact on the construction of a worldview today, and in the past.

Knowledge, however, is not enough. Although she wrote in 1993, what Barbara Wintersgill wrote has relevance for the teacher of religion and worldviews today:

> How religious and secular philosophies are presented to pupils is critical, if the elusive qualities of 'tolerance and respect' are to be developed, and in this context the method of teaching is as important as the content, if not more so. Religious traditions in the hands of an unsympathetic teacher, even if a certain amount of subject knowledge has been acquired, is likely to have the reverse effect. Too often, inappropriate teaching methods foster ridicule, disinterestedness and early dismissal of the claims of religions to be taken seriously.

> (44, emphasis added)

As well as knowing about Judaism, teachers need to understand it and recognize its value in the lives of individuals today. There are many ways that this can be developed for the teacher and within the classroom. The most effective way is, as already mentioned, an engagement with Jews and local Jewish communities. Where this may not be possible then the engagement with authentic voices in preparation and teaching is paramount. The experience of Jews in the local and national community is the first port of call for a teacher. There can be a tendency to show the 'flashy' elements of Judaism, perhaps as practised in India. Consider the showing as an example of Jewish prayer men praying at the Western Wall. This is not wrong, but it gives the impression that Judaism is a religion that happens elsewhere. Much more useful in the RE classroom is the 'Being Jewish' documentary from the BBC that shows ritual in the UK.

> It makes the religion less alien. It may be possible to compare the practices and see what is similar between the two, but when we focus purely on the 'overseas' nature of a religion it is possible that religion is seen to be other. The utilisation of authentic voices

from the local community or from the UK is effective. It enables students to see the reality of lived religion in the UK.

(Holt, 2023c, 282)

The way that is accomplished will differ according to school context. There may be opportunities for visits to local synagogues, and discussions with Jews whether in the classroom or in the shul. Other opportunities might be through live interviews through video call, or through a video conversation, or possibly a film from websites such as TrueTube. The interaction breaks down barriers and helps humanize the 'abstract' religious person. If diversity and accuracy are to be brought into the classroom, and the recognition of individual worldviews then the authentic voice is an important way that this will be accomplished.

Throughout this chapter we have explored the place of Jews in Britain and their experiences of retrenchment and assimilation. At times, the focus is on developing Jewish identity so that the beliefs, teachings and practices are not watered down. On the other hand, Jews are aware of an increasing awareness of their place within, and distinct from, wider society.

As Judaism has developed, there has been the need for Jews to find greater representation of the needs of their communities and the individuals therein. Some of this has happened through the development of representative voices within society, and these are also voices that can be used in the classroom. Groups such as the Board of Deputies of British Jews have sought to raise the profile and awareness of Judaism.

Jews in the public eye have raised the awareness of wider society towards Judaism and Jewish principles. Examples include:

- Sam Mendes (Film Director)
- Vanessa Feltz (TV Presenter)
- Natasha Kaplinsky (TV Presenter)
- Nigella Lawson (TV Chef)
- Gaby Roslin (TV Presenter)
- David Baddiel (Comedian)
- Ronni Ancona (Comedian)
- Sacha Baron Cohen (Comedian)
- Matt Lucas (Comedian and Presenter)
- Craig David (musician)
- Jess Glynne (Musician)
- Amy Winehouse (Musician)
- Jason Isaacs (Actor)
- Miriam Margolyes (Actor)
- Daniel Radcliffe (Actor)
- Stacey Solomon (TV Presenter)
- Ed Miliband (Politician)

The most important examples that we use in the classroom are those from our local area. The diversity of the Jewish experience in the UK is significant and should find expression in our classrooms. Returning to where we started the book with a discussion of what it is to be Jewish, an example such as David Beckham may raise interesting questions about self-definition. His maternal grandfather was Jewish, and remembering this he has suggested:

> So yes, I do consider myself … I was never brought up Jewish, but like I said, my grandfather was, and every time we went to synagogue, I was a part of that.

Reflecting on Beckham and others Rachel Shukert (2016) has taken heart from this:

> But they [celebrities such as Beckham] are all, nonetheless, eager to 'out' themselves as Members of the Tribe. To paraphrase yet again, we've come a long way, baby, from the times when Jewish celebrities were intent on keeping their Jewishness discreet, if not quite entirely secret.

Judaism is a religion that gives an identity to the individual and enables them to repair the world. Sometimes in our writing and teaching we forget that everything in Judaism has its root in the nature of the Almighty in particular. Nothing in the Jewish worldview makes sense without an understanding of the Jewish view of Almighty and existence more widely. Though, in many ways it lies in the background, much like the oxygen we breathe, it is not there but is often the unrecognized sustaining force. It is my hope that as we explore Judaism as a lived religion, it will become more than a list of observable phenomena and that it will reflect the reality of what it is to be a Jew today. It is only then that the richness of Judaism can be understood by those we teach.

Glossary

Aleinu a prayer recited before the returning of the Torah to the Ark.

Aliyah a part of the bar/bat mitzvah the young person is called up to the bimah to read or chant from the Torah.

Amidah the standing prayer. An important part of Shabbat synagogue services.

Aron kodesh ark of the Torah scrolls. Often a closed cabinet with a curtain covering it. This is opened when the Torah scrolls are to be read.

Ashkenazi Ashkenazi Jewish communities spread and developed in Eastern Europe especially in places like Prague and Poland.

Bar Mitzvah coming-of-age ceremony for Jewish boys.

Bat Mitzvah Bat Chayil coming-of-age ceremony for Jewish girls.

Bet ha Knesset/ Beit ha Knesset Shul 'House of Assembly' Henrew root of Greek word 'synagogue'

Beth din (house of judgement) a series of courts which deal with a wide range of legal and religious issues, including divorce and marriage, the laws of kashrut, disputes over financial matters, and conversions.

Bimah a raised platform from which the Torah is read. In an Orthodox synagogue it will usually be in the centre facing the Ark. In a Reform synagogue it will usually be at the front facing out.

Brit Milah circumcision ceremony for young boys, usually performed at eight days. A sign of the covenant with Abraham.

Cantor/ Chazzan a person who chants or sings the various aspects of the services.

Challah bread used in the Shabbat meal.

Chanukiah Menorah the nine branched menorah on which a candle is lit each night of Chanukah

Chanukah a festival that draws on the story of Judah the Maccabee found in the apocryphal texts of the Maccabees

Charedi/ Haredi a group within the Orthodox tradition, sometimes known as the Ultra-Orthodox, though this term does have negative connotations.

Chasidim/ Hasidism one form of Charedi Jews founded by Rabbi Israel ben Eliezer (1698–1760), known as the Baal Shem Tov (Master of the Good Name).

Eruv an eruv is correctly termed an eruv chatzerot. This is a merger of many different areas or domains into one. Essentially making the larger geographic area into one, it has been described as 'a large back garden'.

Gan eden some believe is part of the afterlife. Described as a land of milk, honey, balsam and wine.

Gehinnom some believe is part of the afterlife. The Talmud describes Gehinnom as a hot and fiery place of judgement.

Gemara/Gemarah records of debates and discussions around the Mishnah. Collected together to form part of Talmud.

G'mllut hasadim acts of loving kindness.

Haftara a selection of readings from the Nevi'im, often read in synagogue services or bat mitzvahs.

Haggadah 'telling'. Using refers to a text setting for the order of the seder meal.

Halakhah Jewish law, or the way to behave.

Havdalah Shabbat ends with the Havdalah (separation) ceremony when three stars have appeared in the sky, or if the sky is overcast when a blue thread cannot be distinguished from a white thread when they are held at arm's length.

Israel Jacob changed his name to Israel. Can refer to the land of Israel or the people of Israel (Jews/Hebrews)/

Kabbalah Kabbalah is a school of Jewish mysticism.

Kaddish a prayer using in services, and closely associated with mourning.

Kashrut Kashrut is the name given to the different laws which decide whether meat is kosher or not.

Ketuvim (writings) is a collection of religious writings in the form of poetry, wisdom, story, prayer

Kiddush a prayer/blessing offered over a glass of wine in services and meals such as Shabbat, brit milah and Pesach.

Kippah Yamulkah Skull cap worn by many Jewish men.

Kosher the food which a Jew is allowed to eat is called kosher. The proper way of preparing such food is also called kosher.

Magen David Star of David.

Maimonides twelfth-century rabbi and philosopher. Also known as Rambam.

Mascheach/ Messiah many Orthodox Jews believe in a messiah who will come, gather all his people to the land of Israel, and the resurrection of the dead.

Matzah unleavened bread (soft or hard) is eaten in remembrance of the leaving of Egypt in a hurry, so bread could not rise.

Menorah seven branched candlestick reminding Jews of the menorah that was in the Temple.

Messianic Age this will be an age of peace, an age where the messiah will reign. In this understanding, for many Jews this life is a time to prepare the world for the messiah's arrival.

Mezuzah a container in which is the Shema. Placed 'on the doorposts of your house and on your gates' (Deuteronomy 6: 9), found on all of the doorposts (apart from the bathroom) of the homes of many Jews.

Midrash (meaning study or interpretation of text) is a literary form that is found throughout the Talmud (especially the Babylonian Talmud) and within Jewish culture and tradition. They are imaginative or inspired readings of narratives that reimagine the story.

Mikveh 'a spring or cistern in which water is collected shall be pure' (Leviticus 11: 36). It is with this as a background that the use of a mikveh developed, where a mikveh is used following menstruation or childbirth. There are other traditions that require the use of a mikvah for all Jews, not just women, such as when a person converts to Judaism, before Yom Kippur, and for some Jews before Shabbat.

Minyan or 'quorum', of ten adults. The Shabbat service can only begin when a minyan is present; in Orthodox traditions this is ten men, whereas in other traditions it can be ten adults.

Mishnah judgements passed down by word of mouth. The first record of a written Mishnah, or the Oral Torah is in the late second to early third centuries 200 CE. Forms part of the Talmud.

Mitzvah Mitzvot (pl.) laws. usually believed to be 613 in number.

Mohel official who carries out the circumcision of a boy.

Ner Tamid Eternal Light. Usually found in a synagogue to represent the presence of the Almighty.

Nevi'im Part of the Tanakh. Writings of the Prophets.

Noachide Laws laws based on the covenant with Noah.

Olam ha-ba the world to come.

Parev neutral foods food that is allowed to be eaten with meat or dairy.

Pesach Passover festival celebrating the freeing of the Jews from Israel.

Pikuakh Nefesh the belief that a mitzvot can be broken to save a life. Adultery and idolatry are also excluded from that which a person can do to save their own life.

Purim a festival to remember the story of Esther and the deliverance of the Jews.

Rabbi Rebbe Teacher.

Rosh Hashanah New Year. One of the High Holy Days of Judaism.

Seder meal. Most often associated with Pesach.

Sephardi a form of Orthodox Judaism. Sephardi have their roots in Spain and the Iberian Peninsula.

Shabbat Shabbos festival that takes place on the seventh day, Friday evening to Saturday evening.

Shechinah The Divine Presence. The feminine and immanent aspect of the Divine.

Shema prayer and declaration of faith found in Deuteronomy 6: 4–9.

Shoah 'Catastrophe'. also known as the Holocaust.

Shofar A ram's horn, blown during Yom Kippur.

Synagogue/ Shul house of assembly/ school.

Tallit prayer shawl that will be worn around the shoulders, by men in Orthodox services, possibly by all in a Reform synagogue.

Talmud Oral Torah- combing the Mishnah and the Gemara.

Tefillin/ Phylacteries leather boxes bound on the head and hand containing the Shema. Often worn during prayers.

Tanakh the Torah (law), the Nevi'im (Prophets) and the Ketuvim (the Writings) form the Tanakh

Tikkun Olam the responsibility to repair the world.

Torah The Law. the first five books of the Tanakh.

Tzedakah justice and righteousness. Usually refers to acts of charity.

Yad pointer used in the reading of the Torah.

Yom Kippur Day of Atonement.

Reference List

Aaron, D. (2006, September 9). *Who Is God to Judge?* Retrieved from aish.com: https://aish.com/48961146/

Aaron, D. (2015). *Love Is my Religion. The Spiritual Essence of Judaism*. Jerusalem: Isralight Books.

Adler, R. (1997). In Your Blood, Live: Re-visions of a Theology of Purity. In J. R. Litman, & D. Orenstein (Eds.), *Lifecycles 2: Jewish Women on Biblical Themes in Contemporary Life* (pp. 197–206). Nashville: Jewish Lights.

Allen, A. (2018, October 3). *We Are Created Creative*. Retrieved from Hebrew College: https://hebrewcollege.edu/blog/we-are-created-creative-parashat-beresheit-genesis-11-68-2/

Ammerman, N. T. (2021). *Studying Lived Religion. Contexts and Practices*. New York: New York University Press.

Artson, B. S. (2002, September 26 26). *Mighty Is Love*. Retrieved from American Jewish University: https://www.aju.edu/ziegler-school-rabbinic-studies/our-torah/back-issues/mighty-love

Ashton, D. (2013). *Hanukkah in America*. New York: New York University Press.

Baddiel, D. (2021). *Jews Don't Count*. London: TLS.

Barenblat, R. (2015, December 24). *Who Continually Renews*. Retrieved from Velveteen Rabbi: https://velveteenrabbi.blogs.com/blog/2015/12/who-continually-renews.html

Barnes, N., & Stegmaier, A. (2023). *Eight Nights, Eight Lights*. London: Little Tiger.

Berger, P. (1969). *The Sacred Canopy. Elements of a Sociological Theory of Religion*. New York: Anchor.

Berkowitz, A. (2021). My Body, My Choice: Biblical, Rabbinic, and Contemporary Halakhic Responses to Abortion. *Touro Law Review, 37*(3), 1133–53.

Biala, T. (2022). *Dirshuni: Israeli Women Writing Midrash*. Waltham: Brandeis University Press.

Bloom, C. (2023). *Does Government 'Do God?' An Independent Review into How Government Engages with Faith*. London: Department for Levelling Up, Housing and Communities.

Board of Deputies of British Jews (2024, June 1). *Who We Are*. Retrieved from Board of Deputies of British Jews: https://bod.org.uk/who-we-are/

Bowie, R. A., Panjwani, F., & Clemmey, K. (2020). *Texts and Teachers. Opening the Door to Hermeneutical RE*. Canterbury: National Institute of Christian Education.

Boyd, J. (2023). *A Jewish or a Non-Jewish School: What Lies behind Parents' Decisions about How to Educate Their Children?* London: Institute for Jewish Policy Research.

Boyd, J. (2023a, May 25). *Who Gave Us the Torah? Most British Jews Don't Think It's the Word of God*. Retrieved from Institute of Jewish Policy Research: https://www.jpr.org.uk/insights/who-gave-us-torah-most-british-jews-dont-think-its-word-god

Boyne, J. (2006). *The Boy in the Striped Pyjamas: A Fable*. New York: David Fickling Books.

Buber, M. (1970). *I and Thou*. (W. Kaufmann, Trans.) New York: Scribner.

Bulatao, R. A., & Anderson, N. B. (2004). *Understanding Racial and Ethnic Differences in Health in Late Life: A Research Agenda*. Washington, D.C.: The National Academies Press.

Cohen, S. J. (1999). *The Beginnings of Jewishness: Boundaries, Varieties, Uncertainties*. Berkeley: University of California Press.

Cohn-Sherbok, D. (1989). *Holocaust Theology*. London: Lamp Press.

Cohn-Sherbok, D. (1997). *The Jewish Messiah*. Edinburgh: T&T Clark.

Cohn-Sherbok, D. (2017). *Judaism. History, Belief and Practice. Second edition*. Abingdon: Routledge.

Commission on RE (2018). *Religion and Worldviews: the Way Forward. A National Plan for RE*. London: Commission on RE.

Cooling, T. (2002). Commitment and Indoctrination: A Dilemma for Religious Education? In L. Broadbent, & A. Brown, *Issues in Religious Education*. New York: Routledge.

Cooling, T., Bowie, B., & Panjwani, F. (2020). *Worldviews in Religious Education*. London: Theos.

Council of Christians and Jews (2023). *Why 'Christian Seders' Are Not a Good Idea. A Brief Explainer*. London: Council of Christians and Jews.

Danan, J. (2022). *Farming Tzedakah: The Gleanings and Corners of Your Field*. Retrieved from Wellsprings of Wisdom. The Nature Rabbi: https://wellspringsofwisdom.com/farming-tzedakah-gleanings-corners-field/

Dauvillier, L. (2014). *Hidden*. New York: First Second.

Davis, A. (1981). *The Metsudah Siddur, Metsudah Publications*. Retrieved from Sefaria: https://www.sefaria.org/Shabbat_Siddur_Sefard_Linear%2C_Eiruv_Tavshilin?ven=The_Metsudah_Siddur,_Metsudah_Publications,_1981_-_EN&lang=bi&with=About&lang2=en

Diamant, A. (1997). *The Red Tent*. New York: Macmillan.

Diamant, A., & Cooper, H. (2023). *Living a Jewish Life. Jewish Traditions, Customs, and Values for Today's Families*. New York: William Morrow.

Doniger, W. (1991). Hinduism by Any Other Name. *The Wilson Quarterly, 15*(3), 35–41.

Dosick, W. (1995). *Living Judaism. The Complete Guide to Jewish Belief, Tradition and Practice*. New York: Harper One.

Drazin, I. (2009). *Maimonides and the Biblical Prophets*. Jerusalem: Gefen Publishing House Ltd.

Durkheim, E. (2001). *The Elementary Forms of Religious Life*. New York: Oxford University Press.

Dyson, J. (2009). What's the Use of Stories? Exploring the Place of Personal Stories and Grand Narratives in RE (and Life in General). *Resource, 32*(1), 14–17.

Economist (2024, December 19). *There Is More to Hanukkah Gifts than Meets the Eye: How American Jews Reshaped an Ancient, Minor Holiday*. Retrieved from The Economist: hhttps://www.economist.com/culture/2024/12/19/there-is-more-to-hanukkah-gifts-than-meets-the-eye#

Eden Primary (n.d.). *Our Ethos*. Retrieved from Eden Primary: https://edenprimary.org.uk/about-us/our-unique-offer/our-ethos/

Education, UCL Centre for Holocaust (2016). *UCL Centre for Holocaust Education's Continuity and Change Research Study Third Data Release – The Boy in the Striped Pyjamas in English Secondary Schools*. London: UCL.

Ehrlich, C. (2010). *Judaism*. New York: Rosen Publishing.

Eliach, Y. (1982). *Hasidic Tales of the Holocaust*. New York: Avon Books.

Endlar, D. (2025). *Welcome*. Retrieved from Immanuel College: https://www.immanuelcollege.co.uk/Welcome/

Eskenazi, T. C., & Weiss, A. (2008). *The Torah: A Women's Commentary*. New York: Women of Reform Judaism.

European Union Agency for Fundamental Rights (2018). *Experiences and Perceptions of Antisemitism. Second Survey on Discrimination and Hate Crime against Jews in the EU*. Luxembourg: Publications Office of the European Union.

Fackenheim, E. (1969). Reflections and a Jewish Testimony. In H. W. Richardson, & D. R. Cutler, *Transcendence* (pp. 143–52). Boston: Beacon Press.

Fackenheim, E. (1982). *To Mend the World*. New York: Schocken Books.

Feldman, R. (2017, October 8). *The Bnei Noah (Children of Noah)*. Retrieved from World Religions and Spirituality Project: https://wrldrels.org/2017/10/08/the-bnei-noah-children-of-noah/

Flannery, E. (1985) *The Anguish of the Jews. Twenty-three Centuries of Antisemitism*. (Revised and updated). New York: Paulist Press.

Frankl, V. E. (2004). *Man's Search for Meaning*. New York: Rider.

Friedman, R. (2001). *Commentary on the Torah: With a New English Translation*. San Francisco: Harper San Francisco.

Gafney, W. (2017). *Womanist Midrash: A Reintroduction to the Women of the Torah and the Throne*. Louisville: Westminster John Knox Press.

Gannon, M. (2016, February 5). *Race Is a Social Construct, Scientists Argue*. Retrieved from Scientific American: https://www.scientificamerican.com/article/race-is-a-social-construct-scientists-argue/

Glasson, C. (2025). *The Devils' Gospels. Finding God in four Great Atheist Books*. Croydon: Christian Alternative Books.

Gleitzman, M. (2006). *Once*. London: Penguin.

Glueck, N. (1967). *Hesed in the Bible*. Cincinnati: The Hebrew Union College Press.

Goldberg, J. (2015, April). *Is It Time for the Jews to Leave Europe?* Retrieved from The Atlantic: https://www.theatlantic.com/magazine/archive/2015/04/is-it-time-for-the-jews-to-leave-europe/386279/

Goodman, M. (2017). *A History of Judaism*. London: Penguin.

Graham, D. (2024). *Why This Night Is Different: How and why Do Jews in the UK Celebrate Passover?* London: Institute for Jewish Policy Research.

Graham, D. (2024a). *Shana Tova (Happy New Year): The Observance of Rosh Hashana and Yom Kippur among Jews in the UK*. London: Institute for Jewish Policy Research.

Graham, D. (2024b). *On the Seventh Day: Shabbat Observance and Practices among British Jews*. London: Institute for Jewish Policy Research.

Graham, D., & Boyd, J. (2016). *Charitable giving among Britain's Jews: Looking to the Future*. London: Institute for Jewish Policy Research.

Graham, D., & Boyd, J. (2024). *Jews in the UK Today: Key Findings from the JPR National Jewish Identity Survey*. London: Institute for Jewish Policy Research.

Greenberg, I. (1988). *The Jewish Way. Living the Holidays*. New York: Touchstone.

Greene, M. (2020). *Jew(ish): A Primer, A Memoir, A Manual, A Plea*. Seattle: Little A.

Greenspahn, F. (2009). *Women and Judaism. New Insights and Scholarship*. New York: New York University Press.

Grimmitt, M. (2000). *Pedagogies of RE*. Great Wakering: McCrimmon.

Gryn, N. (Ed.) (2010). *Three Minutes of Hope. Hugo Gryn on the God Slot*. London: Continuum.

Hadran (2025, January 15). *Daf Yomi*. Retrieved from Hadran: https://hadran.org.il/daf/sanhedrin-29/

Hahn Tapper, A. J. (2016). *Judaisms. A Twenty-First-Century Introduction to Jews and Jewish Identities*. Oakland: University of California Press.

haKana, N. b. (n.d.). *Sepher Ha-Bahir*. Retrieved from Internet Archive: https://ia904709.us.archive.org/34/items/JudaismSeferHaBahirBahirEnglishTranslationPdfKabbalahTorahIsrael/%28judaism%29%20Sefer%20ha-bahir%20%28Bahir%29%20-%20english%20translation%20pdf%20-%20kabbalah%20torah%20israel.pdf

Hallet, G. (1967). *Wittgenstein's Definition of Meaning as Use*. New York: Fordham University Press.

Hammer, R. (2005). *Entering the High Holy Days: A Complete Guide to the History, Prayers and Themes*. Philadelphia: The Jewish Publication Society.

Heilman, U. (2012, August 8). *What Reform Jewry Thinks of the Talmud*. Retrieved from Jewish Telegraphic Agency: https://www.jta.org/2012/08/08/culture/what-reform-jewry-thinks-of-the-talmud

Helmreich, W. B. (1976). *Wake Up, Wake Up, to Do the Work of the Creator*. New York: Harper and Row.

Hirt-Manheimer, A. (2021, December). *On God, Indifference, and Hope: A Conversation with Elie Wiesel*. Retrieved from ReformJudaism.org: https://reformjudaism.org/god-indifference-and-hope-conversation-elie-wiesel

Holocaust Educational Trust (n.d.a). *Exploring the Holocaust. A Cross-Curricular Scheme of Work for Key Stage 3 & S2. Teacher's Guide*. London: Holocaust Educational Trust.

Holocaust Educational Trust (n.d.b). *Teaching the Holocaust in English*. London: Holocaust Educational Trust.

Holt, J. D. (2019). *Beyond the Big Six Religions: Expanding the Boundaries in the Teaching of Religions and Worldviews*. Chester: University of Chester Press.

Holt, J. D. (2022). *Religious Education in the Secondary School. An Introduction to Teaching, Learning and the World Religions*. Abingdon: Routledge.

Holt, J. D. (2023a). *Understanding Buddhism. A Guide of Teachers*. London: Bloomsbury.

Holt, J. D. (2023b). *Understanding Sikhism. A Guide fo Teachers*. London: Bloomsbury.

Holt, J. D. (2023c). Religious Education. In N. Majid (Ed.), *Essential Subject Knowledge for Primary Teaching* (pp. 271–90). London: Learning Matters.

Humanists UK (2023, September 19). *Private Jewish School Fails Ofsted Inspection Yet Again*. Retrieved from Humanists UK: https://humanists.uk/2023/09/19/private-jewish-school-fails-ofsted-inspection-yet-again/

International Holocaust Remembrance Alliance (2019). *Recommendations for Teaching and Learning about the Holocaust*. International Holocaust Remembrance Alliance.

International Holocaust Remembrance Alliance's Committee on Antisemitism and Holocaust Denial (2015). *Spelling of Antisemitism*. Retrieved from International Holocaust Remembrance Allianc: https://holocaustremembrance.com/resources/spelling-antisemitism

Jackson, R., Ipgrave, J., Hayward, M., Hopkins, P., Fancourt, N., Robbins, M., et al. (2010). *Materials used to Teach about World Religions in Schools in England*. Warwick: University of Warwick.

Jacobs, J. (n.d.). *Tale of Two Talmuds: Jerusalem and Babylonian*. Retrieved from My Jewish Learning: https://www.myjewishlearning.com/article/tale-of-two-talmuds/

Jacobs, L. (1988). *Principles of the Jewish Faith*. London: Jason Aronson Inc.

Jacobs, L. (1995). *The Jewish Religion: A Companion*. Oxford: Oxford University Press.

Jacobs, L. (1999). *Ask the Rabbi*. London: Valentine Mitchell.

Joffe, L., & Cohn-Sherbok, D. (2022). *Jewish History and Judaism: An Illustrated Encyclopedia of: A History of the Jewish People, Their Religion and Philosophy, Traditions and Practices*. Dayton: Lorenz Books.

Josephus (1999). *The New Complete Works of Josephus. Revised and Expanded Edition*. (W. Whiston, Trans.) Grand Rapids: Kregel Publications.

KeshetUK (2023). *About Us*. Retrieved from KeshetUK: https://www.keshetuk.org/

Kessler, E. (2007). *What do Jews Believe?: The Customs and Culture of Modern Judaism*. London: Bloomsbury.

King, R. (1999). *Orientalism and Religion Postcolonial Theory, India and 'the Mystic East'*. New York: Routledge.

Kirschner, R. (1988). Halakhah and Homosexuality: A Reappraisal. *Judaism, 37*(4), 450–8.

Klawans, J., & Wills, L. (Eds.). (2020). *The Jewish Annotated Apocrypha. New Revised Standard Version*. Oxford: Oxford University Press.

Kolodny, D. (2018, April 16). *Why Israel's Independence Led to an Argument Over the Name of God*. Retrieved from Jewish Chronicle: https://www.thejc.com/judaism/why-israels-independence-led-to-an-argument-over-the-name-of-god-eldd2na5

Kurzweil, A. (2007). *Kabbalah for Dummies*. Hoboken: Wiley.

Labshul (2018). *Storahtelling*. Retrieved from Lab/Shul: http://www.storahtelling.org/

Lawton, C. (2016). *Judaism. GCSE Religious Studies. The Definitive Resource*. London: Board of Deputies of British Jews.

Lessof, C. (2023). *Do Jews in the UK Celebrate Christmas*. London: Institute for Jewish Policy Research.

Lessof, C. (2024). *Antisemitism in Schools: How Prevalent Is It, and How Might It Affect Parents' Decisions about Where to Educate Their Children Post-October 7?* London: Institute for Jewish Policy Research.

Levi, P. (1996). *If this is a Man / The Truce (A Survivor's Journey Home from Auschwitz)*. New York: Vintage.

Lieberman, J. (2011). *The Gift of Rest: Rediscovering the Beauty of the Sabbath*. New York: Howard.

Lopez, D. (1995). *Curators of the Buddha: The Study of Buddhism under Colonialism*. Chicago: University of Chicago Press.

Maccabi, G. B. (2024). *Our Vision and Mission*. Retrieved from Maccabi GB: https://www.maccabigb.org/home

Maimonides (n.d.). *Rambam on Mishnah Sanhedrin*. Retrieved October 2024, from Sefaria: https://www.sefaria.org/Rambam_on_Mishnah_Sanhedrin?tab=contents

Mair, M. (1989). *Between Psychology and Psychotherapy: A Poetics of Experience*. New York: Routledge.

Mashiah, D., & Boyd, J. (2017). *Synagogue Membership in the United Kingdom in 2016*. London: Institute for Jewish Policy Research.

Masorti Judaism (n.d.). *Are Masorti communities LGBT+ inclusive?* Retrieved from Masorti Judaism: https://masorti.org.uk/faqs/are-masorti-communities-lgbt-inclusive/

Masuzawa, T. (2005). *The Invention of World Religions*. London: University of Chicago Press.

Mauss, A. (1994). The Mormon Struggle with Assimilation and Identity: Trends and Developments Since Midcentury. *Dialogue: A Journal of Mormon Thought, 27*, 129–49.

Mayyim Hayyim (n.d.). *About Mayyim Hayyim*. Retrieved from Mayyim Hayyim: https://www.mayyimhayyim.org/about/

McGinty, A. B., & Molk, L. (2022). *A Synagogue Just Like Home*. Somerville: Candlewick Press.

McGuire, M. (2008). *Lived Religion. Faith and Practice in Everyday Life*. Oxford: Oxford University Press.

Mello, R. (2001). 'The Power of Storytelling: How Oral Narrative Influences Children's Relationships in Classrooms'. *International Journal of Education & the Arts, 2*(1), 1–6.

Middleton-Kaplan, R. (2014). The Myth of Jewish Passivity. In P. Henry, *Jewish Resistance Against the Nazis* (pp. 3–26). Washington, D.C.: Catholic University of America Press.

Migration Watch UK (2014, May 12). *A Summary History of Immigration to Britain*. Retrieved from Migration Watch UK: https://www.migrationwatchuk.org/briefing-paper/48/a-summary-history-of-immigration-to-britain

Milgram, S. (1974). *Obedience to Authority; An Experimental View*. New York: HarperCollins.

Moffatt, A. (2017). *No Outsiders in Our School. Teaching the Equality Act in Primary Schools*. Abingdon: Routledge.

My Jewish Learning (n.d.). *What is A Cantor (Hazzan or Chazan)?* Retrieved from My Jewish Learning: https://www.myjewishlearning.com/article/the-cantor/

My Jewish Learning (n.d.a.). *Ketuvim (Writings)*. Retrieved from My Jewish Learning: https://www.myjewishlearning.com/article/ketuvim-writings/

Neuberger, J. (2019). *Antisemitism. What It Is. What It Isn't. Why It Matters*. London: Weidenfeld & Nicholson.

Neumann, E. (2024, December 28). *My Christian Girlfriend Didn't Get Incited to a Jewish Wedding*. Retrieved from Facebook: https://www.facebook.com/share/r/1AkhxK3NrR/

Neusner, Jacob (2014). *What Is Midrash?* Eugene: Wipf and Stock.

Nevins, D. (n.d.). *A Prayer for the Renewal of Creation*. Retrieved from The Rabbinical Assembly: https://www.rabbinicalassembly.org/sites/default/files/2021-04/A%20Prayer%20for%20the%20Renewal%20of%20Creation%20with%20French%20translation.pdf

Newman, L., & Teplow, R. (2024). *Hanukkah*. London: Quarto Publishing.

Newman, T., & Garofoli, V. (2014). *Shabbat Is Coming!* Minneapolis: Bravo.

Nichols, T. (2017). *The Death of Expertise: The Campaign Against Established Knowledge and Why It Matters*. New York: Oxford University Press.

Ofsted (2010). *Transforming RE*. Manchester: Ofsted.

Ofsted (2021, May 21). *Research Review Series: Religious Education*. Retrieved from https://www.gov.uk/government/publications/research-review-series-religious-education/research-review-series-religious-education

Pew Forum on Religion & Public Life (2008). *U.S. Religious Landscape Survey. Religious Affiliation: Diverse and Dynamic*. Washington, DC: Pew Forum on Religion & Public Life.

Pew Research Center (2013). *A Portrait of Jewish Americans Findings from a Pew Research Center Survey of U.S. Jews*. Washington, DC: Pew Research Center.

Plaskow, J. (1991). *Standing against Sinai. Judaism from a Feminist Perspective*. New York: Harper One.

Porton, G. G. (1985). *Understanding Rabbinic Midrash: Texts and Commentary*. Hoboken: Ktav Pub. House.

Pytell, T. E. (2003). Viktor Frankl (1905–1999). In S. L. Kremer, *Holocaust Literature: An Encyclopedia of Writers and Their Work* (pp. 377–80). New York: Routledge.

Ralston, R. (2015, March 4). *5 Principles of Shabbat*. Retrieved from sefaria.org: https://www.sefaria.org/sheets/8314.1?lang=bi&with=AboutSheet&lang2=en

Rapoport, C. (2004). *Judaism and Homosexuality: An Authentic Orthodox View*. London: Vallentine Mitchell.

Rich, D. (2024). *Everyday Hate. how Antisemitism Is Built into Our World and How You Can Change It*. London: Biteback Publishing.

Richter, H. P. (1987). *Friedrich*. London: Penguin.

Robinson, G. (2000). *Essential Judaism. A Complete Guide to Beliefs, Customs and Rituals*. New York: Pocket Books.

Rocker, S. (2014, October 23). *Masorti Approves Single-Sex Marriages*. Retrieved from The Jewish Chronicle: https://www.thejc.com/news/masorti-approves-single-sex-marriages-mwke3hoc

Rosen, M., & Iwai, M. (2006). *Chanukah Lights Everywhere*. Orlando: Voyager Books.

Roth, C. (1964). *A History of the Jews in England (Third ed.)*. Oxford: Clarendon Press.

Rouss, S., & Kahn, K. J. (2013). *Sammy Spider's First Yom Kippur*. Minneapolis: Karben.

Rubenstein, R. (1992). *After Auschwitz. History, Theology and Contemporary Judaism*. Baltimore: The Johns Hopkins University Press.

Rushdie, S. (1991). *Haroun and the Sea of Stories*. London: Granta.

Sacks, J. (2011). *The Great Partnership. God, Science the Search for Meaning*. London: Hodder and Stoughton.

Safrai, S. (1976). The Era of the Mishnah and Talmud (70–640). In H. Ben-Sasson (Ed.), *A History of the Jewish People* (pp. 307–84). Cambridge: Harvard University Press.

Sartori, J., & Rosenbaum, J. (2021, June). *About the Shalvi/Hyman Encyclopedia of Jewish Women*. Retrieved from Jewish Women's Archive: https://jwa.org/encyclopedia/about

Satlow, M. L. (2006). *Creating Judaism: History, Tradition, Practice*. Columbia University Press.

Schama, S. (Director) (2014). *The Story of the Jews* [Motion Picture]. BBC.

Scherman, N., & Zlotowitz, M. (Eds.) (2008). *The Family Haggadah*. (N. Scherman, Trans.) New York: Mesorah Publications.

Schipper, F. P., & Wolberg, S. S. (2022). *A Soul beneath the Earth: A Holocaust Memoir of Faith and Resilience*. USA: Independent.

Schulte, C. (2023). *Zimzum: God and the Origin of the World*. Philadelphia: University of Pennsylvania Press.

Schwartz, A. (2011, July 17). *Is There Life After Death? Jewish Thinking on the Afterlife*. Retrieved from Moment: https://momentmag.com/is-there-life-after-death/

Schwartz, D. (2021, November 25). *Judea versus Judaism: Between 1 and 2 Maccabees*. Retrieved from Torah.com: https://www.thetorah.com/article/judea-versus-judaism-between-1-and-2-maccabees#:~:text=e.,Judah%20Maccabee%20to%20be%20victorious:&text=As%20soon%20as%20Maccabaeus%20got,anger%20having%20turned%20into%20mercy

Shukert, R. (2016, June 21). *David Beckham: I Consider Myself To Be Jewish*. Retrieved from Tablet: https://www.tabletmag.com/sections/news/articles/david-beckham-i-consider-myself-to-be-jewish

Silva, M. (2021). *Kabbalah: The Ultimate Guide for Beginners Wanting to Understand Hermetic and Jewish Qabalah Along with the Power of Mysticism (Jewish Spirituality)*. Independent.

Sinclair, J. (2008, December 18). *Apocrypha*. Retrieved from The Jewish Chronicle: https://www.thejc.com/judaism/jewish-words/apocrypha-vaaypcld

Smart, N. (1998). *The World's Religions, 2nd ed.* Cambridge: Cambridge University Press.

Smith, J. Z. (2004). *Relating Religion: Essays in the Study of Religion*. Chicago: University of Chicago Press.

Smith, M. (1999). The Gentiles in Judaism 125 bce–ce 66. In W. Davies, J. Sturdy, & T. Horbury, *The Cambridge History of Judaism* (Vol. 3). Cambridge: Cambridge University Press.

Sneitker, M. (2015, December 9). *The Goldbergs' Hanukkah Episode Takes Cues from … A Christmas Story?* Retrieved from Entertainment Weekly: https://ew.com/article/2015/12/09/goldbergs-hanukkah-episode-christmas-story/

Spiegelman, A. (1987). *Maus*. London: Penguin.

Staetsky, L. D., & Boyd, J. (2016). *The Rise and Rise of Jewish Schools in the United Kingdom: Numbers, Trends and Policy Issues*. London: Institute for Jewish Policy Research.

Stern, C. (Ed.) (1983). *Gates of Prayer. The New Union Prayerbook*. New York: Central Conference of American Rabbis.

Sugarman, D. (2017, November 6). *Schama, Sebag-Montefiore and Jacobson Unite to Condemn Labour Antisemitism*. Retrieved from The Jewish Chronicle: https://www.thejc.com/news/schama-sebag-montefiore-and-jacobson-unite-to-condemn-labour-antisemitism-g16um4ih

Swanton, M. (1997). *The Anglo-Saxon Chronicle*. London: Routledge.

The Jewish Theological Seminary of America; The Rabbinical Assembly; United Synagogue of America; Women's League for Conservative Judaism; Federation of Jewish Men's Clubs (1988). *Emet Ve'emunah. Statement of Principles of Conservative Judaism*. USA: The Jewish Theological Seminary of America, The Rabbinical Assembly, The United Synagogue of America.

The King David High School (n.d.). *The School and Religious Ethos*. Retrieved from The King David High School: https://www.kdhs.org.uk/ethos.html

The Pittsburgh Platform (1885). Retrieved from Central Conference of American Rabbis: https://www.ccarnet.org/rabbinic-voice/platforms/article-declaration-principles/

The Rabbinical Assembly (2010). *Kol Nidrei and Evening Service of Yom Kippur*. Retrieved from The Rabbinical Assembly: https://www.rabbinicalassembly.org/sites/default/files/assets/public/jewish-law/holidays/mls/mahzor-kol-nidrei.pdf

The Rabbinical Assembly (n.d.). *A Prayer for Our Country*. Retrieved from The Rabbinical Assembly: https://www.rabbinicalassembly.org/sites/default/files/AlternativePrayerCountry.pdf

Tippett, K. (2003, November 20). *Elie Wiesel The Tragedy of the Believer*. Retrieved from On Being: https://onbeing.org/programs/elie-wiesel-the-tragedy-of-the-believer/

UNESCO (2018). *Addressing Anti-Semitism through Education: Guidelines for Policymakers*. Paris/Warsaw: UESCO/ OSCE.

United Kingdom Supreme Court (2009, December 16). *PRESS SUMMARY R (on the application of E) (Respondent) v The Governing Body of JFS and the Admissions Appeal Panel of JFS and others (Appellants) [2009] UKSC 15*. Retrieved from The Supreme Court: https://www.supreme-court.uk/cases/docs/uksc-2009-0105-press-summary.pdf

United States Holocaust Memorial Museum (2024, November 18). *Jewish Population of Europe in 1933: Population Data by Country*. Retrieved from United States

Holocaust Memorial Museum: https://encyclopedia.ushmm.org/content/en/article/
jewish-population-of-europe-in-1933-population-data-by-country

United States Holocaust Memorial Museum (2025, January 10). *Remaining Jewish Population
of Europe in 1945*. Retrieved from United States Holocaust Memorial Museum: https://
encyclopedia.ushmm.org/content/en/article/remaining-jewish-population-of-eu-
rope-in-1945#:~:text=In%20western%20Europe%2C%20the%20largest,from%20eastern%20
to%20western%20Europe

University of Manchester (2007, July 23). *'Majority of Jews Will Be Ultra-Orthodox by 2050'*.
Retrieved from University of Manchester: https://www.manchester.ac.uk/about/news/majori-
ty-of-jews-will-be-ultra-orthodox-by-2050/#:~:text=Ultra%2Dorthodox%20British%20and%20
American,a%20University%20of%20Manchester%20academic

Vaisey, G. (2021). *Belonging and Believing: My Jewish Family*. Blakeney: Books at Press.

Wayland, A. H., & Jorisch, S. (2009). *New Year at the Pier: A Rosh Hashanah Story*. New York: Dial
Books for Young Readers.

Weinfeld, M. (1970, Apr. – Jun). The Covenant of Grant in the Old Testament and in the Ancient
Near East. *Journal of the American Oriental Society*, 90(2), 184–203.

Westminster Synagogue (2011). *Prayer Book for the New Year. The Day of Memorial*. London:
Westminster Synagogue.

Wiesel, E. (1995). *The Trial of God (as it was held on 25 February 1649, in Shamgorod)*. New York:
Schocken.

Wiesel, E. (2006). *Night*. New York: Hill and Wang.

Wigoder, G. (Ed.) (2002). *The New Encyclopedia of Judaism*. New York: New York University Press.

Wintersgill, B. (1993). Learning about World Religions in the Basic Curriculum. In C. Erricker (Ed.),
*Teaching World Religions. A Teacher's Handbook Produced by the SHAP Working Party on
World Religions in Education*. (pp. 42–4). Oxford: Heinemann.

Wintersgill, B. (2017). *Big Ideas in Religious Education*. Exeter: University of Exeter.

Wood, B. (2020). Teaching Worldviews at GCSE. In M. Chater, *Reforming RE: Power and
Knowledge in a Worldviews Curriculum*. (pp. 165–8). Woodbridge: John Catt Educational Ltd.

Yeomans, R. (1978). Religious Education Through Art. In R. Jackson, *In Perspectives on World
Religions* (pp. 51–72). London: University of London, School of Oriental and African Studies.

Zaklikowski, D. (2025). *Why Wear Purim Costumes? On Dressing up and Wearing Masks on the
Holiday of Purim*. Retrieved from Chabad.org: https://www.chabad.org/holidays/purim/article_
cdo/aid/1456808/jewish/Why-Wear-Purim-Costumes.htm

Zalman, S. (n.d.). *Lessons in Tanya*. Retrieved from Chabad.org: https://www.chabad.org/library/
tanya/tanya_cdo/aid/6237/jewish/Lessons-in-Tanya.htm

Zimbardo, P. (2007). *The Lucifer Effect: Understanding How Good People Turn Evil*. New York:
Random House.

Zohar, S. (2021, November 23). *What the 'Friends' Holiday Armadillo Episode Gets
Right about Interfaith Families*. Retrieved from Hey Alma: https://www.heyalma.com/
what-the-friends-holiday-armadillo-episode-gets-right-about-interfaith-families/

Index